Fighting King Coal

Urban and Industrial Environments

Series editor: Robert Gottlieb, Henry R. Luce Professor of Urban and Environmental Policy, Occidental College

A complete list of the series can be found at the back of the book.

Fighting King Coal

The Challenges to Micromobilization in Central Appalachia

Shannon Elizabeth Bell

The MIT Press
Cambridge, Massachusetts
London, England

Set in Stone Sans and Stone Serif by Toppan Best-set Premedia Limited. Printed and bound in the United States of America.

Library of Congress Cataloging-in-Publication Data

Names: Bell, Shannon Elizabeth, author.
Title: Fighting king coal : the challenges to micromobilization in central Appalachia / Shannon Elizabeth Bell.
Description: Cambridge, MA : The MIT Press, 2016. | Series: Urban and industrial environments | Includes bibliographical references and index.
Identifiers: LCCN 2015038405| ISBN 9780262034340 (hardcover : alk. paper) | ISBN 9780262528801 (pbk. : alk. paper)
Subjects: LCSH: Environmental justice–West Virginia. | Environmental health–Social aspects–West Virginia. | Coal mines and mining–Environmental aspects–West Virginia. | Coal mines and mining–Health aspects–West Virginia. | Environmental degradation–Health aspects–West Virginia. | Community activists–West Virginia.
Classification: LCC GE235.W4 B45 2016 | DDC 363.73/1–dc23 LC record available at http://lccn.loc.gov/2015038405

10 9 8 7 6 5 4 3 2 1

for Sean and the people of Central Appalachia

Contents

Acknowledgments

First and foremost, I am deeply grateful to all the individuals whose stories and experiences helped me write this book. Thank you for inviting me into your homes, for answering my questions, for trusting me with your stories, and for patiently helping me try to understand the complicated relationship Central Appalachian communities have with the coal industry. Thank you, especially, to the Photovoice women for being part of a long project and for caring about your communities so deeply.

My research would not have been possible without generous funding support from numerous organizations: the Greater Kanawha Valley Foundation, the Appalachian Regional Commission/West Virginia Development Office Flex-E-Grant Program, the American Sociological Association's Spivack Program in Applied Social Research and Social Policy, the Ohio Valley Environmental Coalition, Cabin Creek Health Systems, Photographic Production Services, the Clay Center for the Arts and Sciences, the University of Oregon (UO) Doctoral Dissertation Fellowship, the UO Center for the Study of Women in Society, the UO Department of Sociology, and the Wasby-Johnson Fellowship. Thank you also to the past and present staff and volunteers at Coal River Mountain Watch and Ohio Valley Environmental Coalition. Special thanks to Vivian Stockman, Patricia Feeney, Maria Lambert, and Patty Sebok, who were particularly instrumental in helping me to identify research communities and recruit participants.

I feel blessed to have had the opportunity to work with an amazing group of scholars while I was at the University of Oregon. Yvonne Braun, Richard York, Ellen Scott, Michael Dreiling, and Carol Silverman, I am grateful to the five of you for believing in me and in the Photovoice project, despite how unmanageable it probably seemed at the start. Thank you for listening to me, for challenging me, for reading my work, for collaborating with me, and for taking me out to lunch (Richard in particular on that last one). I am also grateful to the wonderful network of social scientists who have helped me with my book project since I joined the faculty at the University of Kentucky in 2010. I am particularly indebted to Claire Renzetti and Dwight Billings for being wonderful friends, colleagues, and mentors.

There are also many others who helped make the book a reality: Doug McAdam, who first encouraged me to write a book on the project and mentored me through the proposal process; Beth Clevenger, my acquisitions editor at the MIT Press, and Bob Gottlieb, editor of the Urban and Industrial Environments series, for believing in the value of the book; Tom Shriver and the two other reviewers, whose feedback, critiques, and positivity made the book much stronger; and Miranda Martin and Paul Bethge at the MIT Press, who did much of the behind-the-scenes work.

My amazing network of friends and family have provided wonderful support over the years, from when I was conducting my field work in West Virginia to when I was writing the earliest version of this book as my PhD dissertation. Nancy Reinhart, Jocelyn Gaujot, Courtney Smith, Sarah Cribbs, Shannon Cribbs, Katie Rodgers, Ann Leymon, Ryanne Pilgeram, Miriam Abelson, Shelley Grosjean, Jen Erickson, Christine Metzger, the Friedman Five, and members of the Breakfast Club, thank you—all of you—for the laughter, the love, the support, and the many wonderful (and necessary) distractions you provided.

I must also thank my amazing, generous, and supportive parents, Susan and Tom Bell, for always encouraging me and helping me in extraordinary ways. I am grateful for their love and, support, and for all the times they have rescued me over the years (including driving my car from Oregon to West Virginia in 2006 so I could have it for my first summer of field research). My father is also an amazing proofreader, as is my great-aunt Mary Ellen Collins. Thank you, Dad and Aunt Ellie, for catching my typos and for offering helpful feedback, both on this book and on my first.

And finally, I am more grateful than I can express for the love that my wonderful and patient partner, Sean Bemis, and our big-hearted son, Cedar, have brought to my life. Thank you both for the ways you have cared for me and made me laugh through my many grumpy mornings and late nights. You two are truly the lights of my life.

Introduction

> Different people stood up and told about their water and told about what they believed was happening, and told about the different illnesses—the brain tumors, the gallbladder problems, stomach problems, children's teeth falling out, and all of these things. ... And it's like my whole life flashing before my eyes, because my children had lost their teeth, my parents had had cancer, we'd had our gallbladders removed, and all of these things was, it's just like, oh no, it's not just us—it's the whole community, and we're not even blood related.
>
> —Maria Lambert, West Virginia coalfield resident, as quoted on page 72 of Bell 2013

Maria Lambert lives in the community of Prenter, West Virginia, deep in the heart of the coal-mining region of Central Appalachia. In 2007, residents of Prenter, who had long been plagued by alarmingly high rates of cancer and other serious health conditions, learned that their well water was contaminated with coal waste. Coal waste, also called "slurry" or "sludge," is generated when coal is cleaned to remove non-combustible materials such as sulfur and rock. The liquid waste generated in this process consists of water, chemicals, and particles of coal, which contain a host of heavy metals and semi-metal compounds that can be toxic when ingested or inhaled, including arsenic, beryllium, cadmium, chromium, cobalt, lead, mercury, nickel, and selenium. The large quantity of coal waste that is produced in the coalfields of Central Appalachia is either stored in huge slurry impoundments on the surfaces of flattened mountaintops or pumped underground into abandoned mine shafts. In recent years, increasing numbers of communities neighboring these slurry-injection sites have found that coal waste has leached out of the underground storage chambers into the water table, silently contaminating drinking-water wells in the vicinity.

For many years, individuals living in communities like Prenter did not realize that the brown—or sometimes black—water that ran through their faucets was coal waste; many were told either that they just had a little iron in their water or that dirt was getting through their filters. They continued drinking, cooking with, and bathing in this contaminated water for many years, until they, and especially their children, started getting sick. Residents throughout the coalfields whose water has been contaminated with coal slurry have been found to have high rates of liver, kidney, and brain cancer, as well as gall bladder disease, skin disorders, and even organ failure (Orem 2006; Wells 2006; Bell 2013).

When residents of communities like Prenter find out that their health and safety—and the health and safety of their families—have been jeopardized by a polluting or destructive industry, do they typically rise up to fight for environmental justice and the rights of their communities? The answer to this question is No. In cases of environmental injustice, such as what is taking place in communities like Prenter, there are hundreds of people who choose *not* to participate in local grassroots movements working for environmental justice in their communities, despite being personally affected by these hazards. This is the underlying question this book seeks to resolve: Why do so many of the vast number of people who experience industry-produced environmental hazards and toxics *not* rise up to participate in movements aimed at bringing about social justice and industry accountability?

As McAdam and Boudet (2012) maintain, there is a tendency among scholars of social movements to "select on the dependent variable," beginning with an instance of successful mobilization and then retrospectively studying the factors that have led to collective action and to recruitment into the movement.[1] This tendency creates a skewed picture of social movements, overstating both the frequency of collective action events and the success of mobilization efforts. There are, in fact, many more instances of non-action[2] in the face of injustice than there are cases of action. Even in communities where there are successful social-movement organizations working against local injustices, there are many more people who choose not to participate in collective action than who choose to participate. However, we know very little about the factors that constrain grassroots participation in such organizations. It is within this void in social-movement theory that I situate my study.

This book also seeks to answer David S. Meyer's call for social-movement scholarship that is aimed at the "passionate pursuit of answers to questions that are important to people trying to change the world" (2005, p. 193). Trying to understand why so many unjustly treated individuals do not fight back when given the opportunity is a question that has long plagued organizers of social movements. Figuring out how to recruit people into a movement requires an understanding of the barriers that prevent people from joining it.

I explore the question of non-action through a case study of the coal-mining region of Central Appalachia, where mountaintop-removal mining[3] and the increasing frequency of coal-industry-related flooding, sickness, and water contamination have led to the emergence of a working class, women-driven, grassroots environmental justice movement that is demanding protection from and accountability for the destruction and pollution in coalfield communities. (See Bell 2013 for an account of the local women at the center of this struggle.) The coal industry's impact on local communities has been profound; however, recruiting new local[4] residents to join the movement has proved to be an ongoing challenge. Although there are some very strong local voices at the forefront of this struggle, the number of participants from the affected population is relatively small, despite extensive organizing efforts in the region. This book examines the barriers to mobilization within this context.

The bulk of the data for this book are drawn from 13 months of field research that I conducted between July 2006 and May 2009 in southern West Virginia, the center of the struggle for coalfield environmental justice in the United States. My methods of data collection and analysis included in-depth and semi-structured interviews, participant observation, content analysis, geospatial viewshed analysis, and an eight-month "Photovoice" project with 54 women living in five coal-mining communities. Also included in this book are insights gained from follow-up interviews I conducted with Photovoice participants in 2013.

The chapters of this book are divided into two parts, representing two distinct phases of research. Part I presents four studies that build on existing social-movement theory to examine barriers to coalfield citizens' involvement in the environmental justice movement. Specifically, these studies present and investigate potential barriers to the processes of solidarity building, micromobilization, identity correspondence, and consciousness transformation (or cognitive liberation), which are the critical micro-level factors affecting an individual's propensity to participate in a social movement (McAdam 1988a; Gamson 1992). Through these studies, I identify four major obstacles to local coalfield residents' participation in the environmental justice movement:

- depleted social capital in coalfield communities, indicating that there are high levels of isolation, sparse social networks, and few formal organizations in the region
- the gendering of activist involvement—that is, the underrepresentation of men in environmental justice activism, owing to the coal industry's influence on the local hegemonic masculinity of the region
- the coal industry's ideology-construction efforts to maintain and amplify the perception that coal is both the economic backbone of the state and the cultural identity of the citizenry
- the fact that the majority of the coal industry's environmental destruction is not visible to most local residents.

Are these the only factors constraining local participation in the coalfield environmental justice movement? It is difficult to know because, as McAdam and Paulsen (1993, p. 641) assert, "almost invariably" studies of movement participation "start by surveying activists after their entrance into [a] movement." Thus, our research subjects have typically already overcome whatever barriers to participation may exist among people experiencing injustice. To determine if there are, in fact, other forces hindering local participation in the Central Appalachian case, it is necessary to study a group of individuals who are not yet activists but who are exposed to events and circumstances that could lead to their recruitment into the environmental justice movement.

In part II, I introduce the participatory-action research method of "Photovoice"[5] as a means of studying—in real time—the factors facilitating and constraining involvement in the environmental justice movement. I present the findings of an eight-month Photovoice project that I conducted with 54 women living in five coal-mining communities in southern West Virginia. Forty-seven of the participants in this project had had no previous involvement in environmental justice activism; seven of the participants (one or two from each community) were associated in some way with one of the local organizations fighting the coal industry's irresponsible practices in the region. Through this Photovoice project, I attempted to control for the four barriers discussed in part I while also creating a "micromobilization context"[6] (McAdam 1988a) for the non-activist participants, providing a structure that could serve to facilitate their recruitment into the environmental justice movement. By studying the women who chose to become involved in environmental justice activism during the project and those who did not, I examine the additional social factors that hinder local coalfield residents' participation in the movement.[7]

My analysis of the Photovoice portion of this research suggests that there are two additional barriers to participation in social movements among local residents. The first is the power of members of the local elite, who have direct or indirect ties to the coal industry and who benefit from the maintenance of the status quo. The pressure that these individuals exert to stifle other local residents' willingness to speak out against environmental injustice is a powerful force in these small communities. The second barrier revealed through the Photovoice study is that the collective identity of the environmental justice movement is changing in ways that have made many potential local recruits less likely to view the movement as compatible with their own personal identities. Although the movement was started by local people, in recent years, as mountaintop-removal mining has received increasing national media attention, many "non-local" people have also joined the movement.

My data suggest that the influx of non-local environmental groups, college students, and celebrities into the environmental justice movement, and the protest tactics they have chosen to use, are changing the collective identity of the movement such that many local citizens are now viewing it as an "outsiders' movement." This finding presents a significant dilemma for the future of the environmental justice movement in Central Appalachia. On the one hand, the influx of non-locals into the coalfield region has been positive in the sense that it has helped draw attention to the injustices taking place, and it has given the environmental justice movement a strong and deep base of support. At the same time, however, many supporters of the coal industry have been quick to condemn the newcomers—and the environmental justice organizations by association—as groups of "outsider extremists" who, if successful, will close all the coal mines and leave the "locals" without a source of income to feed their families. Thus, although the environmental justice movement was *started* by local coalfield residents, and those local coalfield residents are *still* central to the leadership of the movement, the influx of non-local people into the region has provided an opportunity for the opposition to capitalize on an "insider-outsider" dichotomy, effectively challenging the collective identity of the movement so that many in the region no longer perceive it as a "local" struggle.

My Positionality within the Coalfields of Appalachia

Although the collection of data for this book officially began in 2006, the seeds of this project were sown more than ten years earlier, when I was a high school student volunteering for a community-service project in the coal-mining region of southwest Virginia. I spent a week during the summer of 1995, and another during the summer of 1997, in Wise County, Virginia, helping to rehabilitate the homes of individuals who could not afford needed repairs. What I thought was simply a community-service trip with members of my church ended up being an experience that shaped the next fifteen years of my life.

I grew up as a fairly sheltered middle-class kid in suburban Maryland, and so my first exposure to coal-mining-related damages and injustices in rural Appalachia was shocking. During my first week of community service, I was startled when I blew my nose and saw black mucous, which, I learned, was the result of coal dust in the air. What, I wondered, did this coal dust do to the lungs of people who actually lived there? I met a number of children who were sick with chronic asthma. I also met retired coal miners, many of whom had frequent coughing spells due to the "black lung" (pneumoconiosis) that plagued their respiratory systems. Many of the homes my group repaired had cracked foundations and warped walls, which, I learned, were attributable to underground coal mining. The people living in these particular houses weren't eligible to receive compensation for their damaged property, because their homes didn't fall within the required angle of the mining operations. The areas in which we worked were extremely impoverished, yet, I was told, billions of dollars' worth of coal were extracted from the region every year. How could that be possible? Why were these communities so poor when they had such wealth buried within their mountains? How could the coal industry so clearly be damaging the health and property of the people living in these communities and not be held responsible?

As a college student, I searched for words to fit what I had seen during those service trips. Exploitation. Corruption. Injustice. I finally began to develop a vocabulary to describe what I saw. Though I would soon learn of many, many other terrible injustices taking place throughout the world, my first "awakening" occurred in the coalfields of Appalachia. That is why, I believe, this particular injustice became "my issue." Many of the papers I wrote during my undergraduate studies explored the history of coal mining in Appalachia and attempted to unravel how that industry had come to possess so much power within the United States and to enjoy such impunity for so many of its destructive actions.

I returned to Central Appalachia between my junior and senior years in college as a Shepherd Alliance Intern and AmeriCorps volunteer at a non-profit health center in rural southern West Virginia. During my eight weeks there, I began to understand that the region's relationship with coal was much more complicated than I had realized. The coal industry was responsible for great environmental and social harm, yet it was also deeply connected to many residents' identities and pride. Even people not employed by the coal industry were often reluctant to speak negatively about it, frequently expressing, "It's all we've got."

After finishing college, I returned to the same non-profit health center in southern West Virginia, working there from 2000 to 2005 in public health and community organizing. During those five years, my education continued. I saw mountaintop-removal coal mining for the first time and witnessed the devastating impacts of this practice on not only the environment but also on the health and well-being of residents living in nearby communities. Flooding, water contamination, structural damage from blasting, and accidents involving overweight coal trucks were all taken as the inevitable costs of living in the communities in which I worked.

I learned that there was a line that I had to toe carefully because of my status as an "outsider." My affiliation with the local health center where I worked (which had been started in the 1970s by the United Mine Workers of America and a group of local residents who had taken out personal loans to pay for the construction of the facility) gave me some credibility and helped me gain the trust of community members. But that was only so long as I didn't overstep certain boundaries—for example, by speaking "too politically" (or too negatively) about the coal industry. I came to realize how important it was to spend a lot of time listening to local people and really *hearing* the complexity of the struggles they and their communities faced. In those long conversations, residents would discuss the hardships they suffered because of the coal industry, but they would also express the pride they felt in their families' and their community's coal-mining history. I would watch as individuals eagerly dug up old photographs of their daddies and grand-daddies, covered in coal dust, standing in front of an underground mine entrance. They would pull out old carbide lanterns that had been used in the mines and pieces of coal company "scrip" that had been used as money in the coal camps where they lived. They shared stories about gruesome mining accidents and explosions that had happened while they were young, and they told me how poor their families had been, always in debt to the Company Store. But they would also tell me that, despite these difficult living circumstances, their coal camp was "the best place that a kid could grow up" because people took care of one another and the community was close-knit.

During our conversations, many people expressed regret that coal-mining practices had changed so drastically in recent years. Very few underground coal mines were left in the area, and even fewer union mines. Although more coal was being extracted from the region than ever before, jobs in the coal industry were difficult to come by. Many people told me how much they hated to see mountaintop-removal mining destroying their mountains and blocking access to many of their favorite hunting grounds and ginseng-digging spots. Some said that they had noticed increased flooding in the area since mountaintop-removal mining began, and some had experienced flood damage to their own homes. Others revealed that coal-related pollution had rendered their creeks unsuitable for fishing or swimming. Many talked about the dangerous road conditions and deadly accidents that had resulted from increased truck traffic to and from the mountaintop-removal mines in their community.

When conversations shifted toward problems related to the coal industry, I often took the opportunity to share information about the work that environmental justice organizations such as Coal River Mountain Watch and Ohio Valley Environmental Coalition were doing to advocate for the rights of coalfield citizens. On numerous occasions, I enthusiastically offered to put community residents in contact with these organizations or to set up meetings with organizers. Most of the time, people didn't take me up on my offers. On a few occasions, residents did express some interest in learning more, but most would not commit to joining or becoming involved in the activities of these groups. Why were they so reluctant? What was keeping coalfield residents who were affected by coal-industry-related pollution and destructive mining practices from participating in a movement that was advocating for their rights? This question has shaped much of my research agenda over the past ten years.

I returned to West Virginia many times to collect data for the various studies that make up this book. During each stint of field research—two months during the summer of 2006, one month during the summer of 2007, ten months in 2008 and 2009, and weekend trips in 2013—the question of local non-participation was the puzzle that tied together my data-collection efforts. Every time I went back into the field, new observations generated additional questions. Thus, the trajectory of the various components of this study wasn't mapped out from the very beginning, but instead unfolded through a series of stages.

Through each phase of the research process and over the years that I was observing, interviewing, reading, and writing about what was taking place (or not taking place) in the coalfields, I saw that there were, in fact, *many* complicated reasons why it was difficult to recruit local people into the environmental justice movement. There is no simple answer to the question, but I hope that I have at least begun to unravel these issues so that others will be able to pick up where I have left off and to expand and refine our understanding of the barriers to participation in environmental justice struggles.

Activist Research and Self-Reflexivity

As my personal history suggests, I situate my work within the tradition of activist research: research that is undertaken with the goal of advancing social justice objectives. Although sociological theory guides my research and I endeavor to make theoretical contributions through my work, theory building is not my sole purpose. I count myself among the number of social scientists who wish to "offer our analytic skills with the aim of improving society" (Pellow 2007, p. 35). Furthermore, I agree with those who contend that this advocacy aim should be a duty within the academy. "A large part of humanity," Greg Philo and David Miller (2001, p. 79) assert, "is being obliterated by the social, material, and cultural relationships which form our world. It can be painful and perhaps professionally damaging to look at such issues and to ask critical questions about social outcomes and power … . But for academics to look away from the forces which limit and damage the lives of so many, gives at best an inadequate social science and at worst is an intellectual treason—just fiddling while the world burns" (quoted in Pellow 2007, p. 35).

Thus, I do not deny that I bring opinions and passions to my research agenda. Instead, I lay them bare and acknowledge how they have shaped the questions I have chosen to ask. The importance of self-reflexivity on the part of researchers is articulated by Sandra Harding and other feminist-standpoint theorists. Harding argues that "all human beliefs—including our best scientific beliefs—are socially situated" (1991, p. 142). Proponents of standpoint theory argue that we researchers should acknowledge that our social locations, our biases, and our perspectives influence all aspects of the knowledge-creation process. According to Harding (1993, p. 69), the underlying and unexamined beliefs that the researcher holds "must be considered as part of the object of knowledge from the perspective of scientific methods." By divulging my personal history, previous observations, and experiences, I hope to contribute to a more open and honest social science.

Organization of the Book

As has already been noted, the book is divided into two parts, part I including four studies that build on existing social-movement theory and part II presenting the findings from the Photovoice study. Before diving into the studies in part I, I first provide (in chapter 1) some contextualization for the Central Appalachian case: historical background on the roots of the coal industry's exploitation of Central Appalachia, the environmental injustices that have plagued the region, and the history of resistance and mobilization against irresponsible mining practices.

In chapters 2–6, I draw on social-movement theory to explain and examine the micro-level processes inhibiting participation in the environmental justice movement among local coalfield residents. In chapter 2, I provide an overview of the sociological literature, focusing on the processes of solidarity building, identity correspondence, consciousness transformation (cognitive liberation), and micromobilization, the four critical micro-level factors affecting an individual's propensity to participate in a social movement

(McAdam 1988a; Gamson 1992). Within this literature, I situate four discrete studies that examine possible barriers to the four micro-level factors in the context of the Central Appalachian coalfields. These four studies make up chapters 3–6. Chapter 3 presents a qualitative study of social capital in a coal-mining community and a demographically similar non-coal-mining community in West Virginia. Through interviews and participant observation, I examine experiences of social capital within the two communities and find that there is a severe depletion in social capital within the coal-mining community. My data suggest that the causes of the coalfield town's social-capital deficit include extensive depopulation and conflicts related to the de-unionization of coal mines in the region. Insofar as both of these processes have been widespread throughout Central Appalachia for more than 30 years, I maintain that this depletion of social capital probably is generalizable to other coalfield communities. A low level of social capital translates to a deficit in social networks and social trust—factors that are integral to the process of solidarity building, the first of the micro-level factors influencing participation in social movements. In addition to inhibiting the building of solidarity, the weak social networks and the lack of organizations in the region also mean that there are few opportunities in the coalfields for micromobilization to take place (i.e. a lack of micromobilization contexts). Thus, I argue that the social-capital deficit in Appalachian coal-mining communities is one reason why relatively few local residents participate in the coalfield environmental justice movement.

The study presented in chapter 4 examines the gendering of participation in the environmental justice movement in Central Appalachia. Of the small proportion of local citizens who are involved in the coalfield movement, an even smaller proportion are men. In order to explore whether there are challenges associated with the process of "identity correspondence" (Snow and McAdam 2000) among local coalfield men, potentially leading to their low levels of environmental justice activism, I conducted participant observation and twenty in-depth interviews with a purposive sample of local environmental justice activists. The analysis of the data (conducted with Yvonne A. Braun) suggests that the differing rates of environmental justice activism among women and men in the Appalachian coalfields may be related to how readily their gendered identities are able to align with the collective identity of the coalfield movement. The findings suggest that the hegemonic masculinity of the region creates a barrier to local men's ability to achieve identity correspondence with the collective identity of the environmental justice movement, in effect removing a major segment of potential social-movement participants from the pool of potential recruits.

Chapter 5 examines the ideology-construction efforts of the coal industry in Central Appalachia and the ways in which cultural manipulation impedes the process of consciousness transformation among coalfield citizens. This study (conducted with Richard York) uses participant observation and content analysis to examine the West Virginia coal industry's faux-grassroots front group Friends of Coal, which was created to construct the image that West Virginia's economy and cultural identity are centered on coal production. I argue that through this campaign, and others like it, the coal industry aims to "greenwash" its destructive practices and to convince the public that being a "true Appalachian" means supporting the coal industry. This industry-created ideology poses yet another impediment to local people's willingness to join the fight to hold the industry accountable for the environmental and social harms it inflicts on the region.

The final study in part I, presented in chapter 6, argues that the process of consciousness transformation is also inhibited among local coalfield residents because the extent of the coal industry's effects on the Appalachian landscape is not readily visible to the majority of the population. This study (conducted with Sean P. Bemis) employs a geographic information system (GIS) in the foremost coal-producing county in West Virginia to quantitatively identify how much of the landscape of the county is visible from transportation corridors. With these data, the local viewshed relative to active and recently surface-mined sites is analyzed to determine whether the effects of mountaintop-removal mining are less likely to be visible than equivalent portions of the landscape. The data reveal that although 47 percent of the total landscape in Boone County is visible from transportation corridors (including U.S. highways, state highways, and county roads), only 23 percent of the surface-mined land mass is visible from these corridors. Removing the county roads (which are remote and largely depopulated) from the analysis makes the findings even more dramatic: only 4 percent of the total area of surface-mined land in Boone County is visible from U.S. and state highways. Thus, these findings support the claims of coalfield activists who contend that much of the coal-mining-related destruction in Central Appalachia is not visible to the majority of the population. I argue that this hidden destruction is another factor blocking consciousness transformation among coalfield residents.

In chapters 8–10 (part II of the book), I seek to address the limitations that are inherent to most studies of social-movement participation, which consistently draw conclusions about recruitment and participation by collecting retrospective data on activists and non-activists *after* their successful (or unsuccessful) recruitment into a movement. By initiating an eight-month Photovoice project with a group of non-activist coalfield women in five communities in southern West Virginia, I attempted to create a micromobilization context that would allow me to study the processes that shape and constrain local residents' entry into the Central Appalachian environmental justice movement. In chapter 8, I introduce the Photovoice process and present an overview of my methods; in chapters 9 and 10, I present the findings from the Photovoice research.

In the concluding chapter, I synthesize the findings from the five research studies that are the subjects of chapters 3–10, examining the barriers to local participation in the coalfield environmental justice movement and reflecting on what these findings mean for the future of this grassroots struggle.

1 Contextualizing the Case: Central Appalachia[1]

Historical Roots of Exploitation

Enduring Stereotypes, Land Theft, and Absentee Landownership

Regarded for more than a century as a "strange land inhabited by a peculiar people" (Shapiro 1977, p. 43), the Appalachian region is burdened with a profusion of stereotypes (Batteau 1990; Whisnant 1983; Billings, Norman, and Ledford 1999; Scott 2010; Fisher and Smith 2012). By some of the more idealized accounts, the region is a pristine frontier, populated by the quaint descendants of white Scots-Irish settlers—individuals who have retained a way of life that has somehow escaped modernity. In other representations, Appalachia is a barbaric, isolated frontier filled with uneducated, backward, and violent "hillbillies" or "white trash" whose impoverishment is a result of their deficient culture. As Scott argues (2010, p. 34), regardless of whether the stereotypes romanticize or degrade the region and people, they are all problematic because the end result is an erasure of "the heterogeneity of Appalachian life."

Over the past three decades, many Appalachian Studies scholars have worked to overturn the stereotypes imposed on the region. (See Billings, Norman, and Ledford 1999; McKinney 1977; Wilhelm 1977; Eller 2008.) For instance, Lewis (1987, 1999), Schifflett (1991), and Turner and Cabbell (1985) have revealed the long history of racial and ethnic diversity that exists in Appalachia, particularly in coal-mining areas, where thousands of immigrants and former slaves flooded the region to work in the coal mines and on the railroads. Even before the coal boom of the early 1900s, Black slaves were brought to West Virginia to labor in the Kanawha Valley salt mines (Dunaway 2003). However, as Lewis (1999, p. 38) reminds us, although the growth of industry in Central Appalachia may have brought about the most dramatic era of racial and ethnic diversity in the region, "we should not lose sight of the fact that African Americans and the racially mixed Melungeons had resided in southern Appalachia since the earliest settlement days, and Native Americans from time immemorial." (See Finger 1986 for a history of the Eastern Band of Cherokees in the region.)

Many scholars have also contested the idea that there is a distinct "Appalachian culture" or subculture (Fisher 1977; Billings 1974; McKinney 1980). In his landmark 1974 study of culture and poverty in Appalachian and non-Appalachian areas of North Carolina, Billings found that attitudinal differences among people living in these regions were very small and were more closely linked to rurality than to a distinct culture or subculture, and that the distinctiveness of an "Appalachian subculture" has been grossly overemphasized. In a similar vein, McKinney (1980) argues that the existence of a culture or heritage unique to the Appalachian Mountains is not supported by history. "While some mountain people certainly share values and lifestyles that differ from those of the vast majority of urban Americans, they are," he asserts, "little different from rural people in the rest of the South, New England, or the Midwest" (ibid., p. 200).

Whereas the Appalachian Mountains are considered to be a geological fact, the existence of the cultural and geographic place of "Appalachia" is not as incontrovertible. A large body of scholarship has argued that the Appalachian region was, in actuality, an "invention" of outside groups with various motives: travel and "local color" writers; journalists; academics; and capitalists seeking to exploit the region for its coal and timber resources (Shapiro 1977, 1978; Whisnant 1983; Batteau 1990; Anglin 1992; Wilson 1995; Billings and Blee 2000; Eller 2008). For example, as Darlene Wilson (1995) has argued, the Kentucky-born author John Fox Jr. perpetuated the idea of Appalachian otherness in a way that directly aided absentee mineral development, particularly in the bituminous coalfields of Central Appalachia.[2]

Central Appalachia's economic, political, and social structures have been strongly influenced by its historical ties to the coal industry. Arguing that Central Appalachia is an "internal colony" (Lewis and Knipe 1978; Weller 1978; Gaventa 1978), an "internal periphery" (Walls 1978), or an "energy sacrifice zone" (Fox 1999; Scott 2010; Bell 2014), many understand it to be a region where the land and much of the population[3] are exploited in order to keep the costs of energy low for the rest of the country. Appalachian stereotypes have served an important purpose in this exploitation. As the Appalachian scholar Rodger Cunningham argues (2010, p. 75), "the material-historical cause of stereotyping Appalachians is, of course, that America wants our land and our resources and must therefore persuade itself that these are not presently possessed by full-fledged human beings." Reid and Taylor (2010, pp. 45–46) support this claim, asserting that the social construction of Appalachia as "premodern" or "savage" has allowed it to serve as a "sacrificial scapegoat" for the atrocities of capitalism, normalizing devastating practices such as mountaintop-removal mining. In other words, Appalachia's status as a sacrifice zone is both a cause and a consequence of its history as an "othered" locale.

The environmental injustices that many coalfield residents are currently experiencing are just the latest within a long history of abuses that began more than 100 years ago, when much of the land in Appalachia was practically (and sometimes outright) stolen from the local people. Although American capitalists knew of the rich mineral and timber resources held within the Appalachian Mountains as early as 1740, it was not until after the Civil War and the birth of the American industrial revolution that the coal and iron deposits of the Appalachians drew large numbers of speculators into the region (Eller 1982). In the late 1800s, eager entrepreneurs from outside Appalachia poured into the mountains, procuring millions of acres of land and mineral rights at exceptionally low prices. Local residents, most of whom had been subsistence farmers up until that point (Haynes 1997), had no idea of the value of the minerals beneath their land. Many are reported to have "'voluntarily' sold [their] land for 50 cents or one dollar an acre" (Gaventa 1978, p. 144); others were duped into various unfair exchanges. For instance, an entire mountain, which in the late 1970s supplied Georgia Power with a million tons of coal per year, was reported to have been traded to a company agent for a hog rifle (Gaventa 1978). Others who refused to sell their land became victims of legal traps, such as being jailed and then offered bond in exchange for their land (ibid.).

The coal industry's control and domination of Central Appalachia has been facilitated both through the political influence of a powerful elite class (Williams 1976) and through corporate ownership of much of the land, a trend that persists even today. The Appalachian Land Ownership Task Force's 1983 study of land ownership patterns in 80 counties in Central and Southern Appalachia found that 72 percent of the 13 million acres of surface land in the study were owned by absentee landholders, and that 46 of the top 50 private owners were corporations. This pattern was found to be even more dramatic in the highest coal-producing regions of Appalachia: four of the five counties with the most corporately held land were in the coalfields of southern West Virginia, and in those counties nearly 90 percent of the land was found to be owned by corporations. A 2013 study conducted by the West Virginia Center on Budget and Policy and the American Friends Service Committee found that absentee landownership is still remarkably high in coalfield counties in West Virginia; not one of the top ten private landowners is headquartered in the state.

The high level of absentee landownership in Central Appalachia has resulted in deficiencies in tax revenue for public services, such as public education. In West Virginia, for instance, farmers and other residents pay more tax money per acre of land than do absentee owners (Rasmussen 1994). Furthermore, as "improvements" are made to the land, such as houses or other buildings, the tax rate increases (ibid.). Again, this benefits absentee landowners, most of whom do not build on or seek to improve the land but rather lease it to coal companies and timber companies for resource extraction. As Rasmussen asserts, this system "continues to shelter the wealth of the absentee and resident owners of corporate nonfarm land and encourages subversion of the process of revenue gathering" (ibid.). The state depends on land-tax revenues to fund public schools and most government services. Some estimates suggest that starting in the 1970s this tax structure has cost West Virginia's public schools more than $150 million a year (Miller 1974, cited in Rasmussen 1994).

The high rate of absentee landownership in Central Appalachia has not only reduced tax revenues but has also effectively blocked other industries from entering the region, preserving this part of Appalachia as a mono-economy for coal production. As Lewis and Knipe assert (1978, p. 19), "it is advantageous for coal mining to operate in isolation without competing companies" because the extraction process is tied to a particular location and the work is hazardous and strenuous. A recent attempt at wind development in southern West Virginia demonstrates the economic stranglehold on the region that the coal industry fights to maintain. In 2006 Appalachian Voices, an advocacy group based in Boone, North Carolina, commissioned WindLogics, a wind energy consulting firm, to explore the wind potential of Coal River Mountain in Raleigh County, West Virginia. The mountain had been approved for three adjacent mountaintop-removal mining permits that would destroy more than 6,000 acres of the mountain once the projects were completed. WindLogics (2006) modeled wind speeds of classes 4 through 7 on top of Coal River Mountain and concluded that the mountain was indeed "viable" for wind energy development. However, if the permitted mining were to take place, they noted, this wind potential would be nearly destroyed. According to a report by Downstream Strategies, LLC (Hansen et al. 2008), the number of jobs that would be generated over the long term by the construction and maintenance of a 164-turbine wind farm on Coal River Mountain would far exceed the number of jobs that would be generated by the coal companies that currently hold the mining permits for the mountain.

The 2009 legislative session in West Virginia seemed to hold promise for gaining political support for the proposed wind farm on Coal River Mountain. Forty-one sponsors and co-sponsors signed on to House Concurrent Resolution 52, a resolution in support of a permanent utility-scale wind farm on the mountain. Four of the five delegates from Raleigh County, where the mountain is located, signed on as co-sponsors of the resolution. The resolution was scheduled to be introduced in the House of Delegates on Tuesday, March 31, 2009. From the events that quickly ensued, however, it became clear that the coal industry was not willing to allow another industry to come into the area and promise new jobs. When the "Resolution in Support of Wind Power on Coal River Mountain" was about to be introduced on the House floor, House Speaker Rick Thompson did not allow the sponsors to speak to the resolution, and it was quickly shunted off to the House Rules Committee without the title even being read on the House floor. It was then killed in committee. Three days later, on April 2, a retaliatory resolution sponsored by 31 senators (and most likely written by representatives of the coal industry) was formally introduced, and fully read, on the Senate Floor. The text of Senate Resolution 50, titled "Recognizing the importance of the coal mining industry in West Virginia and requesting West Virginia's congressional delegation to support the coal industry," read as follows:

> Whereas, The Legislature works tirelessly to improve the quality of life for the citizens of the Mountain State; and
>
> Whereas, Coal mining has been, and continues to be, one of the primary industries responsible for the economic success of West Virginia and its citizens; and

Whereas, Before the national economic downturn, severance tax collections from coal were at record levels, contributing to a budget surplus at the state and county levels; and

Whereas, All 55 counties continue to receive a local share of coal severance dollars to support county, local and municipal budgets; and

Whereas, County governments and county school systems throughout the state rely on the taxes from coal companies and coal miners to fund many valuable programs, including public education, ambulance services and law enforcement; and

Whereas, Thousands of West Virginians are employed, either directly or indirectly, by the coal mining industry which generates payrolls totaling over $2 billion; and

Whereas, The loss of any of West Virginia's coal mines and the loss of any mining-related employment ultimately results in significant harm to all West Virginians; and

Whereas, Surface coal mining, including the practice of mountaintop removal, currently represents forty-two percent of the total coal production in West Virginia; and

Whereas, Engrossed Senate Bill No. 375 provides for master land use plans to be developed in all counties where surface mining takes place, with greater focus provided by the Coalfield Economic Development Office on renewable and alternative fuel sources, highways and residential areas; and

Whereas, Actions and inactions by federal regulatory agencies which have had the effect of closing surface coal mines are more frequent and result in the loss of hundreds of mining and other jobs in West Virginia; therefore, be it

Resolved by the Senate: That the Senate hereby recognizes the importance of the coal mining industry in West Virginia and requests West Virginia's congressional delegation to support the coal industry; and, be it

Further Resolved, That the Senate supports the continued mining of coal in West Virginia, including surface mining by all methods recognized by state and federal law, and is prepared to cooperate with all federal agencies in an effort to resolve quickly any outstanding issues which are preventing the mining of coal and which are contributing to the loss of jobs in West Virginia; and, be it

Further Resolved, That the Senate requests West Virginia's congressional delegation to make every effort possible to assist in securing the needed cooperation from federal agencies to allow the continuation of the mining of coal and to protect the jobs of coal miners and others who derive their employment from the coal industry; and, be it

Further Resolved, That the Clerk is hereby directed to forward a copy of this resolution to the West Virginia Coal Association and West Virginia's congressional delegation.

The resolution was passed quickly, and afterward the West Virginia Coalition on Mountaintop Mining held a celebratory press conference at the Capitol. A similar resolution was also passed in the House of Delegates. This retaliatory measure was a clear attempt by the coal industry and its supporters to assert and protect coal's dominance in West Virginia. Mountaintop-removal mining operations have since begun on Coal River Mountain.

Company Towns and Gender Ideology

As is clear from the example of the failed attempt to gain political support for a wind farm in the coalfields of southern West Virginia, power dynamics that were established and institutionalized more than a hundred years ago still strongly constrain opportunities for diversification of the Central Appalachian economy. Similarly, social structures that were institutionalized when coal was first mined in the region still affect life in the coalfields today. Because a cheap workforce was the foundation of early mining, the operators of coal mines sought to remove the Appalachian people from their land in order to "turn them into a docile workforce" (Haynes 1997, p. 49). As has already been noted, one method of removal was to trick landowners out of their property rights. Another way to ensure a cheap—and captive—workforce was the establishment of company towns.

In the late 1800s and the early 1900s, men were recruited into West Virginia by the tens of thousands to work in the booming mining industry. The population increased tremendously during this period, and hundreds of company towns and coal camps owned and controlled by the coal companies sprung up throughout Central Appalachia. In these towns, the coal companies owned the houses, the streets, the schools, the water systems, the churches, any recreational facilities, the doctor's office, and the company store, which was the only store in the town where one could buy groceries, furniture, and clothes. In addition, most coal companies paid their employees in scrip that could be redeemed only within that particular company's town (Lockard 1998). The use of scrip ensured that the miners and their families were unable to buy fundamental supplies outside the town and that the company store was able to charge monopolistic prices for its goods. The company-store system and the other company-supplied services for which miners were charged, such as tool sharpening, health care, and housing rent, provided additional avenues for the coal company to boost its profits (Cook 2000).

Also integral to maximizing profits was reinforcing the traditional gender ideology regarding the "appropriate" roles for men and women in society, i.e., men as the breadwinners and women as the caretakers of the home.

These social norms, not at all unique to Appalachia, have historically forced households in capitalist economies to subsidize production through the unpaid work of women, allowing businesses to pay laborers wages that fall far below the cost of maintaining and sustaining the household (Dunaway 2001). Through their unpaid cooking, cleaning, washing, child care, and other domestic duties, women have made it possible for capitalism to remain profitable. As Dunaway asserts (2001, p. 22), "if capitalists compensated women for all their externalized costs and unpaid labor, prices would be driven up so high that most commodities would not be competitive in the world economy." Coal towns in Central Appalachia were constructed to exploit and reinforce this gender ideology by placing men in the mines and women in the close-by homes. By intentionally "equating masculinity with a willingness to work in dangerous conditions" and femininity with "domestic labor inside coal camps," the coal industry was able to keep the costs of labor and worksite maintenance low (Maggard 1994, pp. 30 and 18). Not only has this gender ideology had implications for who has historically done what work; it has also meant that men have traditionally been favored as the center of community, work, and politics in Central Appalachia.

The Rise and Fall of the Union and Employment in the Coal Industry

The poor working conditions in the mines and the companies' exploitation of coal miners and their families were not accepted without challenge. An effort to unionize the mines began in the early 1900s and lasted more than forty years. This long struggle is a source of pride among many in the region. Older residents in southern West Virginia often recount stories of the two "Mine Wars" that took place in the state during this unionization campaign, the first in 1913 (the Paint Creek–Cabin Creek Strike), and the second in 1921 (The Battle of Blair Mountain) (Hufford 1999). These Mine Wars arose when workers demanded the right to organize, and both ended in bloodshed. In fact, after the Battle of Blair Mountain had gone on for more than a week, President Harding sent 2,500 troops and fourteen bomber planes to end the West Virginia miners' rebellion (McNeil 2005). The defeat was a tremendous blow to the union, which did not recover its strength until the passage of the National Industrial Recovery Act in 1933 as part of the New Deal (Hufford 1999).

After the coal mines were unionized, miners felt a dramatic improvement in their working conditions, including collective bargaining rights, an eight-hour work day, health and retirement benefits, and safer working conditions (Burns 2007). The union provided more than security and financial benefits, however. It also provided "a measure of power and respect both inside the mine and in the community" (McNeil 2012, p. 86). Citizens of southern West Virginia remember the period of union dominance as one of the few instances in the history of exploitation in the region when the people successfully fought the powers of oppression.

Despite the great success of the unionization movement, many of those gains have been erased since the 1980s. Multinational coal companies have taken a decidedly anti-union stance in the coalfields, causing a dramatic decline in union membership (Burns 2007). The decline in union mines has also brought a loss of the collective union identity—and the collective sense of power—that shaped the people of the region so markedly.

Along with the decline in union mines in Central Appalachia, there has been a decrease in mining employment overall. As will be described further in chapter 5, the increased mechanization of the coal industry and the advent of mountaintop-removal coal mining have drastically reduced the number of mining jobs throughout Central Appalachia, particularly in West Virginia (Burns 2007). This reduction in mining jobs has caused an exodus from the state; since 1950, West Virginia has experienced a net outmigration of 38 percent of its population (West Virginia Health Statistics Center 2013).[4] In 1948 there were 131,700 coal miners in the state; in 2010 there were only 22,599 (West Virginia Coal Association 2011). This decline represents more than a fivefold reduction in the number of mining jobs, even after controlling for the decline in the population.

As the number of mining jobs has continued to drop off, the number of jobs in the service sector has risen, calling into question the coal industry's status as the "backbone" of the state. Furthermore, the technological advances in coal extraction and processing that have led to the need for fewer workers have also led to serious environmental consequences, which have increasingly affected the health, the safety, and the livelihoods of people living in coal-mining communities. Below I briefly describe some of the most serious coal-related threats and place the current struggle for environmental justice within the history of the grassroots movement against surface mining that emerged during the late 1960s and the early 1970s in Central Appalachia. I augment this overview of the coal-related environmental problems with the stories and voices of coalfield residents I interviewed during the course of my field research.[5]

Environmental Injustice in the Central Appalachian Coalfields

The Anti-Strip-Mining Movement of the 1960s and the 1970s

Although surface mining (also called strip mining) has been used as a method of coal extraction since the early part of the twentieth century, not until World War II did technological advances make it cost effective on a large scale (Montrie 2003; Burns 2007). Until the 1980s, contour mining and auger mining were the two most common types of surface mining in Central Appalachia. In contour mining, overburden is removed and the outcrop of a coal seam is mined following the line of the mountainside. Auger mining entails drilling large holes into a coalbed with an auger to simultaneously break the coal apart and bring the broken coal up to the surface (Montrie 2003).

By the 1950s many states had passed legislation to regulate surface coal extraction; however, as strip-mining operations continued to grow, the impacts of the practice became more significant. Strip mining was causing landslides and flooding, threatening underground mining jobs, and jeopardizing agriculture as a competing land use (Montrie 2003). It became clear to many coalfield residents that the state regulatory laws were not stringent enough, and a strong grassroots effort to abolish strip mining emerged. Local people—notably farmers, homemaker mothers and wives, and underground coal miners—initiated and were at the forefront of this struggle (ibid.).

When the formal channels of lobbying and working through the courts did not prove effective, many locals turned to more militant tactics, such as "sabotaging mine machinery with explosives, illegally occupying strip-mine sites, and blocking haul roads" (Montrie 2003, p. 4). Most of this radical action took place in the mid 1960s and the early 1970s, and the movement gained momentum in multiple states. People from outside the region, including national environmental leaders, VISTA workers, and some politicians, joined the struggle to abolish surface mining. However, as the focus of the movement shifted to the federal level, many of the non-local movement participants, particularly national environmental leaders, became increasingly insistent that in order to be "realistic" the movement should abandon its efforts to ban strip mining and should instead work toward passing regulatory legislation for the practice. By the mid 1970s the "middle-class, professional representatives of organizations like the Environmental Policy Center and the Sierra Club … had convinced many strip mining opponents with deeper roots in Appalachia to lend their influence and resources" to the reformist goal of federal regulation policy, rather than abolition legislation (Montrie 2003, p. 156). With this change in focus, the vibrant radical grassroots opposition to strip mining largely dissolved. In 1977 the federal Surface Mining Control and Reclamation Act (SMCRA) was passed, but it was such a weak piece of legislation that many groups called for President Carter to veto it. Even its leading proponents have characterized SMCRA as "a great disappointment" with regard to its ability to control the ecologically destructive impacts of surface mining (ibid., p. 181).

Perhaps the most damaging outcome of this insufficient regulatory legislation was its recognition of mountaintop-removal mining as an approved technique of surface coal extraction. Though mountaintop removal was not particularly common when SMCRA was passed, technological improvements in the 1980s led to a tremendous upsurge and expansion of mountaintop-removal mining in the late 1990s and the 2000s (Montrie 2003; Burns 2007). Mountaintop-removal mining is sometimes called "strip mining on steroids." Its social and environmental impacts have far exceeded those of earlier forms of surface coal extraction.

Mountaintop-Removal Mining and Flooding

Surface mining has affected more than a million acres of land and more than 500 mountains in Central Appalachia (Geredien 2009), and the number of permits for new mines continues to increase. Mountaintop-removal mining, which is the most common—and the most destructive—type of surface mining used today, has become widespread throughout Central Appalachia since the 1990s, particularly in southern West Virginia, eastern Kentucky, and southwest Virginia. Beneath the mountains in these areas lie thin layers of low-sulfur coal, which, the coal industry argues, are too narrow to be mined by more traditional methods of underground mining. In order to reach these coal seams, mining operations remove the "overburden" by clear-cutting trees from ridges and mountaintops and then initiating a series of explosions that blast the portions of the mountains above the coal apart. Once the overburden has been removed, a dragline excavator (a huge earth-moving machine, more than twenty stories tall) scrapes the coal from the newly exposed seam, and this coal is then transported via truck or train to a preparation plant. This method of coal extraction generates a large quantity of what the Environmental Protection Agency terms "excess spoil," namely broken rock, which must be disposed of. Most often, the excess spoil is dumped in valleys that are adjacent to the surface mine, forming "valley fills" (U.S. Environmental Protection Agency 2003). According to the U.S. Environmental Protection Agency's (2005) Environmental Impact Statement on Mountaintop Mining and Valley Fills in Appalachia, mountaintop-removal mining and/or valley fills directly affected 1,200 miles of headwater streams between 1992 and 2002. Additionally, from 1985 to 2001 valley fills *buried* an estimated 724 miles of streams in Appalachia. Now the environmental damage is even more significant.

The expansion of this method of surface coal extraction in the Appalachian coalfields has coincided with considerable increases in flooding in the region. In the steep mountain terrain of southern West Virginia, eastern Kentucky, southwest Virginia, and east Tennessee, most homes have been built in valleys next to creek banks. When the mountains above these homes are deforested and flattened, there is nothing left to stop the rain from washing down the mountainsides and flooding the communities below. A study conducted by the Flood Advisory Technical Taskforce of the West Virginia Department of Environmental Protection found that "mining and timbering impacts [influenced] the study watersheds by increasing surface water runoff and the resulting stream flows," in some cases by as much as 21 percent (Flood Advisory Technical Taskforce 2002, p. 71).

Southern West Virginia communities often refer to the two "500-year floods" that they experienced within a period of ten months between 2001 and 2002 as marking the beginning of widespread and repeated flood events. The first of these floods occurred in July of 2001. The destruction "cut through a swath of southern West Virginia, about 50 miles wide and 100 miles long. ... At least 1,500 families lost their houses, and thousands more had extensive damages" (Loeb 2003). In May of 2002, just as the communities were beginning to rebuild, they were flooded again. Homes, lives, and entire communities were lost. Since 2002, there have continued to be flood events throughout the region. One resident of Boone County whom I interviewed during the summer of 2006 described recent changes he had observed in the river that runs through his community:

> Used to be years ago it would take three or four days of rain to bring this river up. You can take three or four hours of rain now, and it's like a flash flood! You don't have floods anymore, you have flash floods. It's because these mountains now, they don't have anything to hold it back. ... You don't feel comfortable anytime it starts raining real bad. When it starts rainin', you just don't know what's going to happen.

The fear many coalfield residents feel every time it rains is founded in experiences of trauma. One example is the story of Maria Gunnoe, whose family experienced a devastating flood in June of 2003 because of a mountaintop-removal coal mine behind their property. Five acres of their land washed away that night, and the raging water nearly took their house as well. As Maria described, "It was a night that I will never forget. If I live to be a hundred years old, I'll never forget that. ... I literally thought we were gonna die in this house" (Bell 2013, pp. 12-13). The experience of this flood left scars on Maria's family, particularly her children. As Maria poignantly recalled,

> June the fifteenth of 2003 was my daughter's birthday—I'll start there. We had a birthday party, she got her a bicycle for her birthday, had a real good day. The evening of her birthday, it started raining—about 4 o'clock in the evening. And it was, it was a really heavy rain. But honestly, though, we get heavy rains here in the spring—we always have. It started raining about 4 o'clock, and by 7 o'clock, the water was literally running from one hill to the other right here behind me. A stream that you could raise your foot and step over turned into a raging river in three hours' time. I've lived here my whole life, and I've never seen anything like that. ... The stream come up, and when it come up, it just kept coming up, and up, and up. It washed away about five acres of our property. I lost two access bridges, and one of my dogs was killed right up there. He was tied outside the creek and it took him, just tumbled him down the middle of all that flood. My daughter was over here at a friends' house when the flooding first started. And within 20 minutes after it started raining, I left out of here. It was raining hard—I [had to] go get my baby, you know. I wasn't gone maybe fifteen, twenty minutes, and we couldn't get back in.
>
> I threw a rain slicker over her head and threw her over my shoulder and waded the water across. ... Once we got in here, there was no way out. We was surrounded by water. ... All night long, you could hear our structures—pieces and bits of our structures that was on up the holler—you could just hear them twisting and maiming in the water. ... You can imagine the sound of five acres of land washing by you. Nothin' like that had ever taken place here ... .

> [T]he water was eating away at my sidewalk—the end of my sidewalk was standing out in mid-air. My family was in this house. ... I literally thought we were gonna die in this house. We started up the mountain, and the mountain was sliding. So you can't, you can't put your kids on a sliding mountain. ... There was no safe place to go. 911 could not get to me, I couldn't get to them. All I had to do at that point was to hit my knees right there in that sidewalk and pray to God that that water stopped. [Voice breaking] and thank God it did. Because if it wouldn't have, it would have taken the earth that my house was setting on—and me and my family in the process. (quoted on pp. 12–13 of Bell 2013)

Even though her home was flooded seven times between 2001 and 2007, Maria has refused to leave. "My family was here long before they started mining coal," she explained. "And why should we have to leave? Who in the hell are they to think that they can put us out?" (Bell 2013, p. 17). The land on which her family homeplace sits is more than just a place to live; as Maria asserted, it is "our link to who we are, and it's a link to who our children are. We can't allow it to be destroyed. As mothers of future generations of Appalachian boys and girls, we can't allow them to steal this from our children—it's too precious. And it can't be replaced" (ibid., p. 21).

However, Maria's ability to remain in her house after the flood is not a typical experience for most flood victims in the coalfields. After each new flood that ravages communities in southern West Virginia, large numbers of residents are forced to scatter to the homes of relatives and friends living in other parts of the state or even other parts of the country. Those who aren't able to take refuge in the homes of others or to salvage their own residences are relocated to post-disaster housing projects, some built on former mountaintop-removal sites. Beyond losing their homes and their belongings, many flood victims in southern West Virginia have also lost their place in a community.

Coal Waste and Water Contamination

Another major environmental problem associated with mining stems from the storage of coal waste, also called slurry or sludge. Before coal is processed, it must be cleaned in order to reduce sulfur and non-combustible materials present in the coal. The vast quantities of liquid waste generated by this cleaning process consist of "water, fine particles derived from the coal, and chemicals used in coal washing" (Orem 2006). This black chemical sludge is either stored in huge impoundments on the surface of flattened mountaintops or injected into abandoned underground coal mines (ibid.). As of 2005, there were 111 slurry impoundments in West Virginia (Coal Impoundment Location and Information System 2005). Many of these enormous black lakes are situated on mountaintops directly above small communities.

Sometimes these impoundments leak, or completely give way. The 1972 Buffalo Creek Disaster was one such instance. Buffalo Creek Hollow in Logan County, West Virginia, was home to some 5,000 people and was situated downstream of a slurry impoundment holding back 132 million gallons of coal waste. On the morning of February 26, 1972, the dam collapsed, releasing a torrent of black sludge water, which ripped through the hollow, taking with it everything in its path. One hundred twenty-five people died that day, and thousands were left homeless and forever scarred by the devastation they witnessed (Erikson 1976).

A more recent coal-slurry disaster occurred in 2000 in Martin County, Kentucky. The impoundment collapsed, spilling 250 million gallons of coal waste (twenty times the size of the *Exxon Valdez* oil spill), polluting more than seventy miles of West Virginia and Kentucky waterways, killing wildlife, destroying habitat, and contaminating homes. Although there was little coverage in the national news media, the EPA called it "one of the worst environmental disasters in the history of the Southeastern United States" (Eades 2000). As of 2000, forty-five slurry impoundments in West Virginia were considered to be at high risk for failure, and thirty-two at moderate risk (ibid.).[6]

Not all coal waste ends up in slurry impoundments. Instead, some coal operations inject the coal waste underground into abandoned coal mines. This method of "disposal" can create an entirely new set of problems, including contamination of well water and the health problems it can cause, including liver and kidney cancers, colitis, skin disorders, and organ failure (Orem 2006; Wells 2006). People living in some communities in Mingo, Boone, and Logan Counties in southern West Virginia have found their well water to be contaminated with coal slurry from nearby injection sites. Donetta Blankenship of Rawl, West Virginia, is one of the rising number of victims of coal-waste contamination. In our 2007 interview, she recounted the story of her coal-waste-induced illness:

> I started getting sick at the end of February 2005. ... I stayed nauseous, I stayed tired. My urine was changing colors. I started having problems with my eyes. ... The first week of April, I started noticing I could look at my skin and it looked a little yellow.

... I thought maybe it was the sun doing it to me. And, my husband, he kinda noticed it, even getting in my eyes. You know, the white parts of my eyes was lookin' yellow. Then on that Tuesday morning, my kids, I got them up for school, and my daughter looked at me, she said, "Mommy," she said, "What's wrong with you? You look yella." And she got Josh, my son, to look at me, and he agreed with her. And I told him, I said, "Honey, when you look yella," I said, "that means you're about to die." Me not knowing, you know, that I was about ready to ... . I wouldn't have never said anything like that to him if I thought that I was, you know? ... I ended up having to go to the hospital. ... My enzymes—liver enzymes—was up in the—it was close to 10,000. (quoted on p. 62 of Bell 2013)

A normal liver enzyme count is below 50. After a barrage of tests, it was found that the high content of heavy metals (particularly copper) present in Donetta's well water had caused her to come close to liver failure at the age of 38.

There are well-documented medical disorders that result from organic coal compounds in drinking water, most notably diseases of the kidneys and urinary tract. For instance, Balken Endemic Nephropathy (BEN) is undeniably "linked to toxic organic coal compounds from coal in drinking water supplies." It causes "end-stage renal failure," and there is a "high co-incidence of cancers of the renal pelvis or upper urinary tract" associated with this disease (Orem 2006).

Larry Brown lives just a few houses from Donetta Blankenship. At the time of our 2007 interview, he had been pastor of the Rawl Church of God in Christ for almost thirty years. After decades of drinking, cooking with, and bathing in water that he and his family believed was safe, Larry learned that the well that provided water to his house and to his church was contaminated with coal waste. As he recounted:

I really didn't know the full extent—how bad it was. I mean, we'd seen it in our commodes and in our bathtubs and stuff like that, and we wrote it off for years as iron. We wrote it off as iron—that's what we was always told. ... The health department down here in Mingo County come and tested [my] well ... . And the tests, they come back, but he never did give me a report, said it come back with a little bit of iron in it and that was all. That was what I was told. So, we felt there was a cover-up from the beginning on a lot of people's water and wells.

Subsequent tests revealed that Larry's water contained toxic levels of a variety of metals, including arsenic, beryllium, aluminum, copper, manganese, and zinc. He and his wife—and others in the community—had been ingesting this unsafe water for many years, and they were fearful that their health might be compromised because of it.

Jack Spadaro, formerly a top safety trainer for the Mine Safety and Health Administration, argues that the method of cleaning coal that generates a need for slurry impoundments and slurry injections is not necessary, but that the coal industry uses the method because it "saves a dollar a ton in processing." Furthermore, he asserts, "there are other technologies, such as dry filter press systems. Coal impoundments are not at all necessary. There's been technology around since the 1960s … . It would only cost about a dollar a ton more. … Overall the industry simply doesn't give a damn about the people or the environment in this region [of the country]. And I can say that with authority" (Stockman 2006, pp. 6–7).

Researchers have found that, in comparison with the rest of the United States, people living in coal-mining areas of Appalachia suffer higher rates of hospitalization for certain respiratory and cardiovascular conditions, as well as higher rates of mortality, birth defects, cancer, and chronic illnesses, even after controlling for such variables as income and education (Hendryx, Ahern, and Nurkiewicz 2007; Hendryx 2008; Ahern et al. 2011; Hendryx et al. 2012; Hendryx and Ahern 2008; Ahern and Hendryx 2008). It is clear that Appalachian coal communities have a number of unique problems that are tied to the physical environment of this area. Hendryx (2008, p. 9) speculates that "the environmental health impacts of the coal mining industry may operate through water and air transport routes." In addition to coal slurry, another likely source of the region's environmental health problems is coal dust.

Coal Dust and Air Pollution

In certain towns in southern West Virginia, there are no white houses. Though some houses may have been painted white at one time or another, they will have very quickly turned gray. Coal dust doesn't stay inside the mines. At all stages of the mining and preparation process, coal dust is generated, and it often coats nearby towns.

The town of Sylvester in Boone County, West Virginia, is one of the best-known examples of coal dust air pollution in Appalachia. In the late 1990s, the Elk Run Coal Company, a subsidiary of Massey Energy (now Alpha Natural Resources), built a coal-preparation plant adjacent to Sylvester. Since then, coal from mines throughout the area has been belt-lined into the plant, where it is cleaned and then crushed into a fine powder. It is then shipped to coal-fired power plants throughout the region. Ever since the preparation plant was built, the residents of Sylvester have suffered. According to the late Pauline Canterberry, who lived in the town for many years,

> Sylvester was a wonderful place to live up until Massey Energy decided to put in a [coal] preparation plant. They already had a facility over there—an underground [mine]. They cut the bluff off [which was between the mine and the town of Sylvester] and put the processing plant right on top of the ridge where they had cut off the hillside—right in the direct airflow of the town. ... Just as soon as they got it finished and it started into operation, which was in April of 1998, it *instantly* began to cover the town in coal dust. Within one month we were completely covered. It was horrible. ... You couldn't do nothing outside, you couldn't have cook-outs outside, you [couldn't] hang your clothes outside when you wash[ed] them. ... Your filter from your air conditioners and your furnaces are full of it. You have to change them every two weeks or a month—constantly. They're full of coal dust. So that means we're breathing it constantly. (quoted on pp. 28–29 of Bell 2013)

Chuck Nelson, a former resident of Sylvester, described experiencing coal dust problems similar to Pauline's:

> When I'd get home [from work], after my wife had cleaned house, ... I could see [coal] dust, probably a half inch, three quarters of an inch thick, sitting on the kitchen table.

In 2001, 154 residents of Sylvester—more than 75 percent of the town's population (Burns 2007)—filed a lawsuit against Elk Run Coal, the subsidiary of Massey Energy whose operations were responsible for the air pollution. According to Chuck Nelson, the community tried to work out a settlement with the coal company, but "they didn't want to do that. They acted like we wasn't anybody." In response, the citizens began gathering evidence, recording videos of the dust clouds above the community, collecting daily dust samples from windowsills, bird feeders, and cars, and saving dust-filled filters from their air conditioners. In 2003 Elk Run Coal was found guilty of most of the charges filed against it. The company was required to pay damages and court fees and to implement a number of measures for containing coal dust. However, these measures were not sufficient. As Pauline Canterberry and Mary Miller told me (and showed me) during our interviews in 2006 and 2007, they were still fighting a daily battle with coal dust.

One thing that was especially infuriating to Sylvester residents about the coal-dust problem was that the preparation plant could have been built in a way that would have protected the town. As Pauline explained,

We found out through the trial that for ten million dollars, they could have made this perfectly safe over here for us. The technology is available—this could have all been in silos, it could have been covered, it could have been belt-lined with enclosed beltlines, but they chose not to do it. One of their engineers said on the stand [in court], he said, "Well, if we did that, we wouldn't have drawed any bonus." (quoted on p. 38 of Bell 2013)

Pauline believed that there was an even deeper reason, beyond the cost, for cutting corners: "I think that all this was done intentionally in order to drive us out of here." She continued:

Before that preparation plant was over there, there was a mountain bluff that came down that ridge, clear to the river. Their facility was back in that hollow—all of it. When they put the preparation plant in, they come down, they cut the ridge off, flattened it off, and that's where they put the preparation plant. We found out that preparation plant was supposed to have been three hundred feet farther back up that hollow. Because [if it had been] back up that hollow, when [the dust] come up, that mountain would have caught it. It would have landed on the mountain instead of coming in the airflow over the town. (quoted on p. 38 of Bell 2013)

She added:

If they had done what they should've done, we wouldn't have had this problem here. That's the part that makes me really furious, that they really didn't have to do this. But the further I got into this, the further I studied it, [I saw that] what was done to us was done intentionally. Yes, I firmly believe that it was done intentionally. ... I found out that the two mountains behind this area over here, Massey Energy has the mineral rights to them. So, they had to find a way to get over [Sylvester] and get that coal. ... I think they thought we were a group of elderly people here and we wouldn't put up any fight, and they would just run over top of us and they would get their way. (quoted in Bell 2013; p. 38)

Many other coalfield residents have also argued that the coal industry's historical position of privilege in West Virginia provides a measure of impunity for industry-related actions, allowing it to engage in highly destructive mining practices that jeopardize the health, safety, and livelihoods of many residents in coalfield communities. Further, Pauline Canterberry is not alone in her contention that the coal industry uses its power to manipulate local people in its attempts to acquire access to coal deposits. As Chuck Nelson asserted in our 2007 interview, "If they had their way, they'd depopulate the whole river and do as they please. That's *exactly* what they want."

The Movement for Environmental Justice in Central Appalachia

Owing to the seriousness of the environmental problems caused by mountaintop-removal mining since the late 1990s, there has been a resurgence in grassroots mobilization against the environmental and public-health problems caused by the coal industry. Coal River Mountain Watch, the Ohio Valley Environmental Coalition, Kentuckians For The Commonwealth, the Sludge Safety Project, Appalachian Voices, and the more recently formed college movement Mountain Justice are just a few of the organizations that have been engaging in resistance, education, and direct action against certain mining practices. Staging non-violent protests, generating publications, lobbying the legislature, filing lawsuits, blocking new mountaintop-removal mining permits, and working with filmmakers and journalists to expose the devastation coal has caused to the environment and rural communities are a few of the strategies these organizations have used in their attempts to hold the coal industry accountable.

This more recent coalfield movement is connected to, but also distinct from, the earlier resistance movement against surface mining in Appalachia. A few of the same organizations, such as Save Our Cumberland Mountains (now known as Statewide Organizing for Community eMpowerment), were involved in the struggles against strip mining that occurred in the 1960s and the 1970s. However, many newer organizations, such as Coal River Mountain Watch, Ohio Valley Environmental Coalition, and Appalachian Voices, have emerged or joined the movement against irresponsible mining practices within the past two decades. This more recent movement against surface mining in Appalachia is decidedly framed in environmental justice terms and concepts.

Environmental justice movements are distinct from mainstream environmental movements in their attention to social justice. Instead of focusing primarily on nature conservation or preservation efforts, environmental justice movements seek social justice for people who live, work, play, and learn in the most polluted environments in the world (Cole and Foster 2001). Since the first environmental justice movements began to form in the United States in the early 1980s, a tremendous body of empirical research has found that people of color, low-income communities, and people living in the global South are disproportionately burdened with environmental hazards and pollutants (Bullard 1990, 1996; Bullard et al. 2007; Čapek 1993; Pellow 2004, 2007; Faber 2008; Taylor 2014). The coal-related environmental injustices in Central Appalachia, including water contamination, air pollution, flooding, and poor health, are experienced by people living in some of the most impoverished counties in the nation. In the year 2000, the Appalachian Regional Commission classified more than 75 percent of Appalachian coal counties as "economically distressed" (Appalachian Voices 2007). The region also suffers poor educational outcomes—in the eight top coal-producing counties in Kentucky, for instance, the rate of high school completion stands at only 66.7 percent, compared with a rate of 80.3 percent in Kentucky overall, and 84.6 percent nationally (U.S. Census Bureau 2010).

With the increase in coal-related water contamination, flooding, and environmental-health problems in recent years, this latest coalfield movement argues that the coal industry has sacrificed the health and safety of local residents for cheap energy. Like many other environmental justice movements, the current struggle for coalfield justice was initiated in large part by local women fighting to protect their families from toxic substances, flooding, air pollution, and other dangers associated with mountaintop-removal coal mining and coal processing (Bell 2013). Patty Sebok, Maria Gunnoe, Debbie Jarrell, Maria Lambert, Teri Blanton, Lorelei Scarboro, Donna Branham, Donetta Blankenship, Joan Linville, Mary Miller, the late Judy Bonds, the late Pauline Canterberry, and many other Appalachian women have been at the forefront of this movement, speaking out against the injustices the coal industry has brought to their lives and communities. These individuals' leadership in the Central Appalachian environmental justice movement is just one chapter within a long history of women's social protest and activism in the region, however (ibid.). Despite the stereotypes marking Appalachian women as passive, ignorant, and tied to the home, they have led the charge for many social justice causes, such as health care rights, environmental protection, black lung benefits, welfare, unionization, and employment rights (Norris and Cyprès 1996; Cable 1992, 1993; Seitz 1995, 1998; Maggard 1987, 1990, 1999; Hall 1986; Scott 1995; Giesen 1995; Weiss 1993). Appalachian women's repertoires of resistance have ranged from subtle "dissenting practices" within the workplace (Anglin 2002) to collective action and even violence, as was the case during the 1973 Brookside Coal Strike in Harlan County, Kentucky, when coal miners' wives used switches to whip strikebreakers attempting to cross the picket line (Maggard 1987).

Like the anti-strip-mining movement of the 1960s and the 1970s, the recent movement for environmental justice in Central Appalachia was started by local residents of coal-mining communities. However, despite the growing impacts of mountaintop removal and other coal-industry practices, recruiting *new* local participants into the environmental justice movement (as I noted in the introduction) has proved to be an ongoing challenge. While there are some very strong local voices at the forefront of the struggle, relatively few of the citizens in the affected population have chosen to participate in the environmental justice movement, despite extensive organizing efforts in the region. Particularly in recent years, environmental justice organizations have increasingly been forced to recruit constituents from outside Central Appalachia, from non-coal-mining areas, and even from non-Appalachian states. While the numbers of "non-local" recruits to this social movement have increased steadily, mobilization among local people has continued to be difficult. Given the enormity of the coal industry's negative effects on local communities and the increasing political opportunities—in the form of large-scale unemployment, diversification of local economies, and increasing media attention from recent mine disasters and climate change—why are there such low levels of movement participation at the local level? The remainder of this book seeks to answer this question.

I Identifying the Barriers to Participation

2 Micro-Level Processes and Participation in Social Movements

In *Power and Powerlessness: Quiescence and Rebellion in an Appalachian Valley* (1980), John Gaventa examines the history of non-action in Central Appalachia to uncover why, "in the face of massive inequalities," many oppressed communities do not revolt and fight for change. Gaventa argues that in the case of Central Appalachia, and among other dominated groups, "power works to develop and maintain the quiescence of the powerless" because "together, patterns of power and powerlessness can keep issues from arising, grievances from being voiced, and interests from being recognized" (ibid., pp. vi–vii). Although Gaventa's study examines the macro question of why social movements often fail to emerge in the presence of injustice, whereas this book is focused on the micro question of why individuals often choose not to join social movements that have already emerged, Gaventa's findings are still quite relevant to the present study. Gaventa argues that the historical quiescence of Central Appalachia is "a function of power relationships, such that power serves for the development and maintenance of the quiescence of the non-elite" (ibid., p. 4). These power relationships have been repeated and manifested throughout history so that grassroots challenges to the great inequalities many Appalachian residents face have been obstructed, time after time, by the authority and control surrounding and protecting those who benefit from the inequalities. This pattern of defeat has created and reinforced a sense of powerlessness among many in the population, often misinterpreted by outsiders as the "fatalism of the traditional culture" (ibid., p. 254). Gaventa argues that the cumulative experiences of defeat, occurring and recurring throughout history, have taught many in Central Appalachia to anticipate future failure. Thus, the powerful in this region are able to maintain their power precisely because the powerless have learned to remain silent. In other words, "powerlessness serves to re-enforce powerlessness" (ibid., p. 256).

Gaventa's analysis describes power as a macro-level phenomenon that is wielded to suppress rebellion. However, the individual decision to participate in the activities of a social movement is not simply a macro process. As McAdam asserts (1988a, p. 127), "movements may occur in a broad macro context, but their actual development clearly depends on a series of more specific dynamics operating at the micro level." The decision to participate in a social movement is one made by *individual* persons who are situated within a broad political-economic context. Thus, it is necessary to understand both the macro and micro levels operating to facilitate or suppress participation in social movements, as well as the "intermediate theoretical 'bridges'" that connect the two (ibid.).

Gamson (1992) suggests that there are four "central problematics" in the social psychology of micro-level collective action: solidarity, identity, consciousness, and micromobilization. *Solidarity processes* refers to how would-be participants connect with and maintain commitment to the carriers of a social movement (ibid., p. 61). *Identity* functions alongside solidarity such that, before an individual becomes an active participant in a social movement, that individual's personal identity must correspond, or align, with the movement's collective identity (Snow and McAdam 2000). Would-be participants in a social movement must also experience a subjective *transformation in consciousness* that provides the moral impetus moving an individual to take action. Finally, *micromobilization contexts* (McAdam 1988a) provide the settings in which the social-psychological processes of solidarity building, identity correspondence, and consciousness transformation actually take place.

In the literature on social movements, these four processes continually arise as important micro-level issues shaping participation in movements. In the following sections, I synthesize the theoretical and empirical work on these four factors and tie each of the micro processes to the Central Appalachian case. Is the low level of local participation in the coalfield justice movement a problem of solidarity? Of identity? Of consciousness transformation? Of micromobilization contexts? I argue that it is a problem of all four.

Solidarity and Social Capital

As was noted above, *solidarity processes* are the means through which would-be participants connect with and maintain commitment to the carriers of a social movement (Gamson 1992, p. 61). In the absence of a bond with other participants in a social movement, an individual is not likely to become involved in protest activities, even if she or he identifies with the values and aims of the movement. Empirical findings reveal that "the presence of a network tie to someone already engaged in a movement is one of the strongest predictors of individual participation" (Schussman and Soule 2005). For example, McAdam (1988b) found that in the 1964 Mississippi Freedom Summer campaign the existence of pre-existing friendships with other volunteers was the single most significant factor predicting participation in the movement. In addition to interpersonal ties (such as friendship or kinship networks), organizational memberships have been found to be important network factors influencing recruitment into a social movement (McAdam and Paulsen 1993). As Gamson argues (1992, p. 61), the importance of pre-existing social relationships and organizational networks to movement recruitment is so well supported in the literature that it has "become part of our shared knowledge" within social-movement theory.

Why are network ties so important to solidarity and to movement participation more generally? In their examination of the factors that prompt individuals to participate in activities of a social movement, Schussman and Soule (2005) found that having been "asked to protest" was the most significant motive for an individual's movement involvement. It follows that the individuals who are most likely to be "asked to protest" are also those who have network ties to participants in a social movement, either through interpersonal relationships or through organizational memberships. Beyond simply being asked, however, it is likely that *trust* in the people who are doing the asking, as well as *social norms*, or values, encouraging participation, are also among the mechanisms facilitating solidarity with and involvement in a social movement. As McAdam argues (1988b, p. 64), the fact that the students who participated in the Freedom Summer campaign had strong pre-existing social ties to other volunteers was probably why they did not drop out of the movement, as they would have faced "considerable social disapproval for withdrawal."

The three concepts of networks, social norms, and trust are also the major dimensions of *social capital* (Coleman 1988; Putnam 1995; Silverman 2004), a notion that is important to understanding solidarity. Social capital can be thought of as the level of connectedness within a group and the shared resources that emanate from the collectivity.[1] I suggest that an understanding of the intersections and interactions of these three dimensions of social capital (networks, trust, and social norms), and of how they function within communities and groups, may be vital to understanding why social capital and solidarity more generally are so important to individual participation in social movements. It is not simply a matter of whether individuals have network connections with participants in a social movement; it is also the *quality* of those relationships that influences participation. Would-be participants must trust those whom they know in the movement, and they must also share the social norms, or values, espoused by the movement's participants.

Moreover, the types of social capital that are present, and the balance among them, probably influence the potential for collective action. Szreter and Woolcock (2004) argue that there are three types of social capital: bonding, bridging, and linking. *Bonding* social capital is characterized by "thick trust" (Lancee 2010) and cooperation among individuals in a network who share a similar social location, identity, values, or history. *Bridging* social capital denotes cross-cutting network connections among demographically heterogeneous individuals (ibid.; Narayan 1999; Putnam 2000). Whereas both bonding and bridging social capital are experienced among people with similar levels of power and status, *linking* social capital crosses vertical power differentials (Szreter and Woolcock 2004). In other words, linking social capital denotes ties to institutions or people with political influence and authority (Dahal and Adkikari 2008).

All three types of social capital are important for collective action efforts (Dahal and Adhikari 2008; Megyesi, Kelemen, and Schermer 2011). However, it is bonding social capital that has the greatest influence on individual-level participation in social movements, for, as Morrow (2013) argues, bonding social capital is akin to solidarity. Although it is important to note that too much bonding social capital can also have negative effects on collective action by hampering individual choice (Portes 1998; Leonard 2004), in its absence it is highly unlikely that individuals will trust each other enough to take action against a social injustice.

Collective Identity and Identity Correspondence

McAdam and Paulsen (1993) add another dimension to our understanding of the importance of solidarity and social capital through their reexamination of McAdam's (1986, 1988b) research on the Freedom Summer campaign. In that earlier work, McAdam found that a strong pre-existing tie to another Freedom Summer volunteer was the best predictor of participation in this high-risk activism. Through additional analyses that incorporated participants' expressed identification with a particular reference group or community, McAdam and Paulsen (1993, p. 659) found that it was not simply organizational embeddedness or strong ties to another activist that were predictive of involvement in Freedom Summer. Rather, it was the combination of having strong ties to another activist and a "strong subjective identification with a particular identity," such as "teacher" or "civil rights supporter," that led to participation in the movement. This finding has implications for participation in social movements generally, suggesting that it is the *interaction* of solidarity and identity that is important, not simply the presence of one or the other. Gamson (1992, p. 57) also acknowledges the importance of examining the micro-level phenomena of solidarity and identity together, arguing that solidarity functions alongside collective identity to "blur the distinction between individual and group interest" such that individuals within that group feel that a threat to the group is also a threat to them personally.

Collective identity can be defined as "a shared sense of 'one-ness' or 'we-ness'" among individuals who compose a collectivity (Snow and McAdam 2000, p. 42). A large body of social-movement scholarship has pointed to the centrality of identity in shaping individual participation in movement activities (Friedman and McAdam 1992; Polletta and Jasper 2001; Stryker, Owens, and White 2000). It is now widely accepted that before an individual becomes an active participant in a social movement, the individual's personal identity must harmonize with the movement's collective identity (Snow and McAdam 2000). People decide to participate in a social movement "because doing so accords with who they are" (Polletta and Jasper 2001, p. 284) and they feel a shared cultural connection with other activists in the movement. Snow and McAdam (2000) theorize the process whereby a movement's adherents experience this "identity correspondence" between their personal identities and the movement's collective identity. They argue that this occurs mainly through two processes: "identity convergence" and "identity construction." In identity convergence, an individual's personal identity is already aligned with a movement's collective identity so that participating in the movement feels like a natural action (ibid.). However, there are many participants whose personal identities have not always been compatible with the collective identities of the social movements in which they are involved. In these cases, "identity construction" is necessary. For an individual falling into this category, some event or circumstance triggers a change in personal identity to help it become aligned with the collective identity of the movement (ibid.). Experiencing identity correspondence, especially in cases where identity construction is necessary, is facilitated within the context of a network, whether it is a formal organization or an informal network of friends or family members.

Transformation in Consciousness (Cognitive Liberation)

In addition to solidarity building and identity correspondence, there is a third micro-level process that is integral to an individual's decision to become a participant in collective action: a subjective transformation in consciousness wherein the individual recognizes and acknowledges the injustices taking place and comes to believe that something can be done to end those injustices (McAdam 1982, 1988a; Gamson 1992). Radical Brazilian educator Paulo Freire termed this change in awareness and efficacy "concientização," which has been translated as "conscientization" or "critical consciousness."

When individuals undergo the process of conscientization, they learn "to perceive social, political, and economic contradictions, and to take action against the oppressive elements of reality" (Freire 1970 [2000], p. 35). According to Freire, in order to overcome situations of oppression, people must first "critically recognize" the causes of oppression (ibid., p. 47), and they must also overcome the perception that it is impossible to conquer the circumstances standing in the way of freedom. Through the process of conscientization, individuals move from viewing the circumstances as "insurmountable barriers" to recognizing that that the conditions they are experiencing *can* be changed. Once this realization has occurred, individuals may move from passive acceptance of injustice to direct action that is oriented toward change (ibid., p. 99).

Within the sociological literature, McAdam (1982, 1988a) and Gamson (1992) also recognize that a transformation in consciousness is a necessary step toward deciding to participate in social protest. McAdam (1982, 1988a) terms this transformation process "cognitive liberation."[2] He describes it as a "crucial attribution process" (1988a, p. 132) wherein members of the aggrieved population adopt three "cognitions" articulated by Piven and Cloward (1977, pp. 3–4): (1) People stop seeing "the system" as legitimate and begin to believe that the power structures are unjust. (2) People lose their fatalism by moving from believing that the existing power structure and institutional arrangements are unavoidable to demanding change. (3) People come to experience a "new sense of efficacy," progressing from feeling helpless to believing that they have the power to initiate change.

Cognitive Liberation and Ideology

Cognitive liberation is not a simple process, for there are many forces that actively work to maintain the status quo. As Gamson asserts (1992, p. 65), "any change in consciousness involves an uphill symbolic struggle since every regime has some legitimating frame that provides the citizenry with a reason to be quiescent." Critical traditions, from feminism to Marxism, have revealed how those in power actively construct and manipulate ideology to confound the nature of social relations and the causes of oppression in an effort to maintain their power. As the Italian political theorist Antonio Gramsci argued (1971 [2010]), dominant groups retain their hegemony by securing, and actively retaining, the consent of the masses. This process is an active endeavor wherein the power elite integrates values and beliefs held by dominated groups into the public face of its worldview. This ideology is then disseminated through various "hegemonic apparatuses," such as schools, churches, political parties, and the mass media, thereby allowing the dominance to "remain conveniently invisible ... 'naturalized'" as "custom" and "habit" (Eagleton 1994, p. 198). Opposition to the hegemonic order becomes increasingly difficult, for "would-be challengers face the problem of overcoming a definition of the situation that they themselves may take as part of the natural order" (Gamson 1992, p. 68). Thus, attaining cognitive liberation (McAdam 1982), or conscientization (Freire

1970), is particularly difficult because ideology works to mystify the structural causes of injustice.

Micromobilization Contexts

Despite the varied ways by which power holders attempt to thwart cognitive liberation among the groups they dominate, there *are* many people throughout the world who have been able to see beyond the ideologies woven by their oppressors. An important insight into conscientization articulated by Freire (1970 [2000]) is that this process happens through dialectical exchange within a group setting. Critical discourse and reflection allow people to discover, together, that they are "in a situation." Through these group realizations, they are able to "*emerge* from their *submersion* and acquire the ability to *intervene* in reality" (ibid., p. 109).

Similarly, McAdam and Paulsen (1993) argue that group settings are critical precursors to social-movement participation. They contend that these "recruitment contexts" provide the space and opportunity for the necessary intersection of identity and microstructure (networks) among would-be participants in a movement. Social interactions are the spaces in which involvement in contentious activity arises, for humans "live in deeply relational worlds. If social construction occurs, it happens socially, not in isolated recesses of individual minds" (McAdam, Tarrow, and Tilly 2001, p. 131). McAdam (1988a) refers to the small-group settings and interactions that facilitate the social-psychological processes necessary for recruitment as "micromobilization contexts." I also choose to use this term throughout the book (instead of "recruitment contexts") to convey the possibility that some events and interactions that mobilize participants are not solely recruiting efforts on the part of social-movement organizers.

Micromobilization contexts can take a variety of forms: political groups (e.g., unions), groups that are ostensibly non-political (e.g., churches), and informal friendship or kinship networks. According to McAdam (1988a), micromobilization contexts encourage participation in social movements in a number of ways. First, they provide the "rudiments of organization," such as leaders and communication technologies. In other words, micromobilization contexts "provide the established roles and lines of interaction necessary for action to unfold" (ibid., p. 135). They also offer "solidary incentives," which can be defined as the various interpersonal rewards individuals experience when they are involved in any established organization or informal group. These solidary incentives counteract the "free rider problem" (Olson 1965)—that is, the difficulty of recruiting individuals to participate in the activities of a movement when they would reap the benefits without participating. Solidary incentives can be quite effective, for, as Meyer articulates (2007, p. 52), "the sense of stepping into history as a force, in conjunction with people who share your beliefs, is a powerful motivator."

Micromobilization contexts also provide the social settings in which the social-psychological processes of solidarity building, identity correspondence, and cognitive liberation actually take place (McAdam 1988a). Without a social setting, it is very difficult for these group processes to occur. In the case of cognitive liberation, for instance, this process is "both more likely and of far greater consequence under conditions of strong rather than weak social integration" (ibid., p. 50). When citizens are isolated, they are far more likely to see their problems as personal issues rather than attributing them to the system (Ferree and Miller 1985). Furthermore, social integration has been shown to positively influence feelings of efficacy (Neal and Seeman 1964; Pinard 1971). Thus, social bonds with others in a community are important structural resources for overcoming deeply entrenched (and continually reinforced) beliefs that change is not possible.

In the chapters that follow, I present a series of studies enacted in the coal-mining region of Central Appalachia to examine potential barriers to the four "central problematics" of micromobilization outlined above. I first turn to the challenge of solidarity building in coal-mining communities.

3 Depletion of Social Capital in Coalfield Communities[1]

As was discussed in chapter 2, bonding social capital—characterized by deep social trust, close network ties, and shared social norms—is akin to solidarity, the first of the necessary micro-level components influencing participation in social movements. If a high level of bonding social capital in a community translates to high levels of solidarity among the residents, it follows that a depletion in bonding social capital could pose a barrier to participation in social movements by indicating a deficit in local social networks and trust—factors that are integral to the process of building solidarity. In this chapter, I explore whether a depletion of social capital—and bonding social capital in particular—in Appalachian coal-mining communities may be one reason for the low levels of local involvement in the Central Appalachian environmental justice movement.

Past research (Onyx and Bullen 2000; Pena and Lindo-Fuentes 1998) suggests that rural areas have a greater accumulation of social capital than urban and suburban areas. However, West Virginia appears to be an anomalous case, as it is the second most rural state in the United States (U.S. Census Bureau 2000a) but, according to Putnam (2000), it has the eighth lowest level of social capital in the nation. This chapter examines the causes of West Virginia's deficits in social capital relative to other rural areas and theorizes connections between coal extraction and low social capital (low bonding social capital in particular).

Part of my job in the early 2000s at Cabin Creek Health Center in southern West Virginia was coordinating the West Virginia Rural Health Education Partnerships program for Kanawha County. This was a statewide initiative created to provide rural clinical rotations in underserved areas of the state for West Virginia-trained health professions students, and to develop service-learning opportunities to address health-education needs in the communities where the students were placed. As this was a statewide program with thirteen different consortia, I was required to attend meetings, retreats, and events all over West Virginia. Through my position, I became very familiar with most of the state's fifty-five counties and observed a number of regional differences among the rural communities in which I spent time.

One of the greatest differences I noticed was between rural coal-mining communities in southern West Virginia (including the community in which I worked) and rural communities in other parts of the state. Although coal is mined in most of West Virginia's counties, the coal counties in the southern part of the state are often referred to as the "billion dollar coalfields." Here coal dominates life in a way that it does not in the rest of the state. In these communities, people seemed less open and more mistrustful of me as an outsider. I noticed that they had far fewer community organizations and community gathering places. And they didn't seem to have the same level of community cohesiveness as the rural towns in the northern part of the state. At the time, I had not yet begun studying sociology and didn't have a name for what I was observing, but it was a qualitative difference that I felt deeply. Once I was exposed to social-capital theory in graduate school, I wondered if perhaps this concept had something to do with the differences that I had noticed. Did the communities in the southern coalfields of West Virginia have lower levels of social capital than the communities in the northern part of the state? Were these deficits responsible for West Virginia's overall low social-capital ranking? Was the coal industry responsible in some way for depleting the supply of social capital in coal-mining communities? For if there were a depletion of social capital in coal-mining communities—and bonding social capital in particular—then I might have one piece of the puzzle explaining the low numbers of local residents participating in the environmental justice movement.

Studying Social Capital in West Virginia

Most of the research on social capital employs quantitative methods to measure its components. The usual pattern is to conduct statistical analyses on various pieces of data, such as survey responses, membership records, church attendance rosters, and rates of voter turnout. Though some studies—for example, those of Silverman and Patterson (2004), DeSena

(2004), and Smallacombe (2006)—have employed qualitative methods to describe social-capital processes, very few studies have utilized these methods to *measure* social capital. Despite the preference for quantitative methods among social-capital researchers, I decided to design a qualitative study, because I felt that qualitative data would best capture the actual experience of social capital within a community. The multi-dimensional character of social capital seemed to lend itself to interviews in particular, as respondents would have the opportunity to describe what, for example, they believed trusting their neighbors actually meant. One respondent might interpret trust to indicate feeling secure that her neighbor would not try to break into her house, whereas another respondent might interpret trust to mean feeling safe leaving her children with a neighbor for an extended period of time.

Not only does qualitative research provide the opportunity for a more comprehensive picture of individuals' experiences of social capital; it also gives the researcher an opportunity to decipher the *mechanism* by which social capital differs, grows, or declines. It wasn't enough to simply study whether social capital was greater in non-coal-mining communities than in coal-mining communities. I wanted to understand *why*.

During the summer of 2006, I conducted forty semi-structured face-to-face interviews with randomly selected residents of two rural towns in West Virginia, one a coal-mining community and the other a demographically similar non-coal-mining community. My interviews focused on the various components of social capital, including trust, networks, and the social norms of reciprocity, civic engagement, and cooperation. In my analysis, I sought to compare respondents' experiences of social capital within and between these two towns.

Selecting the Study Sites

The selection of the two comparison communities required careful consideration. My criteria for selection were as follows:

- One community should be located in Boone County, the foremost coal-producing county in 2006 (the year of the study), and the other in a non-coal-producing county.
- Both communities should meet the census definition of "rural": 2,500 residents or fewer.

- The communities should have comparable poverty rates, unemployment rates, and rates of educational attainment.
- Each of the communities should be dependent on a major industry.
- Both communities should be incorporated towns, so that census data would be readily available.

Whereas the Boone County community was a simple choice, as it was the best fit for the requirements outlined above, it took a great deal of searching to find a suitable comparison town. Forty-three of West Virginia's fifty-five counties have mineable coal reserves (West Virginia Office of Miners' Health, Safety, and Training 2012[2003]), so more than three fourths of the counties were ineligible from the start. The other major challenge was finding a county that was dependent on another major industry, as there are very few industries in West Virginia that dominate entire communities as coal does.[2]

Hardy County, a rural county in the Eastern Panhandle of West Virginia, is the only county with the aforementioned characteristics. It has no coal operations (or mineable coal reserves) and is dependent on another industry: poultry raising and manufacturing.

I selected a rural town in Hardy County and one in Boone County on the basis of the criteria listed above. I assigned pseudonyms both to the people I interviewed and to the two towns from which I recruited my respondents. "Coalville" is my pseudonym for the coal-mining town in Boone County; "Farmstead" is the pseudonym I use for the non-coal-mining town in Hardy County. As can be seen from table 3.1, at the time of the study both of these towns had very low rates of unemployment (4 percent in Coalville, 2 percent in Farmstead), and they had similar rates of family poverty (23 percent in Coalville, 20 percent in Farmstead), similar rates of high school completion (63 percent in Coalville, 69 percent in Farmstead), and similar median family incomes ($31,500 in Coalville, $28,919 in Farmstead), according to the 2000 census (U.S. Census Bureau 2000b,c).[3] Furthermore, the populations of both counties were more than 90 percent white (Boone 99 percent, Hardy 91 percent).

One striking difference between the two towns that is not reflected in the comparative demographics but that is still very important has to do with their histories of labor organizing. Whereas Coalville has a long and deep history of unionization in the mines, the poultry industry in Farmstead has remained non-unionized. Farmstead residents expressed a belief

Table 3.1
Demographic comparison of Coalville (in Boone County) and Farmstead (in Hardy County).

	Coalville	Farmstead
Census designation	Rural	Rural
Major industry	Coal	Poultry
Population density per square mile	1,244.7	1,457.2
Housing density per square mile	828.2	732.0
Median age	45.0	39.0
Unemployment rate	4.0%	2.0%
Median household income (1999)	$19,250	$24,178
Median family income (1999)	$31,500	$28,919
Per capita income	$13,217	$15,704
Percent of families below poverty line	23.1	19.8
Percent of individuals below poverty line	29.9	21.4
Percent white	99.23	91.4
Percent with high school diploma or higher degree	62.9	69.3
Percent with bachelor's or higher degree	4.8	7.5

Sources of data: U.S. Census Bureau 2000b.c; Workforce West Virginia 2005

that the region was not "culturally" amenable to unionization because of its farming roots. Farming is viewed as an inherently independent profession, very different from the social values of teamwork and "brotherhood" present in the coal mines. But although Farmstead did not benefit from the social-capital-building activities of a strong union in its community, other voluntary organizations (among them the American Legion, the Moose Club, a Veterans of Foreign Wars post, a Committee on Aging, Habitat for Humanity, a bowling league, Little League, a volunteer fire department, and various churches) seem to have filled that role. Coalville had far fewer formal organizations. The only voluntary organizations in the town, aside from churches, were a non-profit grassroots environmental justice organization, a food pantry, a Little League, and a volunteer fire department. Furthermore, although Coalville's history is deeply tied to the United Mine Workers of America (UMWA), at the time of my research there were no union mines remaining in the area and the union hall was boarded up.

I conducted forty face-to-face interviews with randomly selected individuals, twenty in each town. (For a full description of my data-collection methods, including how I used aerial photographs of the towns to obtain a random sample of residents, see appendix A.)

Social Capital as a Lived Community Experience

It was obvious even before I began transcribing and analyzing my interviews that there was a fundamental difference between Farmstead and Coalville with regard to the residents' experiences of "community," and particularly in their levels of social trust. The reception that I (an outsider) received was indicative of this stark difference.

My first interviews took place in Farmstead, the non-coal town. As this was the first door-to-door interview project I had conducted, I was unpracticed and awkward during my first few introductions, not yet sure how to ask a stranger if I could take an hour of that person's time to ask questions about the community. Despite my inexperience, I had a refusal rate of only 23 percent. In Coalville, I had a refusal rate of nearly 40 percent, even though by the time I arrived in the community I had conducted more than twenty interviews and was much more practiced in the art of figuratively sticking my foot in the door and convincing someone that talking to me for an hour or more would be an excellent use of time.

From the beginning, I felt an overwhelming level of mistrust in Coalville. My field notes from my first day in the town (August 3, 2006) indicate feelings of "outsiderness" that were not felt nearly as strongly in Farmstead: "I'm totally conspicuous in every way, as was apparent to me from the moment I ventured outside. My Oregon license plates, even the way I talk—I just don't blend in. And that seems to mean more down here than up in [Farmstead]." Indeed, in order to persuade many of the Coalville interview recruits to speak with me, I had to quickly find a way to "mention" that for five years I had worked "just over the mountain" at a clinic built by the UMWA in the 1970s. In a number of cases, this tenuous connection to a nearby community with a shared history seemed to be the only reason I was granted an interview. However, in many cases this connection was not enough. I had two doors literally closed in my face mid-sentence, and two other refusals happened through the glass of storm doors that were never even opened when the residents spoke to me. None of the refusals I experienced in Farmstead were as harsh as those I encountered in Coalville. At another house with a car parked out front, I was unable to even get to the door to request an interview—a locked chain-link fence surrounded the entire house, and there was a "No Trespassing" sign nailed beside the front door.

Though my experience as an "outsider" in Coalville does not necessarily indicate a lack of bonding social capital between and among residents of the community, aspects of the built environment that I observed *do* seem to indicate a deficiency in the "deep trust" between neighbors that is characteristic of bonding social capital. The number of residents with functional fences in Coalville astounded me (and by "functional" I mean nondecorative; they were usually chain-link fences that surrounded the entire house and had a latching, and sometimes a locking, gate). There were only a handful of functional fences in Farmstead, and most of these were for keeping pets in the back yard. I interpreted Coalville's functional fences as a sign of mistrust and individualism among local residents—characteristics contrary to social capital.

The behaviors of the residents in these two towns also seemed to indicate a qualitative difference in "communityness." In Farmstead there were people out walking, people sitting on their porches, and people working in their gardens. In Coalville I noticed far fewer people on the streets, in their yards, or on their porches. The interviews I conducted in the two communities corroborate my initial observations quite dramatically. Interviewees in Farmstead described a close-knit rural community high in social trust—one in which neighbors exchanged favors regularly and helped one another in times of difficulty. Coalville residents' descriptions of their town, by contrast, painted a picture of a mistrustful community in which neighbors were disconnected from one another and residents were alienated from a sense of "community." Below, to illustrate this difference, I provide a series of excerpts from interviews conducted in Farmstead and Coalville that are representative of the general sentiments within each town. These excerpts are organized into three themes: social trust, interaction with neighbors, and community support of residents in times of difficulty.

As was noted above, Farmstead residents described their experiences of community in ways that suggest a high level of social trust. People indicated that they felt safe and secure, trusting the honesty and integrity of others in their community. Consider the examples that follow, which are drawn from multiple interviews.

SB:

Do you feel like most people trust each other here in your neighborhood?

Bonnie:

Yeah. This is a very nice area—I leave the door open all the time. And I'm not afraid at night by myself or anything like that. Yeah, it's very nice out here.

***

SB:

Do you feel like most people in [Farmstead] trust each other?

William:

Yeah, yeah I do. ... When I leave the house, I never lock my doors. ... I have three cars sitting out here all the time with keys sitting in [them]. I never take the keys out of [them]. So, if I can do that for ten or fifteen years, I feel pretty safe and pretty secure and so forth. I just don't think anybody's going to do anything.

***

SB:

Do you feel safe being outside at night in [Farmstead]?

Mary:

I'm not afraid of the night. In case anything would happen, any of my neighbors I could call on. I mean, I feel more secure living here with it being that way.

The responses of individuals from Coalville differed greatly, as the following examples show.

***

SB:

Do people trust each other in [Coalville]?

Ricky:

Nah, no, people don't.

SB:

What do you see that makes you say that?

Ricky:

It's what you don't see—people out, people talkin', people on the streets. People's in behind their doors guardin' their stuff. They're afraid to leave their homes.

***

SB:

Do you feel safe going outside at night in Coalville?

Robin:

I don't go out unless I go to church. And then they pick me up, and I go and come back here quickly.

SB:

Do you lock your doors?

Robin:

Oh yeah. My doors are locked, I have my gun, all this gun stuff.

***

Ruth:

I won't go out [at night]. Sometimes [my daughter] wants to go sit on the porch at night. I told her that no, I was afraid to because in [the cities], they talk about on the news people shooting people that's out, you know, out in the sides, and they go by and shoot them. I told her they might go by and take a shot at us.

Robin and Ruth from Coalville and Bonnie and Mary from Farmstead are widowed or divorced women above the age of 50 who live alone. This parallel social position makes their differing perceptions of safety in their respective towns all the more telling. Social trust appears to be a strong theme in the Farmstead interviews, whereas social fear appears to characterize Coalville for many residents.

Interaction with neighbors is another aspect of community life that differs dramatically between Coalville and Farmstead. As the following excerpts from the interviews exemplify, residents of Farmstead reported not only knowing their neighbors, but also exchanging favors with them regularly and feeling like a welcome and important part of the neighborhood.

Amber:

You can't go five minutes here without knowing [your neighbors'] names! Because as soon as you move in, they welcome you.

***

Ron:

Since we've moved here, [our neighbors] have done all kinds of things for us.

Liz (Ron's wife):

[They] sent deli trays, fresh rolls, and—that was in July—and then at Christmas, these other neighbors apologized that they didn't get to see us [when we moved here], but they sent this huge basket at Christmastime with all kinds of wine and food and towels—just really nice.

***

SB:

Have any of your neighbors done any favors for you in the past month or two?

Bonnie:

[laughs] Oh, every day! … Oh, they feed me to death. Like I said, I leave the door open, and there's always somebody popping in and out, and if you need anything, all you have to do is call or holler. It's nice.

Residents of Coalville, however, had very different responses to similar questions about their interactions with their neighbors:

Robin:

I've been here three months—there's been no neighbors to see me or nothin' here. … This isn't the town they'll do that. They just don't do it.

***

Ruth:

People used to, they would help each other out, you know, help hoe their fields out. Nowadays nobody don't help each other, I don't know why.

***

SB:

Do you know your neighbors here?

Gloria:

No, not really

SB:

Do your neighbors do any favors for you or have you done any favors for your neighbors that you can think of?

Gloria:

No.

SB:

When you moved here, did anybody come to welcome you to the community?

Gloria:

Not really.

SB:

In the past few years, can you think of a time when people in the community came together to help someone out who was going through a tough time?

Gloria:

No, huh-uh.

SB:

That doesn't really happen very much?

Gloria:

Not here.

The interview excerpts from Farmstead and Coalville illustrate the differences between neighborhood interactions in the two towns. Upon their relocation into a new neighborhood, residents of Farmstead described being made to feel a part of the community through their neighbors' active outreach and welcoming. On the other hand, new or relocated residents of Coalville were left alone, effectively relegating them to an isolated position within the neighborhood. In Farmstead, neighbors exchanged favors regularly, nurturing a strong social norm of reciprocity; in Coalville, neighbors were alienated from one another, independent individuals residing in the same geographic location but not interacting as members of a connected community.

In the last thematic comparison I will make between Farmstead and Coalville, respondents articulated their knowledge of and experiences with their community's level of support for residents going through difficult times. Farmstead residents exhibited high levels of faith in the community support system, speaking proudly of the ways in which residents took care of one another.

Beulah:

If you have a need, and they find it out in [Farmstead] that you have that need, it's taken care of by the community—not by an individual. An individual may start it, or might say, 'Let's go over and help [Beulah],' or 'Let's do this' or 'Let's do that for so-and-so,' but you don't need it in this town if they find out that you have a need—it's taken care of.

***

Harriet:

You just don't think about doing things for people—it's just something that you do. And you don't mark it down on your calendar that you've done it. And you don't think about the fact that you've done it. It's just if someone needs help, you help them. ... I'm on a list to take people to get their chemo or radiation, that sort of stuff. Again, you just do it. ... If it's needed, you just try to pitch in and help.

A few weeks before our interview, the daughter of Ron and Liz's neighbor died, and Ron and Liz marveled at the community's expression of care and support after this sad event.

Liz:

They came in droves with food, and, I mean, she had barely been taken out of the house when there were cars *everywhere*, and it wasn't just family. It was friends, church people, neighbors. And for a solid week, they came everyday with food—it was unbelievable. And everybody jumped in with, you know, helping with the yard work ...

Ron:

And it's important to make the point that it wasn't like a tragic accident. She had been sick for years and years and years and years, so even though she was young and passed away, it wasn't unexpected to happen in the last few years.

Whereas in Farmstead the experience of Ron and Liz's neighbors was one of community support and care during their time of loss and mourning, the experience of a Coalville resident named Sandy after her son died can best be described as alienating and hurtful. More than ten years before our interview, Sandy's 19-year-old son died in a car accident in front of the junior high school. Sandy attributed her family's withdrawal from community activities to his death and the lack of community support during her family's grieving. When asked whether anyone in the community had ever helped her through a difficult time, she responded "Nobody's ever came here." The interview continued as follows.

SB:

Not even when your son died?

Sandy:

No. I remember calling the pastor of the [Coalville] Church at that time, because I didn't know who else to call—because we weren't going to a specific church, but my kids had gone to Sunday School there and went to Bible School there. I was just devastated, and I was trying to talk to him. And he said, "Well, you know, things like this happen." And he said, "I'll be sure to make sure the church prays for you." I thought he would come and see us or something. ... I just felt that that was so cruel. ... A lot of our friends that we had during that time sort of have shied away from us now. They don't know what to say. ... Nobody came to our house except for the friends of my son ... and my family. So I was just trying to find some reasoning for it.

Like Sandy, Elsie (another resident of Coalville) experienced isolation and alienation in a time of need.

Elsie:

I lived here six years by myself. My husband had left. And there wasn't nobody offered me no help. ... All they done was stop me and ask me questions. They didn't want to know how I was—they just wanted to know where *he* was. Just being nosey. People I didn't even know, really.

Farmstead and Coalville respondents consistently answered interview questions and recounted stories in ways that reveal a qualitative difference in residents' experiences of "community" in the two towns. Farmstead residents described being able to count on their neighbors for assistance when they needed it and felt a high level of generalized social trust[4]; residents of Coalville seemed to have the opposite experience in their daily interactions (or lack thereof) with others.

Measuring Social Capital

The differences between Farmstead and Coalville appear to be dramatic; however, in order to simultaneously compare multiple indicators of bonding social capital between and within the two towns, a more comprehensive method was needed. I generated a Social Capital Index (SCI) for that purpose.[5]

The SCI is made up of nine components, which are based both on intended measurements from the literature on social capital and on indicators of bonding social capital that emerged from the interviews. Individuals could be assigned a score of –1, 0, or 1 for each of the nine components. An individual's overall SCI value is the sum of the nine scores, the lowest possible score being –9 and the highest being 9. (For a description of the nine components and what aspects of social capital they measure, see table A.1 in appendix A.)

In order to determine the range of values that indicated various levels of social capital (such as high, moderate, and low), I re-examined the interview transcripts, looking for descriptions and stories demonstrating a shared experience of social capital among respondents. In other words, I was looking for a High Social Capital "type" that was qualitatively different from a Moderate Social Capital "type," and so forth. Through this coding process, I found that my interview subjects exhibited four distinct levels of social capital. I labeled those levels High, Moderate, Low, and Very Low. Next, I examined the SCI values of the respondents in each of those four categories to determine what range of values corresponded to each category.

The SCI values of the respondents in each of the categories fell within the following ranges: High Social Capital = score from 5 to 9; Moderate Social Capital = score from 1 to 4; Low Social Capital = score from –4 to 0; Very Low Social Capital = score of –5 or lower. (Although I have collapsed the SCI values into these categories for interpretive purposes, the statistical analyses are based on the continuous numerical SCI value). I describe the four category "types" in the subsection that follows.

High Social Capital

Respondents falling into the High Social Capital range felt that there were a variety of people in their community they could call on in times of trouble or just for a simple favor. Most of these individuals used phrases such as "close-knit" and "like a family" to describe their town. They also described feeling safe in their town, and some even stated that they felt so safe that they did not lock the doors to their houses or cars. When asked about the benefits they had received from their relationships in the town, subjects offered responses similar to the below reply (from a Farmstead respondent named Nancy):

> Security. Knowing that if you're in trouble you can call any number of organizations or a relative or a neighbor. And, just not having to worry about going out in the street. ... You can walk up and down the street at night and not worry about being jumped at or something like that.

These individuals were also able to provide many examples of favor exchange with their neighbors. For instance, Ann and her husband Skip spoke of a neighbor who regularly checks on their house, waters their flowers, and brings in their mail when they are on vacation. Another neighbor who is away from his home during the day regularly invites Ann and Skip to "hop in [his] pool any time!"—even when he isn't home.

Moderate Social Capital

Individuals experiencing moderate levels of social capital described moderate to high feelings of trust and safety within their communities, and most reported engaging in favor exchange with neighbors. Most of these individuals also described receiving benefits from their relationships with others in the community, such as Amber, who told me: "Being close to people and having my connections [has meant that] they trust me with their children, so [I have gotten] job opportunities" as a day-care provider. The major difference between those experiencing moderate social capital and those experiencing high social capital was in network connections, both formal and informal. Respondents with moderate social capital were less likely to be involved in volunteering or formal organizations, such as a church or a chapter of the Lions Club, and they had fewer locals in their "most important people" network.

Low Social Capital

Individuals falling in the Low Social Capital range experienced low levels of trust in the community and had few formal and informal network connections within the town. However, they were not living in complete isolation from others in their community. For example, Robin, who spoke of her extreme mistrust of neighbors and other community members, was a member of a church outside the community but engaged in some volunteering within Coalville through her church. And Pepe, who had no formal network connections and was not engaged in the community of Farmstead as a whole, exchanged favors with neighbors regularly and had no desire to live anywhere else.

Very Low Social Capital

The Very Low Social Capital range is best described as isolated. People who were asked about the organizations in their community or the events that took place in the town typically responded as Bob did, who admitted, "I don't know what does go on," or like Gloria, who said, "I really don't go out much; I go to work, I come home—that's it." Respondents with very low social capital described having little if any interaction with their neighbors or others in the town, were mistrustful of others living there, and had few or no formal network ties to organizations within the town. Most of the people in their "most important people" network lived outside of the community. These respondents did not engage in any community improvement activities or volunteering, and a number of them spoke of being let down by the community when they were going through a difficult time. Notably, almost all the individuals falling into this category expressed a desire to be elsewhere, such as Elsie, who stated, "I would love to be out of [Coalville]. It's depressing," or Sandy who expressed, "When we do have a weekend off, we leave here. We have a camp in Summers County. So we go there. We don't stay here." These individuals were merely residing in their towns; they weren't members of their communities.

Social Capital in Farmstead and Coalville

An examination of the distribution of respondents in Coalville and Farmstead on the basis of their experiences of social capital reveals some stark differences. Eighteen (90 percent) of the twenty Farmstead residents experienced moderate or high levels of social capital, while only nine (45 percent) of the twenty Coalville residents experienced moderate or high levels of social capital. (See table A.2 in appendix A for the detailed distribution, including residents' ages.) Strikingly, more than half of the Coalville residents experienced low or very low levels of social capital, versus only two in Farmstead. Fisher's Exact Test (using the continuous SCI value) reveals that the difference between the distribution of interviewees' experiences of social capital within the two towns is statistically significant at the 0.05 level. Thus, it is apparent that there is a difference in the experiences of social capital in Farmstead and Coalville. But what is the mechanism?

Clues to the Mechanism

Hints of the possible mechanisms by which Coalville residents differ so substantially from Farmstead residents in their experiences of social capital emerged during the coding process. In the following quotations from Coalville residents, I italicize these clues:

"[Coalville] was good, good town *at one time*. Nice clean little town. Everybody knew everybody, and everybody helped everybody." —Vincent

"I set on the porch a lot, but you don't see very many people *anymore*. ... People just don't socialize *like they used to*." —Elsie

"Ain't no bond. There ain't no bond in town *like there used to be*." —Ricky

These quotations, and others like them, point to a temporal matter: Things changed in Coalville. But what changed, when did the change occur, and why did it happen?

Loss of Population

Part of the story of change in Coalville undoubtedly relates to the long-term effects of the out-migration that had been taking place in West Virginia, particularly in the southern coalfield counties, over the preceding fifty years. West Virginia's net out-migration from 1950 to 2000 was 40 percent, and Boone County has seen negative migration in all decades since 1950 except the 1970s. Cumulatively, Boone County lost 20,193 people to out-migration from 1950 to 2000 (West Virginia Health Statistics Center 2002). This loss in population was due primarily to increased mechanization in the coal mines and the advent of mountaintop-removal coal mining, which has continued to reduce the number of mining jobs throughout the state (Burns 2007). As fewer and fewer jobs have been available in the coal mines, large numbers of young adults have left West Virginia, and especially the southern counties, to find work. This is evidenced in the high median ages for this region. The median age of Boone County residents in 2000, for instance, was 45 years.

Bluestone and Harrison's 1982 study of the effects of deindustrialization on communities offers important insight into the social and economic consequences of dramatic job losses. While the experience of West Virginia is one of mechanization and not deindustrialization, the common outcome of considerable job loss makes these two processes analogous. In the case of deindustrialization, Bluestone and Harrison argue (ibid, p. 67), "what begins as a behind-closed-doors company decision to shut down a particular production facility ends up affecting literally everyone in town, including the butcher, the baker, and the candlestick maker," because the job losses ripple throughout the entire community. Two Coalville respondents described a loss of businesses and services in a similar manner:

> [Coalville] had a stroke just like I did. Well, look at it. All the stores are closed. When I left here in 1989 and moved to Florida, when I resigned as mayor, this town was a-boomin'. We had clothing stores, we had two or three grocery stores, we had five or six restaurants. Now we's lucky to have one of each. —Charles

> We had grocery stores, we had little department stores, we had places for the young kids to go. We have none of it now. Actually, I think we have a flower shop and a carpet store and one restaurant in [Coalville]. And the funeral home [laughs]. That's it."—Tina

Without a doubt, out-migration has had a tremendous impact on the social networks of Coalville residents. This is apparent when one compares the "most important people" networks of Coalville and Farmstead respondents. While Farmstead respondents reported, on average, 5.5 Farmstead residents in their lists of closest friends and family, Coalville interviewees reported, on average, only 2.8 Coalville residents. Furthermore, while only two (10 percent) of the Coalville residents reported membership in a non-religious organization, seven (35 percent) of the Farmstead residents reported membership in at least one formal non-religious organization.

Coalville's population losses have ostensibly led to a disruption of social relations in the town, most likely contributing to a reduction in bonding social capital. However, the loss in population is not the entire story. Social networks are only one aspect of social capital; the breakdown in social trust and social norms in Coalville still requires additional explanation. When I asked respondents about the change they described—the change from a close-knit community where "everybody knew everybody, and everybody helped everybody" to a place where "there ain't no bond" between residents—they didn't point to population loss, which had been a phenomenon occurring in Coalville for more than fifty years. Instead, they shared stories of a particular event in the history of the community: the entry into the area of the A.T. Massey Coal Company (which became Massey Energy and is now Alpha Natural Resources).

"We're Union People"

In 1981 the non-union A. T. Massey Coal Company moved into the heavily unionized Coalville region, opening a non-union mine at what I will call

Division Creek, which is three miles outside of Coalville. In the years that followed, Massey Energy bought out a number of union mines in the area, dismantling the union character of the region. A number of respondents blamed the "change" in the community on Massey. "I believe that if there was no conflict with Massey that things would be pretty much like they used to be," a Coalville resident named Robin told me. "[Massey] came in, everything did change. ... [Massey] come in and start buying all the mines and all the stuff. That did present the big problems. And that's when the conflicts started among the people."

Massey's entry into the community was not met peacefully. Vincent, who was police chief at the time, recalled the "Battle of [Division Creek]," in which 2,000 union miners picketed the newly opened Massey facility:

> If you spoke for Massey, people'd get mad. ... Massey [the owner and CEO at the time] told them when they marched down there on them and burned them out. ... He said, 'I'll own every lump of coal in Boone County and there won't be a union mine in Boone County.' And he kept his word. ... Yeah, [the union strikers] done a number down there. They set the trailers on fire, turned them over—hurt several employees coming out of there in their vehicles. ... One guy got shot down there and he got killed—a security guard.

Sandy, the wife of a Massey coal miner, was also present when the violence erupted. Members of her family found themselves the brunt of some of this community-wide anger:

> Massey's not accepted around here. I was here when it first came to [the area]. ... You still have the union core here which believes it's union or nothing. ... When [my husband] first started workin' up at Massey, we were in constant fear. That was in '81 or '83. Massey opened up [Division Creek] Coal, and he had to go across the bridge every day. They flattened his tires. ... The people that marched on the bridge—the union pickets. And they broke things on the road in front of our house. They called us scabs when we went anywhere. My Avon lady quit comin' to me because she couldn't associate with scabs. It was real bad. My kids were afraid. They broke windows out of his truck. It was really, really bad.

The emergence of such descriptions as a shared narrative among interview respondents points to the union/non-union conflict that ensued when Massey entered the Coalville region as a significant event in the story of this community's ability to access social capital. The history of the unionization movement in the region is central to understanding why this is the case. As has already been noted, the people of this area of West Virginia have a deeply rooted identity as "Union People," having fought for many years to unionize the coal mines. The union provided more than security and financial benefits, however. As McNeil notes (2012, p. 86), it also provided "a measure of power and respect both inside the mine and in the community." These residents remember the period of union dominance as one of the few times in the history of exploitation in southern West Virginia that the people successfully fought the powers of oppression. When Massey Energy came into the Coalville region in 1981 and began to buy out all the union mines in the area, it signaled the end of an era of power for the residents.

The community did not give up without a fight—a fight that caused a bitter conflict within the community between the "union loyalists" who refused to work for a Massey coal mine and those who chose to abandon their shared identity as UMWA members to go to work in the Massey mine in order to provide for their families. Is it possible that the effects of this conflict linger today in the form of depleted social capital?

The Cohort Effect

Examining respondents' ages reveals an interesting difference between Coalville and Farmstead. In Coalville, experiences of social capital appear to depend on age. Most respondents experiencing high or moderate levels of social capital were older than 70 at the time of the study, whereas most respondents experiencing low or very low social capital were 60 or younger. However, this pattern was not replicated in Farmstead. (See table A.3 in appendix A for the disaggregated Coalville and Farmstead results by years of birth.)

Dividing the Coalville results into those born before 1940 and those born after 1940 reveals that experiences of social capital differ by birth cohort. Most of the respondents in the older birth cohort had experiences of moderate and high social capital, while most of those in the younger birth cohort had experiences of low or very low social capital.

The Significance of the Cohorts

Individuals from Coalville born before 1940 share three important characteristics:

• When the Division Creek conflict arose, they would have been working for at least twenty years. Thus, if they or their spouses were or had been union coal miners (as was the case for most), they had met the minimum service requirements to receive the UMWA pension and health-care benefits at retirement, or they were already drawing their retirement benefits.

• In 1981, half of the individuals in this cohort were either already retired or within five years of retirement age. (One can begin drawing benefits from the union at age 55.)

• None of the respondents in this cohort had young children (16 or younger) at home in 1981.

This cohort, which I label the Union Cohort, does not seem to have experienced the same depleted social capital as the rest of the population. They were, in effect, buffered from the conflict, and were able to retain an experience of social capital that is more typical of other rural towns (such as Farmstead).

It appears that those who were in the prime of their working careers (that is, in their twenties or their thirties) during the conflict of 1981 exhibited markedly diminished abilities to access social capital relative to members of the older birth cohort. During the conflict, these were the individuals who had the most to lose when Massey bought out the union mine: they had not yet reached their 20 years of service with the union, they had small children at home, and they were 20 or more years away from retirement. I label this cohort the Conflict Cohort because it was the group most affected by the struggle against Massey.

While Coalville's population losses caused a disruption to the social networks of residents in this community, the Massey conflict caused a breakdown in social trust and shared norms, particularly the norm of reciprocity. These findings are clearly evident in individual components of the Social Capital Index. Sixty-three percent of respondents in the Union Cohort expressed trusting others in the community, whereas only 33 percent of respondents in the younger cohorts expressed a general social trust. Furthermore, though only 33 percent of younger residents talked of favor exchange with neighbors, 75 percent of those in the Union Cohort provided examples of giving and receiving assistance and favors with their neighbors and others in the community. Thus, although everyone in the community, regardless of age cohort, experienced the after-effects of outmigration and the resulting depopulation of the community, those in the Union Cohort did not suffer the aftershocks of the Massey conflict with the same intensity as those in the Conflict Cohort and younger cohorts. The breakdown in social trust and norms of reciprocity in the younger cohorts has meant that their access to social capital has been differentially affected relative to the older residents.

This disparity in access to social capital based on cohort indicates that a community's store of social capital may not be equally accessible to everyone. Events that take place, such as a deep conflict, may negatively affect certain individuals' ability to access social capital in the community, while those not as involved in the conflict are able to continue accessing the store. If that is the case, there are others who should have been buffered from the conflict: those who were not yet born or who were too young to work in 1981, and those who lived elsewhere and thus were not yet members of the Coalville community. Annette, Gloria, and Amy (who were not yet born or were too young to work in 1981), and Ruth (who moved to Coalville in 1994) should have also been buffered from the conflict. As such, they should have also exhibited the higher levels of social capital typical of the older age cohort. However, only one of these residents did. With the exception of Amy, those who became members of the Coalville community after the conflict (either by being in a younger age cohort or by moving there) exhibited lower levels of social capital than those who were born before 1940. Thus, there appears to be a "residual effect" of reduced access to social capital in other groups of people who, in theory, should have been shielded from the conflict: those who were born after 1964 and those who moved to Coalville after the conflict.

Summary and Interpretation of Results

Those who were in the prime of their working careers during the conflict (members of the Conflict Cohort) appear to have experienced a marked decrease in their ability to access, and contribute to, social capital. Those who were in the Union Cohort (born before 1940) seem to have been able to retain a higher level of access to social capital than others in the Coalville community. Additionally, there appears to be a "residual effect" of reduced access to social capital in other groups of people who, in theory, should have been shielded from the conflict: those who were born after 1964 and those who moved to the community after the conflict. Fisher's Exact test of significance confirms this model at the 0.005 level.

These findings suggest that conflicts disrupting certain individuals' access to social capital may have effects that reach beyond the individuals involved in the conflict. A community's store of social capital may remain unavailable even to those who become members of the community after the conflict is over. The Farmstead data support this finding. Table A.3 in appendix A reveals that in Farmstead the age of residents does not predict levels of social capital as it does in Coalville. (Fisher's Exact Test confirms that the differences in age are not statistically significant.)

Conclusion

The concept of Community Anomie introduced by Bluestone and Harrison (1982) may be useful for understanding the loss of bonding social capital in Coalville after the union/non-union conflict of 1981. Bluestone and Harrison found that residents of towns that underwent plant closures suffered more than job losses; they also experienced damage to the "social psyche," wherein the consequences of the closures went far beyond the expected emotional responses of frustration or anger. According to Bluestone and Harrison, individuals "lose faith in the 'system,' leading to a kind of dependency that precludes redevelopment of their communities." Victims feel a sense of overwhelming defeat: "'We put thirty years into building this mill and this community, and it has all come to naught. I can't see that I've the energy to start all over again.'" (ibid., p. 79) Similar disillusionment and hopelessness could be heard in the voices of Coalville residents in their descriptions of their own community:

> You could sit around and see it going down. You could just watch it. You knowed it wasn't going to get any better. It's not never going to get better, I don't think. —Bob

> Well, they've just let the town go down. The buildings up there in town is all dirty on the front. You can't see in the windows, they're so dirty. It just seems like they don't care or something. —Ruth

> There's no heart in this town. It's all about gettin' that coal up and down this road. ... Ain't no pride. Place is dirty, ain't nobody doin' anything about it. —Ricky

The tearing away of the ability of these "Union People" to work for a union mine in their community meant a loss of identity and a breakdown in the community's social trust and social norms. The union served to unite Coalville's residents around a common identity. Once that was taken away, many residents were thrown into a state of community anomie and withdrew from the collective, allowing Coalville to degenerate from a town with a vibrant and caring community life to a town in which residents feel disconnected and alienated from any sort of collective. The continued trend in population loss undoubtedly aggravated this decline. Residents' descriptions of the town reveal the tragedy of this depletion in social capital:

SB:

If you had to describe [Coalville] to someone who had never been here before, how would you describe it?

Ricky:

Dead. ... Dying. Dirty, I don't know. ... Neglected—that's the word.

***

SB:

What's good about living in [Coalville]?

Gloria:

Really nothin'. ... There's nothing up here. It's dead.

***

Elsie:

It's a dead town ... a dead place. I wouldn't advise no one to move into this area.

The transformation of survival in Coalville from the survival of "us" to the survival of "me" exemplifies the difference between union work and non-union work in the coal mines. The forced change in work life may have also affected the social system, re-socializing the community (including those in future generations) from a "we" mentality to an "I" mentality, thus diminishing the store of bonding social capital and the level of solidarity felt among the residents of the town.

This study indicates that Coalville's experience of lost bonding social capital is, in part, due to the ripping away of its union identity and the conflict that this created within the community. The case of Coalville is not an isolated incident; non-union companies have been buying out union companies throughout the coal-mining region of Central Appalachia since the 1980s. The resulting loss of social capital in Coalville, and probably in other coalfield towns, has done more than make certain communities less pleasant to live in. It has also given the coal industry a tremendous amount of power to mine coal in the cheapest and most destructive ways, without a strong social control to keep the industry in check. If people do not feel a sense of solidarity with others in their community, and if they are lacking social networks and organizational connections, they may be less equipped to collectively fight the injustices that this powerful industry imposes upon Appalachia. And perhaps most important, if residents do not trust one another, they aren't likely to feel secure enough to initiate action, for, as Ostrom and Ahn argue (2009, p. 22), "trust is the core link between social capital and collective action."

4 Identity and Participation in the Environmental Justice Movement[1]

with Yvonne A. Braun[2]

Although it is critical to micromobilization, the choice to participate in a social movement is not only tied to whether a person experiences solidarity with members of that movement. Solidarity functions alongside and interacts with another micro-level factor—identity—to influence social-movement participation. A necessary step toward becoming involved in a social movement is the process of identity correspondence, wherein an individual's personal identity becomes aligned with the collective identity of the movement (Snow and McAdam 2000). It follows, then, that if something is blocking the process of identity correspondence in a segment of the coalfield population, there will be lower rates of movement involvement among the members of that group.

The numbers of local women and men who are involved in the Central Appalachian environmental justice movement are quite imbalanced; far more coalfield women have joined the struggle for justice in the region than men. This chapter presents the findings of a study that examines the reasons why there are such differing rates of participation in the movement. Specifically, we[3] investigate whether the deficit in local coalfield men's participation could be tied to difficulties they face in achieving identity correspondence between their personal identities and the collective identity of the environmental justice movement.

The Gendering of Environmental Justice Activism

As has already been noted, the environmental justice movement in Central Appalachia began in the early 1990s and was started in large part by white working-class women fighting to protect their families from water contamination, flooding, air pollution, and other dangers associated with the increasing impacts of mountaintop-removal coal mining and processing (Bell 2013). The women-driven character of the movement in Central Appalachia is not atypical among environmental justice movements. Although women have been found to have lower rates of participation in the mainstream environmental movement than men (Brown and Ferguson 1995; Mohai 1992), a large body of scholarship has found that women "are heavily represented in both the leadership and the membership" of grassroots environmental justice organizations, representing up to 70 percent of the activists in local and state groups (Brown and Ferguson 1995, pp. 148-150; Kaplan 1997; Naples 1998).

In this chapter, we examine the ways in which activism in the Central Appalachian environmental justice movement is gendered,[4] focusing on how men's and women's identities both shape and constrain their activism. Specifically, we ask whether the process of identity correspondence may be more difficult for Central Appalachian men to achieve than it is for women. We explore the ways in which women and men differentially experience the region's complicated relationship with coal—as both polluter and source of pride and identity—and how these gendered relationships shape participation in the environmental justice movement. Our findings suggest that an examination of the influence of hegemonic masculinity in the coalfield region, and the coal industry's role in maintaining the gender order, may be central to understanding why there are so few men involved in environmental justice activism.

Motherhood, Masculinity, and the Gendering of Environmental Justice Activism

Across environmental justice struggles, scholars have found that activist women often describe their motivations and justifications for action as being closely tied to their obligations as mothers or grandmothers (Krauss 1993; Brown and Ferguson 1995; Culley and Angelique 2003; Peeples and DeLuca 2006; Bell 2013; Roberts and Toffolon-Weiss 2001; Braun 2008). For instance, in their study of the environmental justice movement that rose up in response to the Three Mile Island nuclear disaster, Culley and Angelique (2003, p. 454) found that "motherhood as an identity and catalyst for action outweighed any ways in which gender was perceived as a barrier" to activism in the movement. Likewise, Krauss (1993, p. 247) observed that, among the African American, Native American, and white working-class environmental justice activist women she interviewed, motherhood was felt to be "a resource for their resistance." Epstein (1995) suggests that the tendency among many activist women to link their advocacy work to motherhood is connected to the societal pressures that women feel to place their family caretaking roles above all else. Furthermore, drawing on a motherhood identity may even be a strategic choice in some cases; as Shriver, Adams, and Einwohner (2013) note, motherhood can provide women activists with a shield from scrutiny in the wider community, as women acting on behalf of their children are less likely to be considered activists.

While gendered identities—particularly motherhood identities—have shaped and facilitated many women's environmental justice advocacy work, there is evidence that masculine identities have historically stymied men's participation in grassroots environmental justice movements. According to Rome (2006, p. 456), men's lack of grassroots environmental activism can be traced back to the early 1900s, when a "gendered divide" emerged between professional environmental reformers and grassroots environmental activists. Though environmental issues were historically considered the responsibility of women, who were considered to be the "municipal housekeepers," alliances between men and women in environmental-reform coalitions were quite common in the late 1800s. However, this cross-gender cooperation changed with the shift in gender politics that took place between the late 1890s and the early 1910s. During that period, a "masculinity crisis" emerged in response to the significant cultural changes taking place, including the demand for women's suffrage, women's push to enter male-dominated professions, and the closing of the frontier (Rome 2006).

Faced with these threats to Victorian manhood, many men attempted to reclaim their masculine identities by demonstrating "macho" qualities, such as playing football, boxing, and "war-mongering" (Rome 2006, p. 448). Environmental-reformer men also aggressively sought to quash any possible charges of "effeminacy" by distancing themselves from women environmental advocates, both through rhetorical strategies that framed environmental protection using more "masculine" justifications, such as worker productivity and economic benefits, and by explicitly excluding women from environmental and professional organizations (ibid., p. 450).

As is suggested by the ways in which many Victorian men responded to the "manhood threats" of the late 1800s and the early 1900s, masculinity is not a stable identity, but is rather a social construction that is shaped by events taking place in the social world. As gender scholars have long argued, there are actually many masculinities, and some of them are valued more than others. The dominant and "most honored way of being a man" (Connell and Messerschmidt 2005, p. 832) is termed *hegemonic masculinity* and can be thought of as a "pattern of practice" that maintains the dominance of men over women while also producing a hierarchy of masculinities that subordinates some men to others. However, hegemonic masculinity is not static or unchanging; it varies with local contexts (ibid., 840). Thus, what may define "true manhood" in one social or geographic setting may not in another. For example, as Bell, Hullinger, and Brislen explain (2015, p. 289), "the form of masculinity that is hegemonic among bankers on Wall Street looks quite different than the hegemonic masculinity among coal miners in Central Appalachia, or cattle ranchers in Wyoming."

Further, hegemonic masculinity is not automatically maintained or reproduced. As Connell and Messerschmidt argue (2005, p. 844), "masculine domination is open to challenge and requires considerable effort to maintain." Methods of maintenance may include marginalizing or excluding women (Martin 2001) and "policing" other men (Connell and Messerschmidt 2005, p. 844). When hegemonic masculinity is under threat, as it was during the early 1900s, men may engage in "toxic practices" to retain and secure their dominance in the gender hierarchy (ibid., p. 840).

Masculinity and Coal Employment in Central Appalachia

As Bell and York have argued (2010), the hegemonic masculinity of the Central Appalachian coalfields has historically been, and continues to be, tied to coal mining and the coal industry more generally. (Also see Scott 2010.) According to Maggard (1994), the coal industry actively sought from its very beginning to construct a culture in which masculinity was tied to dangerous work in the mines. Coal mining has long been "socially constructed as the epitome of 'men's work'" (Yarrow 1991, p. 286), creating "a context in which 'miner' and 'male' [have] become conflated, a conflation that is so deeply ingrained that it is virtually undetectable" (Beckwith 2001, p. 310).

In much of Central Appalachia, this link between masculinity and coal mining has also traditionally been connected to membership in the United Mine Workers of America. Historically, coal-reliant families held a deeply rooted identity as "Union People," as was noted in chapter 3. However, in recent decades there has been a tremendous decline in union membership (Burns 2007) because of the growth and dominance of multinational coal companies, which have taken a decidedly anti-union stance in the region (Bell 2009; McNeil 2012). The decline in the number of union mines has meant that the union identity, which was once so central to the coal miner's identity (and the masculine identity), is under attack.

As was noted in chapter 1, in addition to the decline in the number of union mines in Central Appalachia, there has been a drastic decline in employment in coal mining overall as a result of technological advances in mining techniques (including mountaintop-removal mining, which requires a fraction of the miners that were once needed to mine the same amount of coal). Service-sector jobs are now the leading sources of employment and earnings in the region (Maggard 1994; Miewald and McCann 2004). With the increase in service-sector jobs and the decline in mining employment, many women are now their families' primary breadwinners—a difficult change for many families (Maggard 1994; Miewald and McCann 2004; Legerski and Cornwall 2010). Miewald and McCann (2004, p. 1054) argue that although the strict gendered division of labor may not be as prevalent in the region as it once was, the associated gender ideology "is still felt." The resulting mismatch between economic reality and cultural beliefs about gender roles has meant that many men are no longer able to live up to the hegemonic image of masculinity that has long pervaded the Appalachian coalfields.

Gender Identity and Activism in the Coalfields

Could coalfield men's masculine identities, and the threats to those identities that they feel, be limiting their willingness to participate in environmental justice activism? To explore this possibility, the first author (SB) conducted 28 interviews with both men and women environmental justice activists in Central Appalachia from 2006 to 2008. The sample was generated by using a list of activists involved in the Friends of the Mountains network (a network of environmental organizations and activists working to stop mountaintop-removal mining in Central Appalachia). A purposive sample of potential respondents was generated to ensure representation from a number of different towns and counties of residence, a range of ages, and both women and men. Men were oversampled so that there would be an adequate number for analysis. For the purposes of this chapter, only the activists who were coalfield residents (individuals who had spent at least half of their lives and/or the majority of their childhoods in the coalfield region and who had a family history of employment in the coal industry) were included in the analysis. This subsample consisted of twenty activists—twelve women and eight men. The median age of the activists in the sample was 52 years for women and 53 years for men. All the respondents were white. Eighty-three percent of the women in the sample and 50 percent of the men were working class (determined by the type of employment and level of educational attainment). (For more details about the interview procedures and analysis, see appendix B.)

The Protector Identity and Women's Activism

Both women and men in the sample of activists recognized the disproportionate number of women at the front lines of the fight for coalfield justice in Central Appalachia. "I definitely see that there are more women on the radical environmentalist side than men," Bill Price asserted. When asked whether he believed that more women than men were involved in speaking out against the coal industry, Nick Regalado stated: "Definitely. Absolutely. Absolutely. I would 150 percent agree with that. ... The women are a lot more vocal than the men, and that is a real dynamic." Similarly, Ed Wiley confirmed: "There's been more women [to] stand up with fire in their eyes and more backbone than what these men got around here, that's for sure ... .There are more women involved [in the movement]."

As is described in Bell 2013 (which includes narratives of the twelve women who are part of this study), the most frequently expressed conviction among the activist women was that their engagement in the environmental justice movement was an "extension of [their] identities—and obligations—as mothers and grandmothers" (p. 168). One example of this pattern is West Virginia activist Maria Gunnoe, whose narrative of entry into the environmental justice movement reflected her motivations for action as having stemmed from her role as a mother and her anger at the compromising of that role. When Maria and her family experienced a devastating flood in June of 2003 because of a mountaintop-removal mine behind their home, her children suffered psychological trauma that lasted long after the flood waters had subsided:

> There is tremendous fear when it rains. ... My daughter went through a, hey, I feel safe in calling it a posttraumatic stress disorder. She would set up at night—if it was raining or thundering, or any weather alerts or anything like that going on on the news, my daughter would not sleep. And I, I didn't notice this to begin with. I was so overwhelmed with everything going on that I never even thought, "What's this putting my kids through?" Until one morning ... . I found out one morning at 3 o'clock in the morning, it was thundering and lightning, and I go in, and I find her sitting on the edge of her bed with her shoes and her coat and her pants [on]. [Pauses, deep breath, voice cracks] And I found out then ... [pauses] ... what it was putting my daughter through. (quoted on p. 13 of Bell 2013)

Her daughter's psychological distress was the provocation that drove Maria to take action:

> That is what *pissed me off*. How *dare* they steal that from my child! The security of being able to sleep in her own bed. The coal companies now own that. They now own my child's security in her own bed. [Pauses] And how can they expect me as a mother to look over that? ... What if I created terror in their children's lives? And that is what it has done to my children. ... All I wanted to do was to be a mother. ... In order for me to be a mother, and in order for me to keep my children safe, ... I've had— it's not an option—I've had to stand up and fight for our rights. (quoted in Bell 2013, pp. 13-14)

Like Maria, many of the women interviewees conveyed a belief that activism against the coal industry was a *duty* that they felt compelled to fulfill, because of their statuses as mothers, grandmothers, or "Appalachian women" (Bell 2013). Some of the activists expressed a conviction that women's leadership in the environmental justice movement was more than an obligation, however. Some, such as Debbie Jarrell, articulated that the preponderance of women in the movement was the result of what they believed to be a deep-rooted "mothering instinct" (ibid., p. 119). "It's the mother's instincts that makes you realize how detrimental what's going on is to our children's future," Maria Gunnoe explained. "But I really don't think that it's in a man's instincts to see that." (quoted on p. 22 of Bell 2013)

Men involved in the environmental justice movement, such as Bo Webb, also echoed the "mothering instinct" justification for women's leadership and involvement in the movement:

> For women—I think it's a natural instinct to protect your children. ... You know, you gave birth to that child. And if someone is going to do some harm to your kids, you're gonna rip their face off. And, I think that brings them to the front—to protect their home, protect their family.

From Bo's perspective, women aren't simply compelled to participate in environmental justice activism because they are more aware of the effects of environmental degradation on children's health. Rather, he expressed a belief that the "mothering instinct" elicits a level of proactiveness—even aggression—among women when their children are under threat.

Regardless of whether biological "instincts" are actually responsible for women's leadership in the environmental justice movement, the cultural protection that such a belief offers to women activists undoubtedly grants them a certain level of freedom to protest—freedom that many coalfield men may not feel. Furthermore, as is described in Bell 2013, although the majority of the women in this study did describe their motivations for action as stemming in large part from their roles as mothers and grandmothers, they also articulated a broader "protector identity" that "encompasses and extends the motherhood identity." Through this broader protector identity, coalfield activist women consider the "moral authority for their activism emanat[ing] not only from a calling to protect their children and grandchildren from irresponsible mining practices, but also from an obligation to protect their communities, their mountains, their heritage, their family homeplace, and their way of life" (ibid., pp. 171–172). Thus, it appears that the work of identity correspondence is readily achievable for coalfield women, as their personal identities as "protectors" align with the collective identity of the environmental justice movement, which seeks protection for children, communities, the physical environment, and the regional culture and heritage. But what about the men?

The Masculine "Culture of Silence"

When the men in our sample were asked why they believed there were so few of them involved in the environmental justice movement, they cited the tie between masculinity and the coal industry. Bill Price remarked: "I think some of that has to do with culture ... . Men were the coal miners, so it's a little harder for them to let go of that sense of, you know, this is how I put cornbread on the table." In other words, many men in the region feel loyalty toward the coal industry. Bo Webb argued that it is more than loyalty to the industry, however. He perceived that there is also a strong "culture of silence" discouraging men from speaking out against coal. He articulated that this silence is linked to peer pressure and the fear of losing status within the community: "They want to be in the old boys' club. And they don't want to mess with the status quo." Men's intimate ties to the coal industry and the privilege these ties afford them within the community may discourage them from taking a critical position against coal-related injustices for fear that such a position could bring marginalization and a loss of status.[5] Women may be less restricted in their challenges to power because their activist challenges are perceived—at least initially—as "less threatening" because they are made by mothers and wives.

Julian Martin confirmed this last point, noting that women seem to have "more protection culturally than the men" when it comes to speaking out against the coal industry. He also suggested that, in order to protect their own status, men publicly disparage or minimize the activist activities of the women in their lives. As an example, Julian described how a man in the coalfields might dismiss his wife's activism to his male peers: "Well, the little old woman is up there raising hell at the Board of Education again. Yeah, she went down there, I couldn't keep her home." A man's joking in this way could allow him to distance himself from his wife's politically contentious actions while also serving to minimize women's challenges to the social order. According to Julian, "the men are forgiven for what their, what the women do ... but the men aren't forgiven for what the men do."

Escaping the Hegemonic Masculinity of the Coalfields

Despite the barriers to coalfield men's environmental justice activism, some local men *have* joined the environmental justice movement in Central Appalachia and have become strong leaders in the fight for coalfield justice, as the men in this chapter demonstrate. How have they been able to overcome the limitations of what Bo described as a "culture of [masculine] silence"? As table B.1 in appendix B reveals, one characteristic that is shared among many of the activist-men in our sample is having spent a substantial amount of time living away from the coalfields.

Six of the eight men in our sample had lived outside the coalfield region for at least five and as long as thirty years. Some of these men specifically cited the significance of their experiences living outside the region in their reflections on why they—and not the other coalfield men in their communities—had chosen to join the fight for environmental justice:

> I left here and I didn't get caught up in the culture of silence. I had been out in the world ... seeing that there are other places, and how this would never be allowed to go on in [those places]. This could not happen anywhere except West Virginia and Kentucky and apparently southwest Virginia. —Bo Webb

> I traveled across the country. ... I'd been to other places, I'd seen other things. ... I was raised here and I'm completely a West Virginian—all of my development really happened here in terms of understanding and ways of the world, but I've—I hate to say it that way, but I've got out of the holler, man, I've actually went farther than [the county seat] to see what the world was like beyond that and see how things operate. —Nick Regalado

Both Bo and Nick suggested that their exposure to other places not dominated by the coal industry allowed them to see the injustice of the coal industry's actions in southern West Virginia in ways that many less traveled residents cannot or will not acknowledge. Similarly, Julian Martin credited his experience as a Peace Corps volunteer in Nigeria—another highly exploited region—as having helped to open his eyes to the problems in West Virginia. After spending two years in Nigeria, Julian stated, southern West Virginia's "similarity to a Third World nation" disturbed him. The experience of seeing his home with new eyes was what prompted him to become involved in fighting for environmental justice.

Whereas six of the eight activist men in our sample had spent five or more years living outside the coal-mining region of Central Appalachia, only four of the twelve activist women had lived outside the coalfields for five or more years. The fact that a considerably larger portion of the men had lived elsewhere further supports the prospect that there is something about the local context of living in a coal-mining community that constrains local men's participation in environmental justice activism. The activist men's broader view of the world and of their place in it may have made them more open to recognizing and being willing to speak out against coal-related injustices in the region.

The other major characteristic placing many of the activist men outside the mainstream masculine identity of the coalfields is that half of them (four of eight) had never worked for the coal industry. (See table B.1 in appendix B.) Larry Brown, a pastor, had previously worked in construction; Larry Gibson had worked for General Motors; Bo Webb had owned a business in the technical field; Julian Martin had been a science teacher. (Gibson, Webb, and Julian Martin were all retired at the time of our interviews.) Three of the four men in our sample who *had* worked for the coal industry at some point in their lives had not spent their entire careers in that line of work. Having other career identities outside of coal employment may have helped create a self-conception that wasn't tied to the coal industry. In addition, working in other environments probably allowed these men to be members of peer groups made up of men (and women) not associated with the coal industry, thus providing additional perspectives and role models.

Chuck Nelson was the one man in our sample of activists who had spent his entire career working as a coal miner and had never lived outside the coalfields. However, his loyalty to the coal industry was destroyed in 2000 when he and his wife joined with other community members who were filing complaints against a coal-preparation plant that was spewing clouds of coal dust onto their homes. The mine in which he worked and the coal-preparation plant adjacent to his community were both owned by the union-hostile multinational coal company Massey Energy. Chuck knew it was just a matter of time before he was fired from his Massey mine, "because you don't work for Massey and speak out against Massey." He was right. After thirty years of experience in coal mining, and with a clean work record, Chuck was forced to quit his job because of a false accusation. He tried to find work at other mines, but he soon realized that he had been blackballed from coal employment entirely. The experience of being forced out of the only occupation he had ever known, coupled with what he perceived to be a blatant disregard for his and his community's health, influenced Chuck's entry into the environmental justice movement. Chuck's personal battles at work and at home made him "see the lack of concern towards citizens and towards communities" that he felt characterized the actions of the coal companies. As a result, he claimed, he became more open to learning about the larger issue of mountaintop-removal mining and joining the fight against it when he came into contact with organizers from the environmental justice organizations.

Although most of the men in the sample did not explicitly draw on a specific identity (such as father or parent) in their descriptions of why they had become involved in the environmental justice movement, many cited protecting their community as a motivation. For instance, Bill Price described "a sense of responsibility to the community he grew up in," believing that he had an obligation to use his skills and knowledge to help people suffering from the consequences of irresponsible mining practices. Similarly, the late Larry Gibson stated that his activist work was in direct response to the injustices the coal industry had perpetrated against Appalachians, whom he called "my people." And Ed Wiley attributed his activism in the environmental justice movement to the guilt he felt from being complicit in working for the industry (and in the very mine) that he blamed for having made his granddaughter sick: "Here I was part of ... setting up something that could kill my granddaughter and all them little kids and possibly the community. I mean, it was just like a sledgehammer hitting me. ... That hurt me. ... That was the wake-up call right there." Thus, although for many men the hegemonic masculinity of the coalfield region may pose a barrier to entry into the environmental justice movement, those men who are able to escape the influence of the local hegemonic ideals of manhood may come to draw on identities that are closely aligned with the protector identities of local activist women.

Summary: Hegemonic Masculinity as a Barrier to Coalfield Men's Activism

This chapter began with a question: Why are there so few coalfield men participating in the Central Appalachian environmental justice movement relative to women? Drawing on interviews with local environmental justice activists, we found that women's and men's differing rates of environmental justice activism in the region may be tied to how readily their gendered identities are able to "correspond" (Snow and McAdam 2000) with the collective identity of the environmental justice movement. Our findings corroborate previous studies that have found that women often draw on their shared and socially sanctioned identities as mothers and grandmothers to motivate and legitimize their involvement in environmental justice activism. In this way, the women discussed in this chapter readily attain identity correspondence between their personal identities and the collective identity of the environmental justice movement because many view their activism as an extension of their roles as protectors of children, community, culture, and heritage.

Alternatively, identity correspondence with the environmental justice movement may be more difficult for coalfield men because of the pervasive belief that masculinity in this region is connected to employment in the coal industry (Beckwith 2001; Yarrow 1991) and because the decline in coal jobs has meant that the coal-related hegemonic masculine identity is under threat. Thus, for local men, speaking out against the coal industry not only means speaking out against a potential employer; it may also mean a further threat to an already vulnerable masculine identity.

Though few local men are involved in the Central Appalachian environmental justice movement, some local men, such as the eight discussed in this chapter, have managed to overcome the gender-specific barriers to activism in the region. Our findings suggest that certain life events and circumstances have affected the personal identities of these men in ways that have rendered the local hegemonic masculinity of the coalfield region less relevant to their self-conceptions. It is these transformations that have allowed for the identity correspondence of these particular men's personal identities with the collective identity of the Central Appalachian environmental justice movement, facilitating their activism. However, it is clear that such shifts are difficult for most men within the social context of coal-mining communities. For many local men, the hegemonic masculinity of the region continues to be a considerable barrier blocking their ability to align their personal identities with the collective identity of the environmental justice movement. Those men who identify with the coal-related hegemonic ideal of manhood may be highly unlikely to *ever* become participants in the environmental justice movement.

5 Cognitive Liberation, Cultural Manipulation, and Friends of Coal[1]

with Richard York[2]

Although the hegemonic masculinity of the coal-mining region of Central Appalachia may be intimately linked to coal production, curiously, this connection no longer has a basis in contemporary conditions. As has already been established, coal employment in West Virginia, the foremost coal-producing state in Appalachia, has declined steadily since the 1940s. In 1948 there were 131,700 coal miners in the state; in 2010 there were only 22,599 (West Virginia Coal Association 2011). There are, of course, also many businesses that support the coal industry's operations, such as trucking companies and manufacturers of mining machinery. Even after accounting for those jobs that the coal industry indirectly provides, however, direct and indirect employment in the coal industry still only totaled about 46,000 jobs in West Virginia in 2008, which was about 7 percent of the total employed civilian labor force (Blaaker, Woods, and Oliver 2012).

As the number of mining jobs has continued to decline, the number of service-sector jobs has increased, calling into question the coal industry's status as the "backbone" of West Virginia. Furthermore, because of the precipitous decline in coal-mining jobs, "achieving" the hegemonic masculinity of the region through a career in the coal industry has become more elusive to men than ever before. In theory, once local people recognized this changing economic reality in West Virginia, and Central Appalachia overall, a political opportunity should have opened up for the environmental justice movement to recruit more local constituents—especially men. When there are so few coal jobs left in the region, and when the mining-related environmental destruction and impacts on local communities are so great, why are there still so few men involved in environmental justice activism?

This chapter argues that part of the answer lies in the coal industry's retaliatory efforts to maintain and amplify the ideology that coal is central to the livelihoods and identities of coalfield citizens, and to the masculinity of coalfield men. The coal industry has not been passive as changing economic realities have threatened its position of privilege in Central Appalachia. This chapter reveals the ideology-construction efforts of the coal industry and the ways in which this industry ideology impedes the process of cognitive liberation—the third micro-level factor influencing participation in social movements—among many coalfield residents.

Coal and the West Virginia Economy

The $3.5 billion that coal mining contributed to West Virginia's real gross domestic product (GDP) in 2011 represented only 6.5 percent of the state's real GDP, ranking behind retail trade ($4.6 billion), manufacturing ($5.0 billion), health care and social assistance ($5.3 billion), real estate and rentals ($5.9 billion), and government ($9.8 billion) (U.S. Bureau of Economic Analysis 2014). Furthermore, mining's contributions to the West Virginia state product began declining in the late 1990s (Witt and Fletcher 2005), and its contributions are forecast to continue declining over the next thirty years (Witt and Leguizamon 2007). The tax revenue generated from coal severance tax[3] represents 9 percent of the General Revenue Fund for the state, whereas personal income tax represents 39 percent (State of West Virginia 2014), and a continuing decline in coal severance tax revenue is expected (McIlmoil et al. 2010). Very little of this coal severance tax actually goes to coalfield towns, which must bear the brunt of the varied social, economic, and environmental injustices related to coal-mining practices. The town of Sylvester, for instance, which sits next to the enormous Elk Run coal-preparation plant and beneath a mountaintop-removal coal mine and an enormous slurry impoundment with the capacity to hold 769 million gallons of coal waste, received only $860 in coal severance tax during the 2011 fiscal year (West Virginia State Treasurer's Office 2014). Furthermore, in their analysis of the revenues from and costs associated with the coal industry, McIlmoil et al. (2010, p. x) found that the coal industry "actually costs West Virginia state taxpayers more than it provides." The expenses associated with the coal industry include the direct costs of overseeing mining activities, environmental protection, restoration, maintaining coal haul

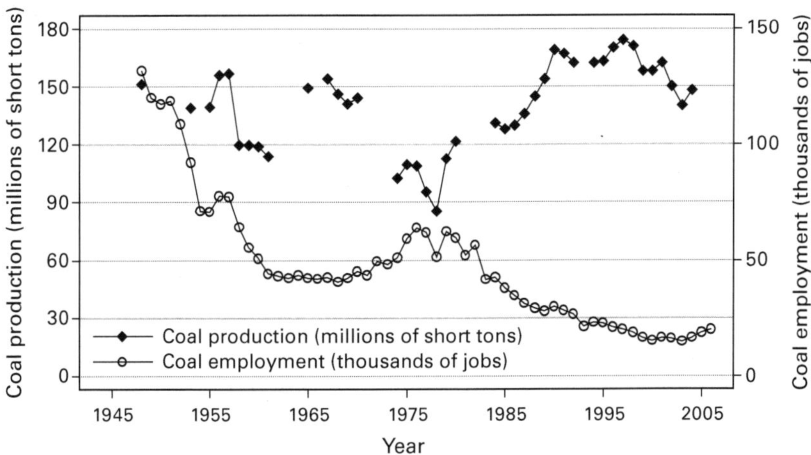

Figure 5.1
West Virginia coal employment and production.Sources: Workforce West Virginia 2000a, 2000b, 2001, 2002, 2003, 2004, 2005, 2006, 2007; Energy Information Administration 2002, 2004, 2006; U.S. Census Bureau, *Statistical Abstract of the United States* 1961, 1971, 1981, 1991, 1994, 2000, 2005.

roads, and the loss of revenues from exemptions, credits, and reduced tax rates. After accounting for all the direct and indirect benefits from the coal industry, McIlmoil et al. found that the coal industry cost the state $97.5 million in fiscal year 2009.

As figure 5.1 shows, coal employment in West Virginia has declined substantially since the 1940s. The reduction in mining jobs has caused a considerable exodus from the state. Between 1950 and 2010, West Virginia experienced a net out-migration[4] of nearly 38 percent of its population. Depopulation was most pronounced in the southern coalfield counties, which suffered a net out-migration of nearly 70 percent (West Virginia Health Statistics Center 2013).

As was noted above, the coal industry directly or indirectly employed 46,000 people in 2008, which accounted for 7 percent of the total employed civilian labor force that year (Blaaker, Woods, and Oliver 2012). Health care, hospitality services, retail trade, professional and business services, and local, state, and federal government were all far more significant employers within the state than coal (West Virginia Bureau of Employment Programs 2005).

Most of the decline in mining jobs since the middle of the twentieth century has not been the result of a reduction in the scale of coal production. Although coal production has declined in recent years, because of a number of factors described below, the productivity of coal mines at the beginning of the twenty-first century was about the same as it was in the late 1940s. (See figure 5.1.) Rather than reductions in productivity, job losses between the late 1940s and the early 2000s clearly were due to the ongoing process of the treadmill of production[5] (Schnaiberg 1980), in which workers are replaced by machines. Owing to changes in the methods of coal extraction, the same amount of coal can be extracted in the twenty-first century by employing only one-sixth as many workers as were required in the middle of the twentieth century. Coal *was* central to the building of West Virginia's economy. However, with the advent of the continuous mining machine, the longwall mining machine, and (most recently) mountaintop-removal mining, a huge workforce of coal miners is no longer needed.

The periodic reductions in coal production shown in figure 5.1 correlate with a number of important events—particularly the implementation of various environmental laws in the late 1960s and the 1970s, among them the Coal Mine Safety and Health Act, the Clean Air Act, the Federal Water Pollution Control Act, and the Surface Mining Control and Reclamation Act. The significant decline in production from 1970 to 1978 can be attributed in part to the much stricter sulfur dioxide emissions standards for coal-fired power plants, which made Western (e.g., Wyoming) coal, which is very low in sulfur, the "most cost effective choice for meeting sulfur dioxide limits without the installation of expensive equipment retrofits" (Bonskowski, Watson, and Freme 2006, p. 2). This change in the standards caused a decrease in the use of Appalachian coal in the 1970s. However, as figure 5.1 shows, the trend was only temporary; Appalachian coal production soon began to rise again to keep up with the demand for energy in the United States.

Although the declines in coal production described above have undoubtedly affected employment, the primary driving force behind job losses has been technological changes in mining practices (Burns 2007). This is evidenced by the trend, seen throughout the 1980s and in the early 1990s, in which jobs continued to decline despite sharp increases in coal production. (See figure 5.1.)

Coal production peaked in Central Appalachia in 1997 and has slowly declined since then. McIlmoil et al. (2013) point to a number of forces causing the decline in production, including competition from cheaper low-sulfur coal from the western United States, new environmental regulations, increasing production costs because the easy-to-reach coal seams have been depleted, and the upsurge in cheap and plentiful natural gas (made cheap by hydraulic fracturing, which uses huge amounts of freshwater and generates an abundance of liquid toxic waste).

Industry Ideology: The Birth of Friends of Coal

According to coal analyst Richard Bonskowski (2004), grassroots efforts at resistance were another factor contributing to the decline in coal production within West Virginia, and in Appalachia as a whole, during the late 1990s and the early 2000s. Efforts relating to litigation and permitting delays for new mountaintop-removal mines and stricter enforcement of coal-truck weight limits and license fees were especially influential. Not surprisingly, the coal industry did not stand idly by in the face of these challenges. This became especially apparent in the coal industry's strategy to win one of the most contentious legislative debates in West Virginia in recent years: limits on the weight of coal trucks. In its efforts to win this battle, the West Virginia Coal Association constructed a countermovement to the environmental justice movement, calling the fake grassroots (or "astroturf") organization it created Friends of Coal. This corporate front group has engaged in elaborate framing efforts to maintain and enhance coal's status as the economic identity of West Virginia (and now, other Appalachian states).

In 2002, in response to a string of fatal accidents involving overweight coal trucks (some that were carrying loads more than twice the legal limit), Delegate Mike Caputo (D-Marion) introduced a bill in the West Virginia legislature to increase enforcement of the weight limits on coal trucks. Legislators supporting the coal industry quickly introduced retaliatory legislation that would have raised the maximum legal weight limit for coal trucks from 80,000 pounds to 132,000 pounds (with a 5 percent variance) (Nyden 2002). Neither bill passed, but legislative efforts on both sides continued to stir controversy in the state.

During the summer of 2002, as the coal-truck debate was raging, board members and officers of the West Virginia Coal Association held a strategic planning meeting to discuss ways to improve public relations (Shanghai Zoom Intelligence Co., Ltd. 2006). The outcome of that meeting was the birth of Friends of Coal, which was to be a "grassroots organization" that would be "dedicated to informing and educating West Virginia citizens about the coal industry and its vital role in the state's future" (Friends of Coal 2007). According to Bill Raney, president of the West Virginia Coal Association:

> For many years ... we have claimed that coal represents many more West Virginians beyond the thousands directly employed by the industry. Friends of Coal clearly indicates that this is the case. ... With Friends of Coal, we are making an effort to count, organize and mobilize these people. It's time to clearly demonstrate to public officials, to media representatives and to the general public, just how many lives are touched in a positive way by the coal industry (Shanghai Zoom Intelligence Co., Ltd. 2006).

In addition, according to *Coal Leader: Coal's National Newspaper*, "one of the aims of the new organization 'Friends of Coal' is to reverse the perception that coal mining has declined in importance in West Virginia and the country" (*Coal Leader* 2003). Although Friends of Coal boasts that it is a "grassroots organization," its funding comes from the member companies of the West Virginia Coal Association (Hohmann 2005). Furthermore, Bill Raney was reported to have said that the campaign was created as an effort to "remove 'impediments' to coal mining" ("Nehlen to Pitch for Coal Group," *Charleston Daily Mail*, December 13, 2002), clearly exposing the agenda of the organization.

In January of 2003, the West Virginia Coal Association contracted with the West Virginia-based firm Charles Ryan Associates to "provide public relations, advertising and internet services for Friends of Coal" (Shanghai Zoom Intelligence Co., Ltd. 2006). This step proved to be a strategic one in terms of timing, for it came just before the 2003 West Virginia Legislative Session, during which the issue of weight limits for coal trucks would be re-examined. As Bill Reid, managing editor for *Coal Leader*, asserted, the passage of Senate Bill 583, which raised the legal limits on the weight of coal trucks, "occurred just a few short months after the introduction of the West Virginia Coal Association campaign Friends of Coal" (Reid 2003). "There is no doubt," Reid continued, "that Friends of Coal had a significant impact on the passage of the Coal Truck Bill." This was particularly significant, for, as Reid argued, increasing weight limits would "provide a much needed boost for the coal industry in southern West Virginia by removing some of the question marks regarding the future of coal trucking and giving greater stability to both coal producers and trucking companies" (ibid.).

The passage of the weight-limit increase was only the beginning of Friends of Coal, however. Since 2003, the organization has launched a full-scale campaign within West Virginia (and nearby coal-mining states) to reconnect the citizenry to an industry that can no longer truly be characterized as the "lifeblood" of the economy. The focus of the empirical analysis in this chapter is on the activities that this organization undertakes and the messages it imparts to West Virginians. We[6] argue that the underlying strategy of Friends of Coal is to attempt to counter the coal industry's loss of citizens' employment loyalties by constructing an ideology of dependency and identity through a large-scale public relations campaign.

Data and Methods

In order to uncover the primary strategies that Friends of Coal uses in its attempt to maintain and amplify a bond between coal and West Virginia communities, we use two approaches: content analysis and field observations. Data for the content analysis were gathered from four sources:

- regional and national newspaper articles during the period 2002–2007 that mention Friends of Coal
- articles mentioning Friends of Coal in *Coal Leader* during the period 2003–2006
- the Friends of Coal website (http://www.friendsofcoal.org), accessed once in 2005 and then again in 2007
- the website of the West Virginia Coal Association (the parent organization of Friends of Coal), accessed in 2008.

The regional and national newspaper articles were located through the Lexus-Nexus Academic database by entering the search term "Friends of Coal" and searching between 2002 (the year of the organization's inception) and 2007. The data set from this source consists of 207 newspaper articles. The articles from *Coal Leader* were found on that publication's website. Only issues printed between 2003 and 2006 were available. The data set from this source consists of four articles about Friends of Coal. The websites of Friends of Coal and the West Virginia Coal Association, our third and fourth sources, provided particularly illuminating data: four 60-second television commercials and two 30-second television commercials promoting Friends of Coal and the coal industry in general. These commercials were transcribed and coded both for visual themes and spoken words. In addition, all of the content posted on the Friends of Coal website was included in the analysis.

The coding was undertaken in an inductive manner: reading through the documents and then creating (1) a list of actions that Friends of Coal has taken since its inception during the summer of 2002 and (2) a list of themes and messages that it is attempting to impart to the West Virginia public.

In addition to content analysis, observations from the first author's (SB) field research in southern West Virginia during the summers of 2006 and 2007 were utilized. While the interview data are not explicitly used here, general knowledge gained from the interviews and the field observations inform the analysis.

"Coal Is West Virginia"

The coding process revealed that Friends of Coal's main strategy to reinforce a bond between coal and West Virginia communities centers on attempting to present coal mining as the defining feature of the state. The statement "It is likely that no state and industry are as closely identified with one another as West Virginia and coal," which appeared on the Friends of Coal website in 2005, imparts exactly the message this organization hopes West Virginians will continue to believe, despite the coal industry's declining contribution to employment in the state. Content analysis and field observations reveal that Friends of Coal employs two strategies to maintain its standing as the identity of West Virginia: (1) appropriating West Virginia cultural icons and (2) creating a visible presence in the social landscape of West Virginia by means of stickers, yard signs, and sponsorships.

Strategy 1: The Appropriation of West Virginia Cultural Icons

Even before securing Charles Ryan Associates as its public relations firm, Friends of Coal recruited a spokesperson: Don Nehlen, a popular retired football coach of the West Virginia University Mountaineers and a recent inductee into the College Football Hall of Fame. Nehlen was soon joined by two other spokespersons: retired Marshall University football coach Bobby Pruett and professional bass fisherman Jeremy Starks. In addition, retired Air Force general "Doc" Foglesong has appeared in at least one television commercial speaking on behalf of Friends of Coal. Each of these spokespersons represents an important West Virginia "cultural icon" that signifies the historic and present hegemonic masculinity of the region. (We define "cultural icons" as representations of cultural or regional identity that resonate with individuals of a particular area or community.)

The Winner Icon

Coaches Nehlen and Pruett together represent the two Football Bowl Subdivision (formerly Division 1) teams in the state and thus represent the two sets of football fans that exist in West Virginia: fans of the Mountaineers (West Virginia University) and fans of the Thundering Herd (Marshall University). In a state with a population of only 1.8 million, these two football teams are important cultural icons. By securing the two coaches with the most wins in the history of these two teams, Friends of Coal has attempted to appropriate football—and winning—as a part of its identity. To further this end, in 2006 Friends of Coal initiated and became the corporate sponsor of a seven-year series of football games between the Mountaineers and the Thundering Herd. Before 2006, the two teams had played each other only once since 1923. College football fans in West Virginia had waited for many years for the in-state rivals to play each other. The so-called "Friends of Coal Bowl" quickly became a raging success, further solidifying the cultural association between Friends of Coal and college football in West Virginia.

Friends of Coal further reinforced the connection between the coal industry and football with two 30-second television commercials promoting the Marshall University Thundering Herd and the West Virginia University Mountaineers. The first commercial begins with a chorus singing "When we go down deep through the dark today, we come up with the light for America." Next, the narrator announces:

> Champions are born of hard work and determination, and just like the Thundering Herd, coal miners are a championship team. During this 2008 season, the Friends of Coal honor our coal miners and our Thundering Herd—all champions indeed.

A chorus of voices concludes the commercial by exuberantly singing "COAL IS WEST VIRGINIA!" (This chorus was subsequently made into a cell-phone ringtone available for downloading on the West Virginia Coal Association's website). The second commercial is worded similarly, praising coal miners and the West Virginia University Mountaineers for both being "championship team[s]."

Friends of Coal also added the NASCAR driver Derek Kiser to its "winner icon" by becoming his primary corporate sponsor. Kiser drives a race car with the Friends of Coal logo prominently positioned across the hood. By associating itself with the winning football coaches and the winning NASCAR driver, Friends of Coal asserts that the coal industry is a winner too.

The Provider and Defender Icons

The provider icon and the defender icon are closely intertwined within Friends of Coal propaganda. This becomes particularly apparent in two Friends of Coal television commercials. In the first of these commercials, called "American Hero," "Doc" Foglesong, a retired Air Force general, narrates as images of hard-working coal miners (all men) flash across the screen.

Doc:

You could say the West Virginia coal miners are modern-day pioneers. Men and women of courage, pride and adventure, who safely go where no one's been before and harvest the coal that powers our nation. ... In fact, if these miners didn't produce coal, our nation would be in trouble. More than half of the nation's electricity is generated by coal. West Virginia is the national leader in underground coal-mining production, and America needs that energy—today more than ever. So if you know a West Virginia coal miner, say "Thanks." Not that he or she is doing it for the thanks. They're doing it for their family and for our future. I'm retired Air Force General Doc Foglesong. Friends of Coal salute the pioneering spirit of the West Virginia coal miner. Why not join us and do the same?

Within the text of this commercial, the coal *industry* becomes synonymous with the coal *miner.* Thus, the coal industry is presented as a provider—both for West Virginia's families and for the nation's energy demands. As Doc states, "America needs that energy—today more than ever," and it is the West Virginia coal industry that is to be thanked for meeting those energy demands.

The working-class provider icon is a decidedly masculine image. Although Doc calls coal miners "men and women of courage," not a single woman can be seen among the fifteen coal miners who appear throughout the one-minute commercial. This is in line with traditional mainstream ideologies of "the provider" in American society, and in Appalachian coal communities in particular. As was noted in chapter 4, Beckwith (2001, p. 310) argues that the historically male-dominated coal-mining workforce of Central Appalachia has created "a context in which 'miner' and 'male' become conflated, a conflation that is so deeply ingrained that it is virtually undetectable." In fact, not until the late 1970s were women granted the right to work in the coal mines. Even that legal victory was largely empty, however. Once women became coal miners, they were the first to be pushed out when technological changes "shrank the size of the labor force, leaving only those miners with seniority" (Maggard 1999, p. 186), and of course, those miners were men. Thus, by reinforcing the hegemonic image of the working-class provider as a man, and a particularly *masculine* man, the images in this commercial lubricate the process of the coal industry's becoming synonymous with the family provider.

Underlying this commercial is the image of the West Virginia coal industry (as represented through the face of the coal miner) as the "defender" of the country: "If these miners didn't produce coal, our nation would be in trouble." The choice of a retired military general as the narrator of this commercial is particularly telling of the messages that Friends of Coal seeks to present: the coal industry defends the "American way of life" just as the military does. Thus, coal is more than an energy source—it is a *patriotic* energy source!

The "coal industry as defender" trope is also apparent in a Friends of Coal television commercial called "Tracking the Source." In that one-minute piece, the narrator states:

> [W]ithout West Virginia coal, our nation's economic status as a leader would be in jeopardy. It may seem like a daunting task to supply the nation with energy. But clean coal technology continues to gain momentum, helping us reduce our dependence on foreign oil and creating jobs for the men and women who proudly call themselves coal miners.

Thus, according to this commercial, the coal industry is responsible for defending the United States from economic disaster and foreign conflict over oil. Again, in this section of the commercial, it is only men who are depicted in the images relating to the coal-mining process, reinforcing mainstream images of a working-class man as provider and the true face of the coal industry. This image works within the historical gender structure of Appalachia and thus makes this association more "natural."

Through appropriating the cultural icons of the provider and defender as being ultimately represented within the workers of the coal industry, Friends of Coal is able to again construct a connection between the increasingly isolated "coal industry" and the local communities. The coal industry's approach fits with Habermas's (1975) observation that efforts at legitimation typically draw on existing cultural institutions, providing continuity with tradition. The coal industry, in its development of the provider and defender icon—linking coal to the military, a symbol of patriotism and strength—is clearly trying to embed coal mining in deep cultural traditions. It connects its legitimation efforts with those of the state, which has long worked to build the image of the military as a noble institution upon which all Americans depend.

The Outdoorsman Icon

Hunting and fishing are important traditions to many West Virginians. Many pride themselves on being avid outdoorspeople, a value that often stands in contradiction to the destructive ecological practices of the coal industry. Mountaintop-removal mining has caused the destruction of vast tracts of land once used for hunting, digging ginseng root, gathering morels, and collecting other types of medicinal herbs, such as black cohosh, bloodroot, and mayapple. Many streams in which West Virginians used to swim and the fish habitat they provided have been buried under valley fills or polluted with acid mine drainage and coal waste. Thus, Friends of Coal needed to address this contradiction to make the coal industry appear to also value the outdoors, as a large number of West Virginians do. This they attempted to accomplish by becoming the primary corporate sponsor of professional bass fisherman Jeremy Starks and by bringing him on as an official spokesperson for Friends of Coal in 2006. Adding even more to his credentials as an "environmentally conscious" spokesperson for Friends of Coal is the fact that Starks serves as a representative on the Bass Angler Sportsman Society's "conservation team," which meets with government officials to discuss conservation issues.

Starks appears in two one-minute Friends of Coal television commercials, in the first alongside Nehlen and Pruett and in the second on a stream bank fishing with five children. In the first commercial, Starks, Nehlen, and Pruett are fishing from Starks's 21-foot bass boat, which has a panoramic photo of West Virginia mountains and the Friends of Coal logo emblazoned across its side. As the three men fish in a West Virginia stream, they discuss the West Virginia coal industry:

Nehlen:

Thousands of tons of coal are mined in this area

Starks:

And scientific tests have shown

Pruett:

That the water is clean, clear, and a strong provider for wildlife. And the coal-mining industry is proud of that.

Nehlen:

And of their role in making sure that it stays that way.

In his second commercial, Jeremy Starks continues with this theme of clean streams as images of him standing on a stream bank fishing with young children alternate with images of coal mining.

Starks:

Hi. I'm Jeremy Starks—a Friend of Coal and a pro fisherman who's concerned about the environment. … This clear stream is proof that sustaining water quality is a big part of the reclamation process. Scientific tests have shown that this water quality is better now than it's ever been. And this is after 22 million tons of coal have been mined in nearby land. Our need for energy is greater than ever. And with responsible practices in place, we can safely mine coal while restoring our land for future generations. …

From the mouth of self-proclaimed conservationist Jeremy Starks, we are assured that coal extraction and a clean environment can coexist (much in the same way that the rhetoric of "clean coal" is aimed at countering coal's reputation as a "dirty" fossil fuel). We are even told that the coal industry *improves* water quality! It is through this assertion that Friends of Coal attempts to identify itself as the quintessential West Virginia "outdoorsman."

By appropriating some of the most potent cultural icons of the region, such as football, the military, race car driving, the accomplished outdoorsman, and the working-class provider, Friends of Coal has attempted to amplify the connection between West Virginia and coal so that this industry appears to be more than a provider of jobs; it embodies all the characteristics of the archetypal West Virginian.

It is no coincidence that this "archetypal West Virginian" is clearly constructed to be a man. With the changing economic realities in West Virginia, wherein coal is no longer the main source of employment or earnings, the gendered division of labor, and related gender ideology, is under attack. As described in chapter 4, with the rise in service-sector jobs and decline in mining employment, women have increasingly entered the workforce, while greater and greater numbers of men have been forced to leave, threatening men's status as their families' sole breadwinners (Maggard 1994, Miewald and McCann 2004). As Maggard (1994, p. 31) relates, "the Appalachian coalfield region is witnessing the disassembling of a nearly century old economic and domestic arrangement." In many cases, this has translated to turmoil at home, including divorce, depression, domestic violence, and even suicide (Miewald and McCann 2004). Paradoxically, the very industry that created the hegemonic masculinity of the region in the first place is also responsible for preventing most coalfield men from achieving it. Because of this ideological connection between the male provider and the male coal miner, it is necessary for the coal industry to convince residents that men are still the breadwinners of their families if it is to convince them that coal is still the backbone of the economy.

Strategy 2: Becoming Pervasively Visible within the Social Landscape of West Virginia

The second major way in which Friends of Coal endeavors to become the identity of West Virginia is through its attempts to be seen virtually everywhere in the state. The organization accomplishes this in three major ways: (1) distributing hard-hat stickers, window decals, buttons, yard signs, and ball caps at nearly every major public event; (2) sponsoring sporting events, community-improvement projects, cultural happenings, scholarships, and various other venues that provide opportunities for the Friends of Coal logo or name to be in the public's attention; and (3) infiltrating the school system through the Coal Education Development and Resource program of southern West Virginia.

The Friends of Coal Logo

Revealing Friends of Coal's goal to pervade the visual landscape with its presence, Warren Hylton, a member of the West Virginia Coal Association Board of Directors, was quoted in Shanghai Zoom Intelligence Co. in 2006 as having said: "This logo will be the visible proof that there are Friends of Coal all over West Virginia. ... The more you see of this symbol, the more you can be sure our message is getting across." Friends of Coal has made concerted efforts to distribute its stickers, hats, buttons, and yard signs widely throughout West Virginia and other Appalachian coal-mining states. Membership in Friends of Coal is free, and there are no participation requirements. Simply putting a Friends of Coal decal on the back of one's pick-up truck is a contribution to the organization's goal to paint the landscape with Friends of Coal logos, providing a strong visual image of solidarity and "grassroots support" for the coal industry.

Figure 5.2
A Friends of Coal decal on a car in southern West Virginia.

Friends of Coal Sponsorships

Connected to the wide distribution of Friends of Coal logos is the extensive list of events, places, and services that Friends of Coal sponsored during its first five years. Those that we identified through our data are presented in the box on the next page.

Friends of Coal's far-reaching campaign to have its name attached to everything from soccer fields to auto fairs to the state capital's Fourth of July celebration to volleyball games to theater performances is a clear attempt to broaden its base of support among people who may not care about football or fishing and who may not come from a working-class background. Through appearing to sponsor everything and anything, Friends of Coal gives the impression that the coal industry is still acting as the backbone of the state, regardless of whether it provides many jobs or contributes significantly to public services. Thus, these diverse sponsorships serve to perpetuate an ideology of dependency: without the coal industry, West Virginians would not only be without jobs, but they would also be without sporting events, soccer fields (see figure 5.3), cultural events, and community centers.

Figure 5.3
Example of a Friends of Coal sponsorship: soccer fields in Charleston.

Events, Buildings, Places, and Professionals Sponsored by Friends of Coal

Events

Friends of Coal Bowl A yearly football game between the two Division 1A teams in West Virginia: West Virginia University and Marshall University.
Friends of Coal Day at the Legislature A day-long event that has taken place every March since 2004. On the first Friends of Coal Day at the Legislature, the state Senate and House of Delegates passed concurrent resolutions designating March 4, 2004 as Friends of Coal Day.
Friends of Coal Auto Fair An annual three-day event with live music, carnival rides, games, food, and, of course, cars.
Friends of Coal Blue-Green Volleyball Classic An annual NCAA Division I volleyball event featuring West Virginia University and Marshall University.
Paint the City Green Presented by Friends of Coal An annual pep rally and tailgate party for Marshall University alumni and fans.
Fifth Third/Friends of Coal West Virginia-Ohio All-Star Basketball Game An annual high school all-star basketball game.
Tiskelwah Community Center Fundraiser An event to raise money for a new heating system in the Tiskelwah Community Center.
West Virginia University Band Fundraiser An event to raise money for new band uniforms.
Independence Day Celebration in the Capital Contributed $20,000 to Charleston's Independence Day celebration.
***The Odd Couple* Theater Performance** Sponsored a performance of *The Odd Couple* at the Clay Center for Arts and Sciences in Charleston.
Hall of Fame Tribute for Don Nehlen Sponsored a tribute dinner for former West Virginia University football coach (and spokesperson for Friends of Coal) Don Nehlen when he was inducted into the College Football Hall of Fame.

Facilities

Friends of Coal Soccer Fields Contributed $1 million to the construction of a six-field soccer complex in Kanawha County in 2004.
Attempted (without success) to purchase naming rights for the new Class A baseball stadium in Charleston.

Sports Professionals

Jeremy Starks A professional bass fisherman, born in West Virginia, whose main corporate sponsor is Friends of Coal.
Derek Kiser Friends of Coal Racing is the main sponsor for this up-and-coming NASCAR driver, a native of West Virginia.

Coal Education in the Schools

In his study of social cohesion in liberal democracies, Mann (1970) found that the most common form of "manipulative socialization" by the state does not attempt to *change* the values of the working class, but instead seeks to *perpetuate* the values that hinder the working class from interpreting "the reality it actually experiences." This insight fits with our observation that the coal industry actively works to maintain and amplify its status as the state's economic identity in order to prevent the working class from recognizing the coal industry's role in the economic and environmental degradation of coalfield communities. Furthermore, Mann cites studies that reveal the school system's crucial role in the manipulative socialization of children, particularly those from working-class families. In this same way, the coal industry, with the blessing of the state, endeavors to socialize school children in the southern coalfields to an "understanding of the many benefits the coal industry provides in daily lives" through the Coal Education Development and Resource program, which consists of special educational materials and curricula created by the West Virginia Coal Association (West Virginia Coal Association 2007).

Teachers in the counties of Boone, Logan, Wyoming, Mingo, and McDowell (some of the leading coal-producing counties in West Virginia) are offered grant money to create and implement classroom study units on coal using the curriculum materials, and the three teachers at each grade level (from kindergarten through grade 12) with the best "performance" have the opportunity to win cash prizes (ibid.). Furthermore, each school has a principal-appointed Coal Fair Coordinator, whose duties are to organize a Coal Fair at the school so that each student has the opportunity to enter a project on coal in one of seven categories: Science, Math, English-Literature, Art, Music, Technology-Multi Media, and Social Studies. The winners of each local Coal Fair are invited to enter their projects in a regional Coal Fair, at which cash prizes are given to those who come in first, second, and third in each of the seven categories in three age groups. Additionally, nine cash prizes are awarded to the overall winners in each age group (ibid.). Finally, the program offers ten $1,000 scholarships to students from the five participating coalfield counties to be used at one of the Southern West Virginia Community and Technical College campuses (ibid.).

Through its presence in the school systems of many of the leading coal-producing counties in the state, the coal industry attempts to manipulate the loyalties of citizens as young as 5 years old. As quoted in an article in *Coal Leader,* the Coal Education Development and Resource Program "is working toward securing coal's future TODAY by educating our leaders of TOMORROW!" ("Cedar of Southern West Virginia" 2005). By engaging students and teachers in coal education, encouraging participation in coal fairs, and offering college scholarships, the coal industry is working to ensure that the future citizenry of southern West Virginia is socialized to believe that coal is indispensable to the life, culture, and economic future of their communities and their state.

Summary: Ideology Construction as a Barrier to Cognitive Liberation

The drive for profit accumulation is a defining feature of capitalism and is central to the treadmill of production. This drive has always generated a fundamental tension, however, because activities that increase profits also frequently degrade the environment and undermine social well-being. These circumstances create legitimation problems for the owners of the means of production. The social and environmental costs of coal production have resulted in increasing opposition to the industry's often unrestrained access to natural resources. This rising tide of protest, challenging the power of the coal industry, has increasingly led to backlash against the industry, which struggles to cling to its power despite its declining contributions to the economy and employment.

One way the coal industry maintains its power is by actively constructing ideology that furthers its interests. The changes in coal production in West Virginia illustrate how industry works to retain community loyalty when it no longer serves as a major source of employment. When the number of jobs it provided declined as a result of changing mining practices, the coal industry faced a significant challenge to its hold on political power. The industry's response to this ongoing threat has been to engage in cultural manipulation, attempting to construct a pro-coal ideology that will shape a community's economic identity. Its strategies center on the appropriation of West Virginia cultural icons and the infusion of coal-industry ideology into a variety of social arenas. The intended effect of these efforts has been to (re)construct the identity of West Virginia as both economically dependent on coal and culturally defined by coal.

A recent study by Blaaker, Woods, and Oliver (2012) provides empirical evidence of the degree to which the coal industry has been successful at convincing West Virginia residents that coal contributes more to the economy than it actually does. Analyzing data from a survey of 494 students at a large university in West Virginia, Blaaker et al. found that approximately 98 percent of the students surveyed provided vastly inflated estimations of the proportion of the jobs in the state that are provided by the coal industry.

The pervasive ideology-construction efforts of the coal industry are likely to pose a tremendous barrier to the process of cognitive liberation among would-be challengers to the coal industry's power. The coal industry attempts to maintain its position of privilege through engaging in ideology construction and manipulation that leads to what Gramsci (1971) terms "cultural hegemony." Through cultural hegemony, the values of the power elite infiltrate the everyday, commonly held beliefs and practices of the entire social structure such that those who are dominated unintentionally participate in the perpetuation of their own domination. Ongoing ideology construction and maintenance ensures that "would-be challengers face the problem of overcoming a definition of the situation that they themselves may take as part of the natural order" (Gamson 1992, p. 68). Thus, attaining cognitive liberation may be particularly difficult in the coalfields because this ideology functions to conceal and confound the structural causes—and the extent—of injustice.

6 Cognitive Liberation and Hidden Destruction in Central Appalachia

with Sean P. Bemis[1]

As was discussed in chapter 5, the coal industry's efforts at cultural manipulation include "greenwashing" strategies that attempt to counter widespread claims that the coal industry is environmentally destructive and polluting. However, it is unlikely that the coal industry's greenwashing efforts could be successful if the extent to which Central Appalachia has been impacted by mountaintop-removal mining were visibly obvious. Thus, necessary to the coal industry's ideology-construction efforts—and to its capacity to block cognitive liberation among local residents—is an industrial landscape that is out of sight from most local residents.

Though no official records are kept on the total number of "disturbed acres" that have resulted from surface mining (U.S. Government Accountability Office 2009), Geredien's (2009) geospatial analysis of high-resolution imagery data from the National Aerial Imagery Program reveals that between 1.05 million and 1.28 million acres of land and more than 500 mountains in West Virginia, Kentucky, Tennessee, and Virginia have been surface mined.[2]

The number of permits for new surface mines in this region continues to rise, and the overwhelming majority of land that has been permitted for surface mining is highly concentrated (U.S. Government Accountability Office 2009). In West Virginia, 48 percent of the 245,200 acres of land under open permit is concentrated in just three counties: Boone, Logan, and Mingo (ibid., p. 20). Likewise, in eastern Kentucky 44 percent of the 420,900 acres under open permit is concentrated in three counties: Pike, Perry, and Knott (ibid., p. 18). Collectively, the acreage under open permit in these six counties accounts for 17 percent of the total land mass of these counties (ibid., pp. 20, 22). It is important to note that this percentage does not include "released" land (reclaimed) or "forfeited" land (land that the coal companies abandoned before fully reclaiming).

Mountaintop-removal mining has also had significant negative effects on water resources in Central Appalachia. According to the U.S. Environmental Protection Agency's 2005 Environmental Impact Statement on Mountaintop Mining and Valley Fills in Appalachia, mountaintop-removal mining and/or valley fills directly affected 1,200 miles of headwater streams between 1992 and 2002. Additionally, from 1985 to 2001 valley fills *buried* an estimated 724 miles of streams in Appalachia. Today, these numbers are even higher, as these figures do not account for the permits that have been approved since 2002.

Despite the vast tracts of land and water that have been, and continue to be, affected by mountaintop-removal mining and valley fills, many local residents do not realize the extent of the destruction taking place around them. "Even though I lived here all my life," Chuck Nelson (a former coal miner) said in our 2007 interview, "I didn't really know the scope of how big mountaintop removal was, because it's not nothing you can ride up the road and see everywhere. It's more or less back away from the highway where people can't see it unless you get in a plane. … It's a whole different world once you get up and you can see that." The coalfield resident and activist Maria Gunnoe echoed Chuck's account in our 2007 interview:

> Throughout my lifetime I literally watched the horizons around me disappear. Without realizing the widespread destruction that was taking place—sitting down here in the valleys and watching it take place on the mountains is one thing, but when you get up there and you see how huge it is, that's something else. I never realized it was so bad. My first fly-over was with SouthWings [non-profit aviation organization], and that right there is really what fired me up. When I got off the plane that day, I cried all the way across the tarmac, all the way home, and when I pulled in my driveway, I sat there and just literally felt a sense of fear that I could not, I could not overcome this sense of fear. After seeing this and then driving back into it, thinking "My God, I live in the middle of it," and not knowing it until I done that fly-over. I mean, you feel the blasting and you see all the dust, all the trucks, but you don't really see the impact of it over time. I guess maybe the human mind doesn't have the capacity to accumulate all that without major research. It happens, and people don't even know that it's happening. (quoted on pp. 14–15 of Bell 2013)

Chuck's and Maria's reflections are supported by the authors of the U.S. Government Accountability Office's 2009 report:

Despite the public scrutiny that surface mining in mountainous areas has received, the public is limited in its ability to access information on the scope of these operations—their size, location, and how long they have been in operation—and on what the mountain can be expected to look like after mining operations have ceased and the land has been reclaimed.

Why is the extent of this destruction unknown to so many people who live in the midst of it? An important piece of this puzzle is the fact that a considerable proportion of land in Central Appalachia is owned by absentee corporate landowners (Appalachian Land Ownership Taskforce 1983; West Virginia Center on Budget Policy and American Friends Service Committee 2013). In fact, five of the six West Virginia counties in which only ten landowners own more than 50 percent of the land are located in the southern coalfields (West Virginia Center on Budget Policy and American Friends Service Committee 2013). With such a high rate of absentee and corporately held landownership in the region, it would be entirely possible for large tracts of land to be mined without local residents' knowing, or seeing, how much of the land is being disturbed.

Is a significant portion of surface mining, in fact, "hidden" from local residents? To investigate this possibility, we examine the spatial relationships between the effects of mountaintop-removal mining and the roads in Boone County, which was the foremost coal-producing county in West Virginia at the time of our study. Specifically, we use a geographic information system (GIS) to quantitatively identify the portion of the total landscape of the county that is visible from the roads (the viewshed). Using geospatial data on surface mine permits in Boone County, we analyze the local viewshed relative to active and recently surface-mined sites and find that the locations of the effects of mountaintop-removal mining are, in fact, less visible than equivalent portions of the landscape. We argue that the low visibility of mountaintop-removal mine sites is yet another factor limiting local residents' ability to experience the consciousness transformation that is necessary for micro-mobilization against the injustices of the coal industry to take place.

Constructing a Viewshed Analysis

Our analysis focuses on Boone County, the leading coal-producing county in West Virginia in 2010 and one of the counties with the highest concentration of corporate landownership in the state. In Boone County, 59.1 percent of private land is owned by ten corporations (West Virginia Center on Budget Policy and American Friends Service Committee 2013).

We obtained publicly available geospatial data for Boone County through the West Virginia GIS Technical Center (http://wvgis.wvu.edu/index.php). The required data include a 3-meter-resolution digital elevation model (DEM) for Boone County and contiguous counties and statewide data on roads and on the boundaries of mining permits. Using the Spatial Analyst extension in ArcGIS 9.3, we performed a viewshed analysis using the 3-meter-resolution DEM of Boone County. For this analysis, we included a 2-kilometer-wide buffer of the DEM beyond the perimeter of the county in order to reduce the influence of any edge effects created by county lines.[3] We ran separate viewshed analyses for U.S. highways, state highways, and county roads within Boone County. (There are no interstate highways in the county.) To speed processing, we used a 9-meter output cell. The output of the viewshed analysis is a (raster image) map of the county showing which areas are visible from the roadways and which areas are not.

The available geospatial data for mined areas of West Virginia are based on mining permits; however, these permits include various non-surface-mining permit classifications. In order to distinguish the regions of Boone County affected by active and recent surface mining, we eliminated permit classifications for activities related to underground mining and quarrying, and we eliminated permits for surface mining in locations where excavation had not yet begun. We intersected the resulting areas of active and recent surface mining with the viewsheds to calculate the visible area of surface mining from the various classifications of roads.

Seeing (and Not Seeing) Surface Mining

The total land mass of Boone County is 1,302 square kilometers. Our findings indicate that 232 square kilometers (18 percent) of that land mass is affected by recent or active surface mining. Figure 6.1 shows the active surface-mining sites in the county.

Of the 1,302 square kilometers of land in the county, 609 square kilometers (47 percent) are visible from a U.S. highway, a state highway, or a county road. (See figure 6.2.) In figure 6.3, we have overlain the active surface-mine sites onto figure 6.2. Figure 6.4—a simplified version of

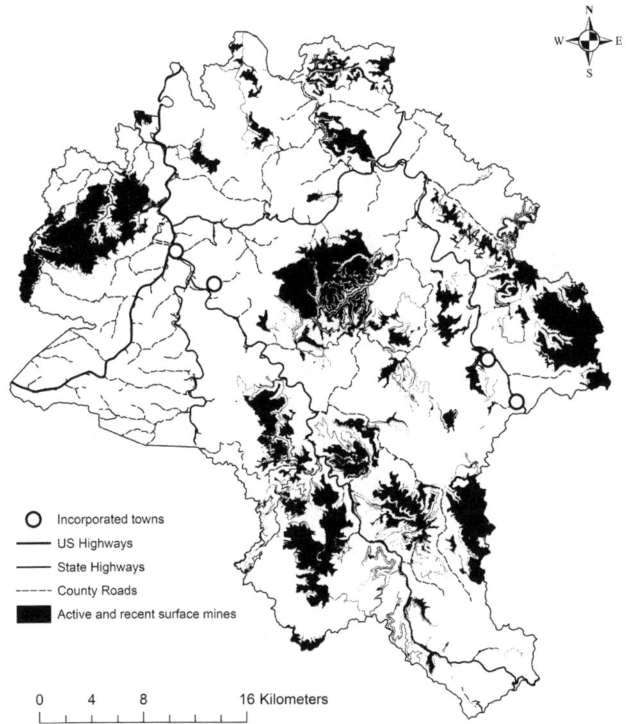

Figure 6.1
Active and recent surface-mining sites in Boone County.

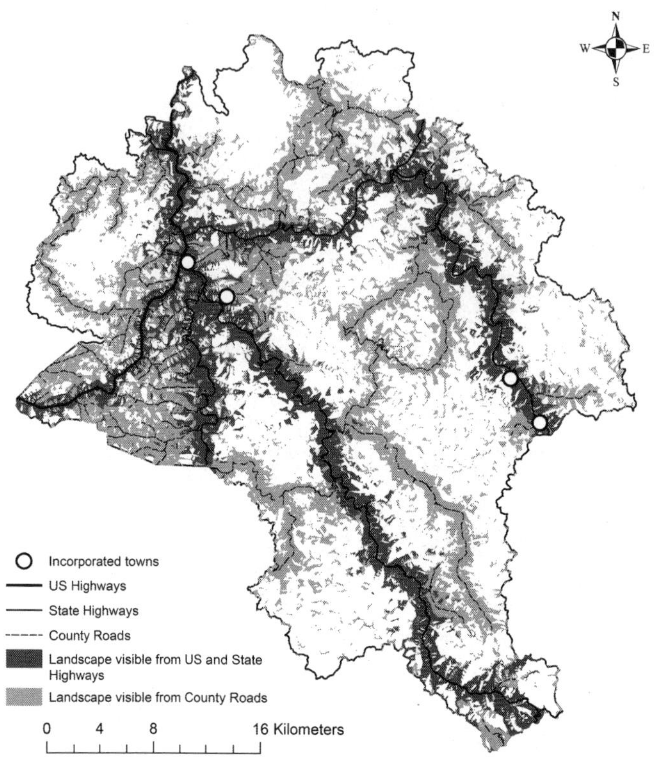

Figure 6.2
Landscape in Boone County that is visible from all roads in Boone County.

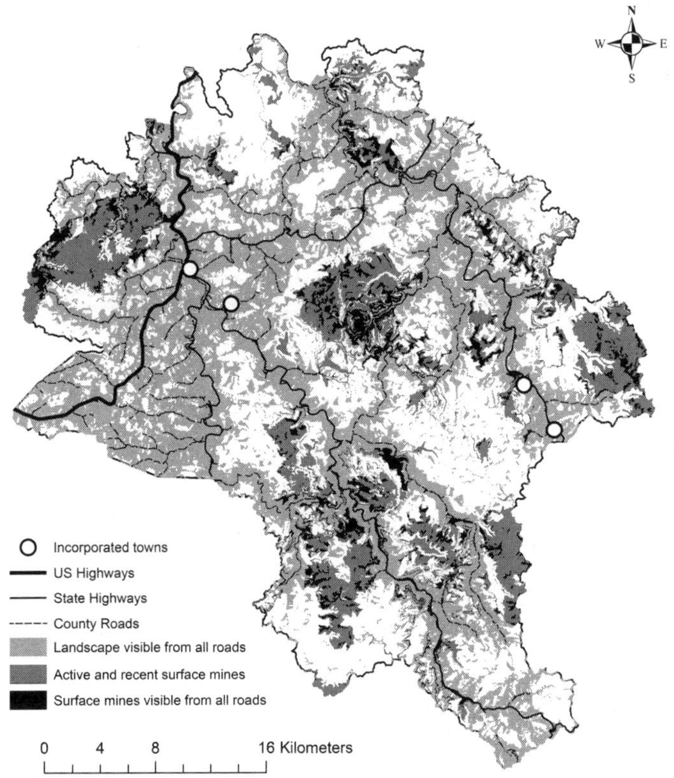

Figure 6.3
Total landscape visibility, total active and recent surface mines, and surface mines visible from all roads in Boone County.

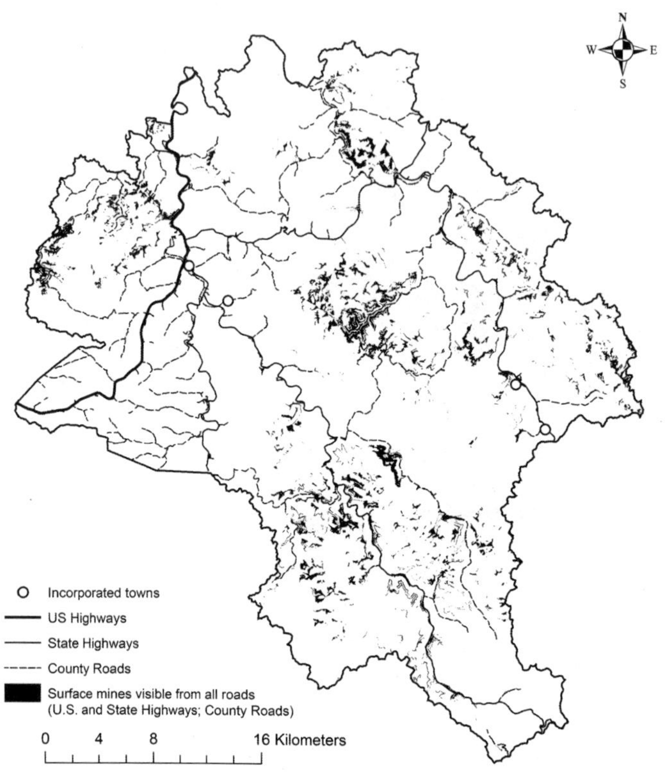

Figure 6.4
Visibility of active and recent surface-mining sites from all roads in Boone County.

figure 6.3—shows only the portions of the surface mines that are visible from the highways and roads.

The analysis reveals that of the 232 square kilometers of active surface mines in Boone County, 54.2 square kilometers are visible from highways and roads in the county. Thus, while 47 percent of the land in Boone County is visible from these transportation corridors, only 23 percent of the active surface mines are visible.

Figure 6.5 extracts the surface mines that are visible from U.S. and state highways. By excluding the mines that are visible only from the less traveled and often depopulated county roads, we find that only 4 percent of the surface mining taking place in Boone County can be seen from the U.S. and state highways in the county.

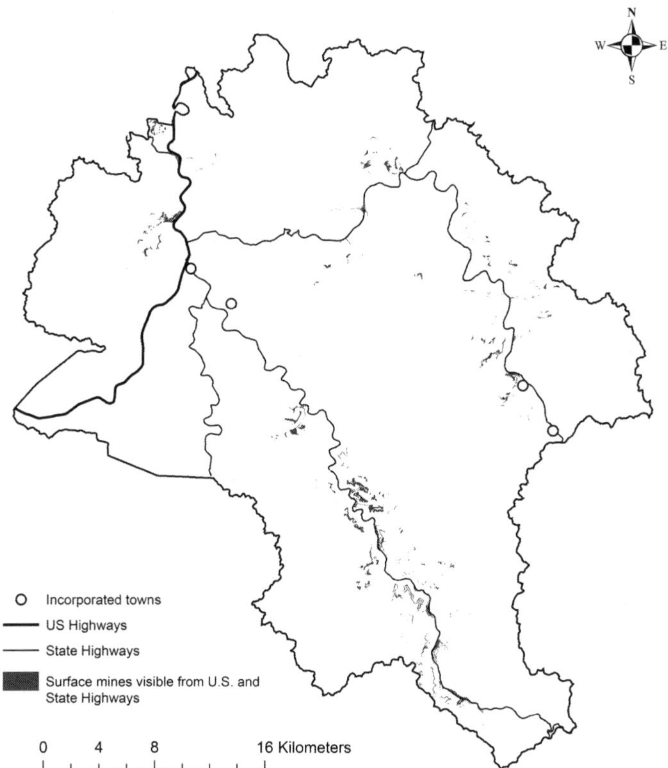

Figure 6.5
Active and recent surface-mine sites visible from U.S. and state highways in Boone County.

These findings support the claims made by many local coalfield residents, such as Chuck Nelson, who maintained that mountaintop-removal mining is "back away from the highway, where people can't see it." In light of the high rates of absentee landownership in the region, it is possible for mining to take place in areas that are out of view for the majority of local residents. The data presented in this chapter suggest that much of the coal-related destruction is, in fact, not within sight of local residents and others traveling the roads through this heavily mined county, and probably through other such counties. Because the impacts of the coal industry appear to be far less extensive than they actually are, the hidden character of surface mining in the region is another likely factor stymying the process of cognitive liberation among the general public.

7 Summary of Part I

The studies presented in chapters 3–5 have pointed to four major factors suppressing local participation in the environmental justice movement in Central Appalachia:

• depleted social capital in coalfield communities, indicating that there are high levels of isolation, sparse social networks, and few formal organizations in the region (chapter 3)
• the gendering of activist involvement—that is, the underrepresentation of men involved in environmental justice activism, attributable to the coal industry's influence on the local hegemonic masculinity of the region (chapter 4)
• the industry's ideology-construction efforts to maintain and amplify the perception that coal is both the economic backbone of West Virginia (and the region more generally) and the cultural identity of the citizenry (chapter 5)
• the fact that the majority of the coal industry's environmental destruction and pollution is hidden from the view of most local residents (chapter 6).

These four factors function to hinder solidarity building, identity correspondence, cognitive liberation, and micromobilization, which are the critical micro-level processes affecting an individual's propensity to participate in a social movement.

Are these the only factors constraining local participation in the Central Appalachian environmental justice movement? This is a very difficult question to answer, made even more complicated by the fact that most studies of participation (or non-participation) in social movements are retrospective (McAdam and Boudet 2012). Though much can be gained from retrospective studies, much can also be lost or dismissed as irrelevant. Gaining a deeper understanding of the barriers limiting participation is best done through actually *observing* the process of becoming, or not becoming, an activist. However, finding individuals who are, as McAdam and Boudet designate them, "at risk" for activism can be difficult. I needed a group of individuals who weren't yet activists, but who were exposed to events and circumstances that could potentially lead to their recruitment into the environmental justice movement. This, I believed, would provide a window into the nuanced social dynamics and events that might not be observable in a purely retrospective study. Creating such a social setting, or micromobilization context, is what I set out to do in part II of the book, in which I introduce the feminist participatory-action research[1] method of "Photovoice" as a means of studying—in real time—the factors facilitating and constraining involvement in the environmental justice movement in the coal-mining region of Central Appalachia.

II Creating a Micromobilization Context

8 Creating a Micromobilization Context through Photovoice

The findings presented in part I provide a snapshot of the social factors inhibiting micromobilization against the myriad coal-related injustices affecting many Central Appalachian residents. To provide a more complete picture of "non-action in the face of injustice," though, I felt it necessary to find some way to study non-activists who seemed to be primed for activism by virtue of their living in a community affected by problems caused by coal extraction and processing (i.e., a community with significant grievances against the coal industry) and who shared certain social characteristics making them more likely to become involved in the environmental justice movement. I recognized that my approach needed to address the problems with micromobilization identified in part I (depleted bonding social capital, the difficulties of recruiting local men into the movement, and inhibited cognitive liberation, resulting from the coal industry's manufacturing of pro-coal ideology and the extent to which the majority of land disturbances from mountaintop-removal mining are not visible to most residents). I also knew that my method needed to create an appropriate "micromobilization context" (McAdam 1988a) for the non-activists in my study in order to connect them with the environmental justice movement in a meaningful way. I believed that the feminist[1] participatory-action research method of Photovoice could fulfill these needs.

In 2008 I initiated an eight-month Photovoice project with 54 women living in five coal-mining communities in southern West Virginia. Forty-seven of the women I recruited had had no previous involvement in environmental justice activism; seven were associated in some way with one of the local organizations fighting the coal industry's irresponsible practices in the region. Through this Photovoice project, I attempted to control for the four barriers discussed in part I while also creating a micromobilization context for the non-activist participants, providing a structure that could serve to facilitate their recruitment into the environmental justice movement. By studying the women who chose to become involved in environmental justice activism during the project and those who did not, I sought to identify the additional social factors hindering local coalfield residents' participation in the movement.

The Photovoice Method

Most often used in human service fields, particularly public health, Photovoice is a process that involves using participant-produced photography and narratives as a way to give voice to and facilitate "empowerment education" among participants (Wang and Burris 1994; Wang et al. 1998). Participants are given cameras in order to take photographs that represent important aspects of their lives and communities. They gather for regular group reflection meetings to share their images, discuss common themes, build social bonds with other participants, and examine the underlying problems, concerns, or assets represented in their images. After discussing their photographs, participants write short narratives about their pictures, creating "photostories." Typically, a part of the Photovoice process is organizing community exhibits, presentations, and other actions emanating from ideas presented in the photostories.

Through regular group reflections, narrative writing, and public presentations, Photovoice provides the opportunity for participants to record and reflect on their community's strengths and issues of concern, to deepen a shared understanding of the causes and potential solutions to problems facing their community; and to inform policy makers of the community's true needs (Wang and Redwood-Jones 2001). The Photovoice method was developed to engage those who are not typical "community leaders." People from disadvantaged groups or people who do not usually have a chance to participate in decision making in a public or even a private forum are usually sought out as participants in Photovoice projects. Thus, it is often women, members of marginalized racial and ethnic groups, children, and people of a lower socioeconomic status that become community-based photographers through Photovoice. The Photovoice process allows these individuals to become their own documentarians, with the power to decide how their lives and communities should be represented, instead of allowing outside photojournalists to make those decisions for them.

Photovoice has been used throughout the world to empower local residents and groups to identify community concerns and communicate those needs to others (see www.photovoice.org). The method has been used extensively in the field of public health as a health-promotion strategy (see Catalani and Minkler 2009 for a review of this literature) and has been used as a way to document and gain insight into the experiences and everyday challenges of marginalized groups, such as homeless populations (Walsh et al. 2014; Fortin et al. 2014), sex workers (Capous-Desyllas 2013; Oliveriraa and Veary 2015), indigenous populations (Jennings and Lowe 2014; Krieg and Roberts 2007), low-income African-American women (Ducre 2012), and queer and transgender youth (Holtby et al. 2015). However, insofar as it can be used as a means of studying social change, Photovoice has been largely under-utilized. I argue that this method of visual feminist ethnography holds the potential to contribute to multiple types of social investigation, particularly research questions that require studying transformations in individuals' perceptions, concerns, or actions over time.

In the study described here, I employed the Photovoice method to create a micromobilization context that would allow me to observe the factors facilitating and constraining local coalfield residents' participation in the environmental justice movement in Central Appalachia. Recognizing the potential that the Photovoice method holds for creating a micromobilization context emerged from insights I gained while conducting an earlier, smaller Photovoice project in 2003 and 2004 in the coal-mining town of Cabin Creek, West Virginia. As I describe in Bell 2008, through this earlier Photovoice project

> I witnessed participants' understanding of community needs evolve from an individualistic view of problems to an awareness of the structural roots of many issues. In addition, I found that participants felt an increased sense of efficacy through the experience of being respected and listened to in a group setting, many for the first time in their lives. Within their group, the participants experienced a sense of community that many had expressed not feeling within their town otherwise. Finally, participants became more civically engaged, taking action through planning community improvement projects, communicating with elected officials, and reporting community problems to the appropriate authorities (p. 38).

Although my initial intention for this earlier Photovoice project was for it to serve as a type of "needs assessment" that would facilitate the communication of Cabin Creek residents' shared concerns, needs, and ideas for change to policy makers, the unanticipated outcomes of the project reveal that the small-group setting and intimate interactions that are integral to the Photovoice process could also provide an excellent micromobilization context for facilitating the micro-level processes of solidarity building, identity correspondence, and cognitive liberation (consciousness transformation) among participants.

It is important to note that the Photovoice process is not merely about creating visual images, nor is it only about group discussions of community problems. The power of Photovoice to serve as a catalyst for bringing about changes in participants' lives lies in the synergy it creates between visual images and network building among participants. Photographs are often able to spark emotions and discussion in a way that facts and figures cannot. Furthermore, as was described in chapter 2, social integration is central to the emergence of the social-psychological processes necessary for participation in social movements. Thus, simply having participants take pictures in solitude would not be a sufficient way to initiate change in their lives. Through creating communities of Photovoice participants located in areas where environmental-justice organizing was already taking place, I attempted to create micromobilization contexts – social settings that held the potential for Photovoice participants to be recruited into the environmental justice movement.

My intentions for this Photovoice project were not purely academic. I also sought to create a project that could be beneficial to my research participants by providing them with a venue to draw attention to community needs, celebrate the resilience and the assets in their communities, and share their ideas for change with policy makers and others with political influence. By designing my project in such a way that it could benefit my research participants and their communities, I sought to challenge a widely held notion that participatory-action research (PAR) "cannot be integrated with conventional academic standards" (Cancian 1993, p. 96). I contend that it is possible to use the same PAR project for both academic and activist purposes.[2] As I note on page 51 of Bell 2015, "creating two agendas within the same project (one that the research participants control and one that the researcher controls) is one way to avoid the bind of choosing between the two social worlds of activism and academia." However, because in this book I focus on the academic questions that the Photovoice project sought to answer, my discussion of the community empowerment goals and the advocacy outcomes of the project is very limited. For a more thorough overview of that side of the project, see Bell 2015.

The Southern West Virginia Photovoice Project

In July of 2008, I began the recruiting process for an eight-month Photovoice project in five coal-mining communities in southern West Virginia.[3] I recruited 54 local women for the project, 47 of whom had had no previous involvement in the environmental justice movement and seven of whom were associated in some way with one of the environmental justice organizations in the area.

In September of 2008, I held a Photovoice orientation meeting in each community. I provided the participants with digital cameras and asked them to take pictures to "tell the story" of their communities, including the problems and the positive aspects of life. I facilitated meetings approximately every three weeks in each of the five communities during the eight-month project, providing an opportunity for the women to share their photographs, discuss common themes, create photostories, and openly discuss and question the underlying structural causes of the community problems they identified. In addition to the local meetings, I held two regional Photovoice meetings in which women from all the groups came together to meet one another and to share their images and stories. The Photovoice groups also held public exhibits and presentations of their photostories, helped create a website, communicated their communities' concerns to state legislators, and developed projects to initiate change in their communities.

Through using Photovoice as part of this research, I attempted to create a micromobilization context in each community and also to control for the barriers to movement participation that I identified in part I of the book.

The first barrier is the region's depleted social capital—that is, high levels of isolation, sparse social networks, and few formal organizations. I attempted to address this barrier through enacting the Photovoice project in a group setting, with regularly scheduled meetings that employed a community-building format.

The second barrier is the gendering of activist involvement, wherein men are underrepresented in environmental justice activism, owing to the coal industry's influence on the local hegemonic masculinity of the region. I controlled for this barrier by recruiting only women for the Photovoice groups.

The third barrier is the coal industry's ideology-construction efforts to convince the public that coal is the cultural identity of West Virginia. I attempted to address this barrier by recruiting one or two local women in each community who were already critical of the coal industry (the "activist participants" in the project) and through creating a meeting environment in which dialogue and questioning were encouraged. Because of their critical views of coal, it was likely that the activist recruits would take photographs of the industry's destructive practices and share those photographs and their opinions during the Photovoice meetings (although I did not specifically ask them to do so, because I wanted the participants to have autonomy). I anticipated that the discussions the activist participants initiated during our meetings would help the non-activist Photovoice women become more open to questioning the coal industry's irresponsible mining practices.

The fourth barrier is the fact that much of the coal industry's environmental destruction and pollution is not readily observable. This hidden destruction means that many local people are simply not aware of the extent of the devastation taking place around them. Again, I addressed this barrier by placing at least one participant who was already critical of the coal industry in each of the groups. It was my hope that these individuals would take photographs exposing the coal industry's hidden practices and would share those photographs with the other women in the group setting.

It is important to recognize that structural availability, or what McAdam (1986, 1988b) terms "biographical availability," poses a major constraint on individual participation in *any* social movement. However, because the Photovoice project required that participants commit to taking photographs, writing about the photographs, and attending regularly scheduled local and regional meetings over the course of eight months, individuals who weren't "structurally available" were likely to self-select out of the study early on, or not to have joined the project in the first place.

By gathering data over the course of this project in the form of pre-project and post-project questionnaires with intervention and control groups, participant observation in each of the meetings, the participants' chronologically ordered photostories, and post-project interviews, I was able to assess what factors constrained and facilitated Photovoice participants' willingness to (1) criticize the coal industry's practices in a public setting and (2) participate in the environmental justice movement.

In the remainder of this chapter, I will provide a detailed overview of my recruitment procedures, a description of each Photovoice community, and an explanation of my data-collection methods.

Selection of Communities

During July of 2008, I enlisted the help of grassroots environmental justice organizations Coal River Mountain Watch and Ohio Valley Environmental Coalition to identify five coal-mining communities in southern West Virginia that would be suitable locations for the Photovoice project. The selection criteria for each community were as follows:

- Irresponsible mining practices were negatively affecting local residents.
- There were low rates of environmental justice activism among local residents.
- Environmental justice organizers had at least a few pre-existing connections in the community.

In the pages that follow, I refer to the communities selected for the project as Community A, Community B, Community C, Community D, and Community E. I have also assigned pseudonyms to the Photovoice participants. The first letter of each participant's pseudonym matches the pseudonym of that individual's community—for instance, "Alice" is from Community A and "Betty" is from Community B.

After selecting the communities, I asked environmental justice organizers to identify local women in each of the selected communities who had been recently involved in some way with the environmental justice movement and who might be willing to participate in the Photovoice project. "Involvement" could have meant attending one or more meetings, testifying against a permit for mountaintop-removal mining at a hearing, attending a protest, or participating in an educational event sponsored by one of the environmental justice organizations. I refer to these individuals as "local activist participants" or simply "activist participants." My goal was to recruit two such individuals into each Photovoice group in order to make it more likely that during the reflection meetings at least one person in each group would share photographs and initiate discussions that were critical of the coal industry. I intended to observe whether these individuals would draw attention to the industry's harmful practices and whether what they shared would help to "normalize" discussing these issues in the group setting. Though it was my aim to recruit two of these local activist participants for each of the five groups, I was able to meet this goal only in Community A and Community B. In the remaining three communities, I was able to recruit only one activist participant for each of the Photovoice groups.

Recruiting Non-Activist Participants

After at least one activist participant had committed to taking part in the project in each community, I asked those individuals to help me identify the two largest churches in their communities, one that would be the site for recruiting non-activist Photovoice participants and one that would be the site for recruiting a control group. Churches were used for recruitment because they are the only formal organizations in many rural areas of southern West Virginia, largely because of the depletion of social capital discussed in chapter 3. In addition, the high level of church participation in this region provided access to a large portion of the population.

I telephoned the pastors of the churches that had been selected for Photovoice participant recruitment to introduce myself and to give a brief overview of the Photovoice project. After explaining the project, I asked them whether they would allow me to recruit Photovoice participants through their congregations. All of the pastors agreed. The pastors of the churches in Communities A and C allowed me to give a twenty-minute PowerPoint presentation about the Photovoice project after a church service. In Community E, I gave the presentation before a church council meeting. In Communities B and D, instead of a formal PowerPoint presentation, the pastors opted to have me announce the project and distribute recruitment flyers after a church service. For each Photovoice group, my goal was to recruit twelve women above the age of 18 who were not active members of any environmental justice organizations in the area (I refer to these individuals as "non-activist participants"). I had varying levels of success recruiting participants in each of the communities. I was able to recruit eleven non-activist participants in Community A, three in Community B, eleven in Community C, twelve in Community D, and twelve in Community E. I discuss the recruitment challenges in these communities—particularly Community B—below.

In addition to the Photovoice participants, in each community I also recruited a group of women who were not part of the Photovoice project to serve as a control group. These individuals completed the same pre-project and post-project questionnaires that the Photovoice participants completed, but they did not participate in Photovoice. Administering questionnaires to the five Photovoice groups and the five control groups at the beginning and at the end of the project provided me with a way to compare changes in Photovoice participants over time and also to control for community events not related to Photovoice that could have also caused changes in local residents' perceptions and behaviors.

My goal was to recruit between eight and ten participants for each of the control groups; however, as with the Photovoice groups, I had varying levels of success meeting this goal in each community. To recruit participants, I contacted the pastors of the control-group churches in each of the communities and asked for permission to attend a church service to recruit people to fill out my questionnaire. Through a partnership with a local non-profit health center, I was also able to offer free blood-pressure and glucose screenings (performed by health professional students completing clinical rotations at the health center) at each of the churches. Though the health screenings were open to anyone in the church regardless of whether they completed the questionnaire, most of the women who came to the screening also filled out the questionnaire. The number of Photovoice participants and control-group participants I recruited in each community and how many remained in the project for the duration of the eight months are noted in table 8.1.

The Photovoice Communities

In the subsections that follow, I provide a brief overview of each of the five Photovoice communities. Each of the "communities" is, technically, a collection of small towns (usually former coal camps). As has already been noted, the coalfield region of southern West Virginia has been severely depopulated, and many "towns" have very few residents. Each of the "communities" is served by one high school and has a common regional identity. People often refer to each of these collections of towns by a common name, often one associated with a creek or a river along which the towns are scattered. For instance, what local people call "Cabin Creek" (where I organized my first Photovoice project in 2003–04) is technically a

Table 8.1

Photovoice participants and control-group participants.

	Photovoice participants							Control group		
	Non-activists		Activists		Total					
	Start	End	Start	End	Start	End	Total attrition rate	Start	End	Total attrition rate
Community A	11	11	2	2	13	13	0%	5	4	20%
Community B	3	3	2	2	5	5	0%	8	5	38%
Community C	11	8	1	1	12	9	25%	11	9	18%
Community D	12	6	1	1	13	7	46%	9	9	0%
Community E	10	5	1	0	11	5	55%	8	4	50%

collection of towns spread along a stretch of road, about ten miles long, that parallels the waterway named Cabin Creek.

Community A

Community A is in a rural area located in the county with the highest coal production in West Virginia. In recent years, mountaintop-removal coal mining has become more pervasive in the area, and some residents have experienced structural damage to their homes from blasting. Less than a year before I began the Photovoice project, residents of a segment of this community learned that their well water was contaminated with coal waste from an underground slurry-injection site. High rates of cancer, skin rashes, thyroid problems, teeth problems, and various other maladies were reported by local residents. Since the fall of 2007, environmental justice organizations had been working to recruit residents in this area to collect water samples for testing, to speak out at public hearings, and to lobby state legislators and other political leaders for clean water in this community. When I began the Photovoice project, the group was trying to raise money to purchase a water truck and refillable water barrels for all the residents in this area. Their ultimate goal was to have the closest municipal water line extended into the community so that residents would have access to a public water supply.

Agnes and Alice were the two local activists I recruited to the Photovoice project in Community A. Agnes had been involved in the environmental justice movement since the late 1990s. Her participation began when overweight coal trucks speeding down the road in front of her house were endangering the lives of her family and neighbors. Agnes began as a volunteer and later became a paid employee for one of the environmental justice organizations working in her area. Agnes's husband, a coal miner for many years, had recently become very sick. Agnes believed that the contaminated water that she and her husband had long been drinking had caused his illness. Because of her husband's condition, Agnes was unable to commit a large amount of time to the Photovoice project, but she did participate intermittently during the eight months of the project.

Alice had become involved in the movement only recently, having attended her first meeting about the water contamination in October of 2007. Since attending that first meeting, she had been writing letters telling legislators, county commissioners, Department of Environmental

Protection officials, and the governor about the problems in her community. Alice was also regularly attending hearings of the local water board and offering her home as a gathering place for community meetings of the environmental justice organizations. Alice had been a homemaker for most of her life, and her husband had worked in the coal mines for many years.

In August of 2008, Alice introduced me to her cousin Adah, who was a member of the largest church in the community. Adah helped put me in touch with the pastor of her church. After he granted permission, she scheduled a Photovoice presentation to follow a Wednesday night church service. I recruited eleven non-activist Photovoice participants through that church network. The pastor agreed to allow our group to hold meetings in the church's fellowship hall.

Community B

Community B is located in a remote and depopulated rural area in the same county as Community A. Entering this part of the county, one is oppressively surrounded by reminders of the coal industry's presence. Driving the twisting, narrow roads, one passes beneath and beside abandoned coal tipples and other dilapidated coal-industry structures no longer in use. Boarded-up buildings, abandoned vehicles, and overgrown lots cover the landscape. Community B has seen enormous population losses. As one drives along the main road to the most isolated and depopulated parts of the community, some mountaintop-removal mining operations become shockingly visible from the roadways. The mining operations of Massey Energy (now Alpha Natural Resources) have slowly crept down the valley, selectively buying out residents who are in their way. Others have moved away on their own to escape the coal dust and the blasting. Many of those who remain living in this area are older and poorer residents who do not have the resources to leave or the power to demand that the coal company buy them out. A few stay to spite the coal industry.

When I began recruiting in this community, there were organizing efforts taking place in the part of the community closest to the mining operations, where Massey was selectively offering to buy out certain people. Organizers with the environmental justice movement were attempting to unite residents of this isolated and depopulated town around the common goal of community relocation. Instead of allowing the coal company to selectively offer to buy out certain people in the town, activists were advocating for a buy-out and relocation of all the residents in that area. The destruction of community is the silent tragedy that occurs in southern West Virginia regularly. People are not compensated for the loss of community or for the loss of social capital that occurs when individuals in a town are forced to scatter to different places.

My hope was to recruit people from the area of Community B in which the organizing efforts for mass relocation were taking place. However, recruitment proved extremely difficult in Community B, especially in the area where the organizing attempts were happening. My first contact in Community B was Betty, who lives in a slightly less isolated part of the community but who has still suffered great losses from irresponsible mining practices. Betty became involved in the environmental justice movement in 2003, when a breach in an above-ground slurry impoundment on the mountain above her home flooded her property and caused extensive damage to her house and land. She believed that the flood had contaminated her well water with coal waste, and that the contamination caused her husband's death from cancer. Betty introduced me to Belinda, another resident of Community B who had also been involved in environmental justice activism in the area. Both Betty and Belinda agreed to participate in the Photovoice project.

I attempted to recruit non-activist Photovoice participants in Community B through Betty's church. I attended two services with her, handed out flyers, and gave a brief overview of the project during the announcements at the end of each service. The pastor's wife (Brandy) and stepmother (Barbara) were the only two women who expressed interest in participating in the project. Because of my limited success with Betty's church, I also attended a service at a different church in Community B, in the area where the community organizing efforts were taking place. The pastor of that church also allowed me to hand out flyers and give an overview of the project during the announcements. Though a number of the women in the church took the flyers, none of them signed up for the project. The only other non-activist participant I was able to recruit for the project in Community B was Betty's daughter Bonnie, who lived next door to Betty but did not attend a church. We held our meetings in a church fellowship hall on the same street on which Betty and Bonnie lived.

Community C

Community C is located in the coal-mining region of a large county that contains one of the biggest metropolitan areas in the state. The coal-mining region of the county is rural and low-income, and residents feel that this area is neglected and "forgotten" by politicians and business leaders. Community C borders West Virginia's most productive coal-mining county (the county in which Communities A and B are located).

Community C, like Communities A and B, has experienced a great deal of out-migration in the past fifty years. With a number of very large mountaintop-removal mining operations scattered in the mountains around the community and a coal load-out facility very close by, residents of Community C must deal with a tremendous volume of coal-truck traffic on their winding, narrow roads. In recent years, a number of fatalities have been caused by overweight, speeding coal trucks.

As is the case in other communities with large coal reserves, there is a very high rate of absentee landownership in this community. There are a number of people living in the community who do not own the land that their houses occupy. In the early 2000s, residents in an entire "hollow" in Community C were given thirty days to leave their homes because the coal company that held a mining permit for that area planned to mine the land beneath their houses. One of the many consequences of such high rates of absentee landownership is that many in the community fear losing their homes if they speak out against the coal industry. Even when a settling pond that the coal industry had created breached and flooded the houses and property of a number of residents, the residents declined to speak out against the company because they feared losing their homes.

My primary "activist" contact in Community C was Carolyn. Carolyn and her husband had recently become involved in the environmental justice movement after discovering that coal slurry was being pumped into an abandoned underground coal mine in the mountain above their house. Carolyn and her husband came across the injection site while riding an all-terrain vehicle in the mountains. They became very angry that no one had informed them that slurry injection was taking place so close to their home. Soon thereafter, they had their well tested and found that it was contaminated with coal slurry. Although by that time their house was receiving water from a municipal line, they had been watering their vegetable garden with contaminated well water for many years and feared the potential health consequences.

Carolyn was a member of one of the largest churches in Community C, and we decided to recruit Photovoice participants through that church. She helped me pass out flyers and make an announcement about the project during church services and adult Sunday School. Through this church network, eleven non-activist women were recruited to participate in the Photovoice project. We held our Photovoice meetings in the church's fellowship hall.

Community D

Community D is located in the least productive coal-mining county of the four counties represented in the Photovoice project. In contrast with the other three counties, farming makes up a significant portion of the economy in this county. In recent years, however, coal operations have increased significantly in the portion of the county in which Community D is located, as have the impacts of the coal operations. At the start of the Photovoice project, one of the environmental justice groups had recently begun organizing in this community in response to some residents' fears of water contamination and to the problems they were experiencing from mine blasting in the area. However, the coal industry's practices did not seem to be affecting life in this community quite as dramatically as it was in Communities A, B, and C.

My first contact in Community D was with Diane and her two sisters. Earlier that summer, members of Diane's family had sought out one of the environmental justice organizations in order to ask for help holding the local coal company accountable for mining-related water contamination, blasting damage to their homes, and landslides caused by a "mine blowout" adjacent to their farm. Diane and her sisters had only recently become involved in speaking out against the coal industry. I invited Diane and her sisters to participate in the Photovoice project, but Diane was the only one of the three who had time to participate. Diane did not attend a church in the community, but she encouraged me to talk to members of the local Crime Watch group because she knew a number of the members attended churches in the area. I called the president of the group and asked him if I could give a presentation to the group at their next meeting; he agreed. During my presentation, one of the members of the group offered to pass out my flyers at his church and to tell the women in his congregation about my project. Dixie, the pastor's daughter, called me soon after my meeting with the Crime Watch group and told me she was interested in the project. She invited me to give a presentation to the women in her church after a service the next Sunday, and I did. I recruited twelve non-activist participants in Community D, both through this church connection and through word of mouth. We held our Photovoice meetings in the local community center.

Community E

Community E is located in the third largest coal-producing county in West Virginia. Although residents of Community E had not yet discovered coal-waste contamination in their well water, residents of nearby communities had. Community E was similar to Community D in that the effects of mountaintop-removal mining were just beginning to be felt there. Some residents were acutely aware of problems associated with coal mining, such as increased flooding and overweight, speeding coal trucks; others were quick to defend the coal industry, arguing for the industry's importance to the economy of the area.

Eve, my first contact in Community E, had become involved in the environmental justice movement fairly recently, having just joined one of the environmental justice organizations during the summer of 2007, a year before I began the Photovoice project. Her involvement stemmed from her efforts to fight against a permit for a mountaintop-removal mine on the mountain behind her house. Eve and her husband, a retired union coal miner, had a small farm where they grew vegetables and fruit, raised chickens, and kept honeybees. Eve worried that the mountain stream they used to water their crops and chickens would be destroyed by the mining operation. She was also very concerned about the dust that would be caused by blasting, which almost certainly would affect her husband, who was already suffering from black lung disease. Since the beginning of her involvement with one of the environmental justice organizations in the area, Eve had become active not only in fighting the permit for the mountaintop-removal mine behind her house but also in promoting the idea of wind farm development in her county as a source of "green jobs" for local residents.

Eve was not a member of a church during the recruiting phase of my project, but she offered to call the pastor of the largest church in her community on my behalf. While I was visiting her at her house, she called the pastor, told him a little about the Photovoice project and about me, and then handed me the phone so I could fill in additional information and answer his questions. I asked the pastor if he would allow me to give a presentation on the project to members of his church. He agreed, and we scheduled my presentation to take place before a church council meeting on a Tuesday evening. I gave my PowerPoint presentation to a group of about eight people, two of whom signed up to participate in the project. They helped me recruit other women for the project through the church and through their community networks. In all, I recruited ten non-activist participants for the Photovoice project in Community E. We held our Photovoice meetings in the church fellowship hall.

Data-Collection Procedures

In September of 2008, the Photovoice project began. I held an orientation meeting in each of the five communities during the week of September 8. The purpose of that meeting was to train participants on the Photovoice process and to collect baseline data about their lives, experiences, and attitudes. At the start of the meeting, I asked the women to complete a questionnaire, which I also administered to the control groups at a separate set of meetings in September and October. At the end of the project, in April and May of 2009, I again administered the same questionnaire to the Photovoice and control groups. Questions centered on participants' behaviors, experiences, and cognitions relating to coal, the state, their own sense of efficacy, their levels of civic involvement, and their participation in social protest. Most questions were drawn from a number of established national and international questionnaires, including the General Social Survey, the Social Capital Community Benchmark Survey, and the World Values Survey. I drew on pre-existing questionnaires to increase the validity of my research instrument. Questions were selected to provide a way to assess participants' status in relation to the three aspects of cognitive liberation identified by Piven and Cloward (1977) (detailed in chapter 2) and to measure their levels of community involvement.

After administering the questionnaires at the orientation meeting, I conducted a training on the Photovoice project. This training had four goals: to introduce the Photovoice process and offer examples of previous Photovoice projects, to engage participants in a discussion about the ethics of

Photovoice, to teach participants about the technical and creative aspects of their cameras, and to gain informed consent for their participation in this research project. During this orientation, I instructed participants that they should simply take pictures to "tell the story" of their community, including positive and negative aspects of life and things they would like to see changed. They were not asked to document coal-related problems or any other specific topics.

Our first reflection sessions were held three weeks after the orientation meeting, during the week of September 29. I planned for these local meetings to take place approximately every three weeks in each community (with a break over the winter holidays). During the weeks we held meetings, Community C met on Monday afternoons at 1 p.m., Community A met Mondays at 6 p.m., Community D met Tuesdays at 5 p.m., Community E met Wednesdays at 6 p.m., and Community B met Thursdays at 1 p.m.

The Photovoice reflection meetings provided an opportunity to unify the participants around common concerns and solidify group interconnectedness. I brought my laptop computer, a multimedia projector, and a relatively lightweight color laser printer to each meeting. During these sessions, I downloaded the previous three weeks' worth of photographs from each participant's digital camera onto my computer. With the multimedia projector, I projected the Photovoice participants' images onto a wall. As I scrolled through each person's set of photographs, I led that individual through a process of sharing and discussing the significance of the photographs she took. I used the questions shown in the box on page 141 to direct the discussion and the sharing, although in many cases (particularly later in the project) the participants took the lead in explaining their photographs and did not require additional probing.

It is also important to note that participants often shared their photographs in such a way that a series of photos were related to one issue or theme. Thus, participants did not usually talk about every single photograph they scrolled through, only about those that represented different topics. After each participant shared her photographs, I used my laser printer to print as many as fifteen of the photos she shared. Participants wrote narratives about their photographs on the pages I printed (to create "photostories") and kept those photostories in the binders that held their orientation manuals.

Discussion Questions Used to Guide Sharing of Photos During Reflection Meetings

1. [Name], can you please describe this picture to us?
2. Why did you decide to take this picture in this particular way?
3. What does this picture represent to you?
4. What does this picture tell us about life in this community?

IF THE PICTURE IS OF A PROBLEM ...

5. Why do you think this problem exists?
6. How could this picture educate the community or policy makers?
7. What can we do about this problem? (Open this question up to everyone.)

IF THE PICTURE IS OF A STRENGTH IN THE COMMUNITY ...

8. Do you think most people in the community know about this (strength/asset)?
9. Do you think people outside this community know about this (strength/asset)?
10. Do you have any ideas for how to build on this (strength/asset) to improve life in this community? (Open this question up to everyone.)

IF THE PICTURE IS ABOUT AN IDEA FOR CHANGE ...

11. How do you think life here would be different if we could make your idea happen?
12. What do you think we need to do in order to make this idea become reality? (Open this question up to everyone.)
13. Is there anything else you would like to say about this picture?

In addition to taking field notes and audio recording each of the meetings, I created a chronologically ordered digital archive of all the photographs each participant shared throughout the course of the project so that I would be able to trace changes in the subject matter of the participants' photographs over time. As others have noted, visual images produced by research participants provide important insight into those individuals' experiences, relationships, and ideologies and their perceptions of themselves and of the environment in which they live (Frohmann 2005).

After each local meeting, I wrote up a record of the themes and topics the women discussed. I distributed the record to the members of the group at the beginning of the next reflection meeting. Across the five communities and over the eight months of the project, I held forty-three local Photovoice meetings (including the orientation meetings). In Communities A and B I held eight local meetings, and in Communities C, D, and E I held nine.

As was noted earlier, throughout the course of the project each participant selected a subset of her own photographs about which to write short narratives, creating "photostories." In preparation for the first regional Photovoice meeting, which was held January 24, 2009, I asked participants for copies of the photostories they had created over the first four months of the project. I used these photostories to create a PowerPoint presentation for the regional meeting. The goals for this regional meeting were for the women to meet the members of the other Photovoice groups for the first time, to share their communities' stories with one another, to realize and articulate their communities' assets, and to discuss projects or initiatives that they might be able to start in their communities to address some of their major concerns. Through this meeting experience, I hoped that each Photovoice group would come to see that many of the problems they were experiencing in their own communities were actually shared issues across the entire region. In addition, I invited an organizer from a local environmental justice organization to present information about water contamination and other coal-related problems in southern West Virginia, thus creating an opportunity for the Photovoice women to connect with the environmental justice movement.

Throughout the remainder of the project, Photovoice participants continued to turn in photostories to me as they created them. I photocopied all of their photostories and returned the originals to them to keep in their binders. In the sixth month of the project, we began preparing for the local Photovoice exhibits, which were held in March and April of 2009. Each Photovoice group selected a central location for a public exhibit and presentation of their work. (In four of the communities this central location was a school; in one community it was a community center.)

Each woman selected ten of the photostories she had created to be enlarged and mounted for the local community exhibit. I also asked each participant to select the three photostories that she wanted to have included in the regional Photovoice exhibit that was to be held in Charleston (West Virginia's capital city) in April of 2009. The photostories that the women selected for these public displays (and those that they did not) offered important insight into which community problems they were willing to publicly acknowledge. I was particularly interested in observing which participants and which communities chose to include photostories that were critical of the coal industry in the public exhibits.

In addition to selecting photostories, each Photovoice group prioritized the community problems and project ideas that they wanted to present at their public exhibit. During the local Photovoice meetings held in February, I led each group through this prioritization process. As has already been noted, after each Photovoice meeting I created a written record of the major community problems the women discussed, and of any ideas for community projects that were mentioned. I compiled all the problems and ideas that had been discussed in each community and created a form for the Photovoice participants to use to prioritize the problems and ideas, indicating which ones they most wanted to see the Photovoice project try to address.

Using the prioritized lists and the women's ranked photostories, I created a draft of a PowerPoint presentation for the women to collectively present at their local community exhibits. During our March reflection meetings, the participants refined the presentations and decided who would read which slides at their community's event. For many of these women, this presentation would be their first time giving a public talk of any sort. It is important to note that the Photovoice presentations didn't focus only on the problems in these communities; each PowerPoint presentation began with photostories depicting the community's strengths, beauty, and the unique characteristics that made it a special place to live.

As has been mentioned, we also held a regional Photovoice exhibit. Each of the Photovoice participants, from all five of the communities, selected up to three photostories to be displayed at the Clay Center for the Arts and Sciences in Charleston on April 15–19, 2009. A reception for the Photovoice women was held on Friday, April 17.

On May 2, after all the local exhibits and the regional exhibit had taken place, I held a final regional Photovoice meeting. The women from the five communities again came together to share their successes and to plan for the future of the project. I gave the groups their enlarged and mounted photostories to keep, with the hope that they would plan future public exhibits on their own. This meeting was also another opportunity for connections to be made with environmental justice activists. Three organizers attended this meeting (as did two state legislators and one representative of a legislator). This meeting marked the "official" end of my research intervention, although I hoped that the women would continue to meet, plan exhibits, and work on their project ideas.

In addition to the "official" and planned-for aspects of the project—the local meetings, regional meetings, and exhibits—a number of informal events occurred during the eight months of the project that were important opportunities for participant observation and informal interviews. In the process of building rapport with the Photovoice participants, I attended numerous church services, visited their homes, had countless phone conversations, and had informal social interactions with other people in their communities. In addition, some of the Photovoice women asked for my help in organizing meetings with their state legislators during the 2009 legislative session. I accompanied two of these women on their first trip to the state capitol to meet with policy makers. Three women from another Photovoice group helped one of the environmental justice organizations with a visit from a reporter and photographer from a prominent national newspaper, who wanted to talk to residents affected by mountaintop-removal mining. I went along on the community tour of mountaintop-removal sites the women organized for the newspaper reporter and photographer. Thus, my participant observation activities are not limited to "Photovoice events," and I draw on these other experiences in my data analysis.

In September of 2009 (four months after the project ended), I conducted follow-up phone interviews with Photovoice participants. I asked what they had done since the end of project, whether they were still in contact with other women from the group, whether they had held any additional Photovoice exhibits, what they believed were the most important outcomes from the project, and if they believed that Photovoice had affected their lives or their communities in any particular ways. In addition, in order to gather long-term reflections on what happened and what did not happen during the Photovoice project, I interviewed a sample of Photovoice participants in August and September of 2013, four years after the end of the project.

To summarize, then, data for this portion of my study include the following:

- pre-project and post-project questionnaires with Photovoice participants and a control group in each of the five communities

- field notes and audio recordings from forty-three local Photovoice meetings and two regional Photovoice meetings
- field notes from five local Photovoice exhibits and one regional Photovoice exhibit
- a chronologically ordered digital archive of all the photographs each participant in each Photovoice community shared throughout the course of the project
- all the "photostories" that each participant submitted to me, and which of those photostories the participant chose to include in the local and regional Photovoice exhibits
- each community's prioritization of the problems and project ideas discussed at reflection meetings throughout the eight-month Photovoice project
- participant observation of other non-Photovoice events and interactions I witnessed or experienced in the Photovoice communities
- follow-up phone interviews that I conducted with Photovoice participants four months after the end of the project
- follow-up in-person interviews that I conducted with a sample of Photovoice participants four years after the end of the project

9 Photovoice in Five Coal-Mining Communities

Through using the Photovoice method with five groups of women living in the coal-mining region of southern West Virginia, I attempted to create a micromobilization context, providing a structure that could serve to facilitate the non-activist participants' entry into the environmental justice movement. Recruiting one or two local women who were already critical of the coal industry to join each group increased the likelihood that photographs would be shared during the reflection meetings that focused on the effects of the coal industry's most destructive practices. This, I hoped, would serve two purposes: increasing the non-activist participants' awareness of the coal-related problems in their communities and creating a space in which it was safe, possibly even encouraged, to talk about these problems openly.

In this chapter, I examine the story of the Photovoice project in the five communities. I describe the significant events and micro-level interactions that took place during and outside the Photovoice meetings in each community, providing an analysis of how those events and interactions influenced the likelihood that group members would publicly acknowledge their concerns with certain industry practices or become involved in environmental justice activism. In chapter 10, I examine the stories of the five individuals who became involved in the environmental justice movement in some way during the Photovoice project. Before delving into the micro-level stories of these communities, however, I believe it useful to first provide an overall picture of how the Photovoice project influenced participants' views of the coal industry and a comparison of measurable indicators of coal-critical attitudes across the five groups.

A Broad Look at the Five Photovoice Communities

As I described in chapter 8, I administered identical questionnaires to participants in the five Photovoice groups at the start of the project and then again at the end of the project, and I also administered the same questionnaire to members of five control groups from the same communities at the same two times. The questions focused on respondents' histories of civic involvement and social protest, their feelings of self-efficacy, and their behaviors, experiences, and cognitions relating to the coal industry and the state. The purpose of administering the questionnaire to the Photovoice groups and the control groups before and after the project was to allow me to identify changes in Photovoice participants' attitudes and behaviors over time, while also providing a way to control for extraneous community events not related to Photovoice that could have also caused a change in local residents' attitudes or behaviors (for example, a major mining accident or a corruption scandal). By having the control groups in each community to serve as a comparison, I was better assured that any changes that I observed among members of the Photovoice groups were attributable to their participation in the project.

In order to measure whether Photovoice participants became more critical of the coal industry as the project progressed, I included four questions in the pre-project and post-project questionnaires that served to assess respondents' attitudes toward the coal industry. Combining these four questions into a "Coal-Critical Index" enabled me to compare participants' attitudes toward the coal industry over the course of the project. Specifically, I assessed the following:

- whether the non-activist participants in the Photovoice groups became more critical of the coal industry during the time period of the project
- whether members of the control population[1] became more critical of the coal industry during the same time period
- whether the non-activist participants in the Photovoice groups became more critical of the coal industry than the members of the control population during the time period of the project.

My statistical analysis of the difference between the pre-project and post-project questionnaires reveals that there was a statistically significant increase in how critically non-activist Photovoice participants viewed the

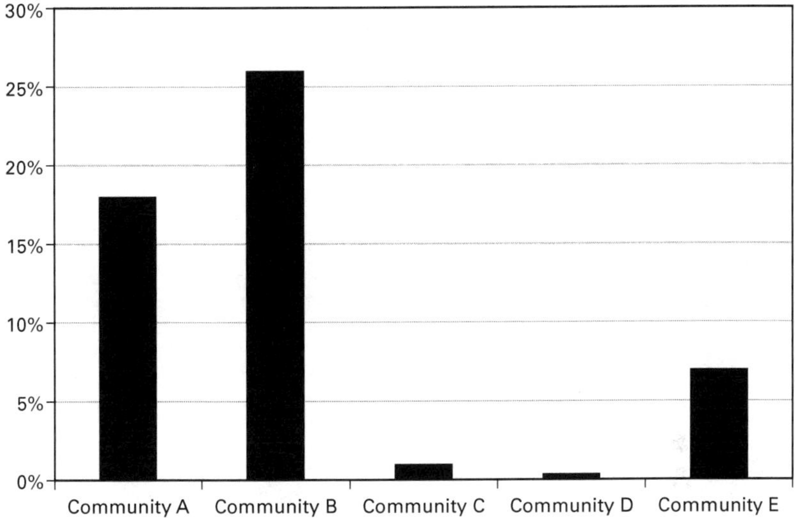

Figure 9.1
Coal-critical photographs as a percentage of total photographs shared across the five Photovoice communities.

coal industry during the project, while there was no such increase among those who did not take part in Photovoice. (See appendix C for the details of the analysis.) From these results it can be inferred that, as a whole, the Photovoice groups provided a venue that exposed participants to knowledge about the coal-related problems in their communities, leading to increased levels of disapproval toward the coal industry. But, were Photovoice participants compelled to share these feelings publicly during meetings or community presentations? And, taking it a step further, does being critical of the coal industry mean that those participants chose to become involved in the environmental justice movement when given the opportunity? The remainder of this chapter examines these questions.

Comparisons across the Five Groups

When comparing the number of coal-critical photographs shared during Photovoice meetings and the number of coal-critical photostories created for the local public exhibits, Communities A and B seem to have become the most successful micromobilization contexts of the five groups. As is revealed in figure 9.1, members of these two Photovoice groups shared and

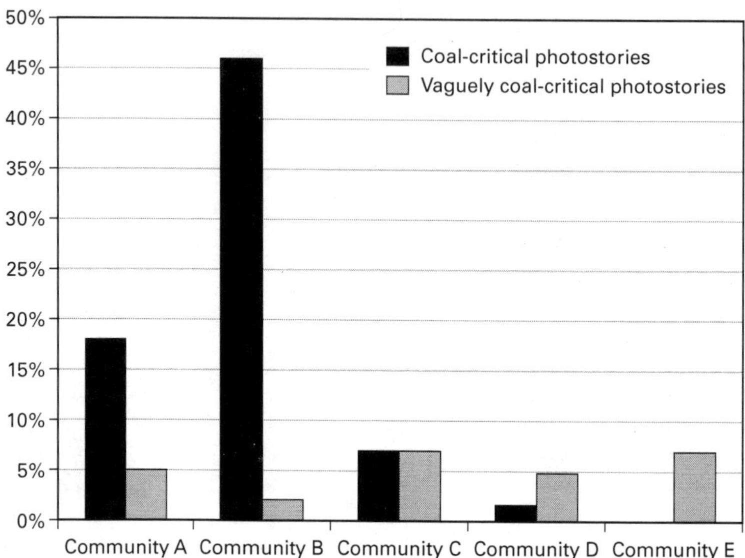

Figure 9.2
Percentages of explicitly coal-critical and vaguely coal-critical photostories as a percentage of total photostories selected for display at the local public exhibits.

discussed the largest number of photographs that were related to problems with the coal industry. Furthermore, these two groups also created the largest percentage of photostories for their local public exhibits that were explicitly critical of the coal industry. (See figure 9.2.) In addition, four of the five "non-activist" Photovoice women who began participating in activities associated with the environmental justice movement during the course of the project were from these two groups.

Communities C and D were not, for the most part, successful micromobilization contexts, at least with regard to issues related to the coal industry. Though a few participants in Community C did talk about problems with the coal industry's practices during reflection meetings, and some even created coal-critical photostories, no one in that group chose to take political or public actions to address coal-related problems. Of the five communities, Community D had the fewest discussions about the coal industry; in fact, of the 1,179 photographs that were shared during the eight-month project in that community, only three focused on problems with the coal industry. Interestingly, though, one of the five Photovoice participants who became involved in the environmental justice movement was from Community D. I discuss her case in chapter 10.

The outcomes in Community E were completely different from those in the other four communities. An *anti*-mobilization context seems to have emerged. On a number of occasions when certain participants spoke negatively about the coal industry, their opinions were suppressed, both during interactions I witnessed and probably also during many interactions that I did not witness. What unfolded in Community E provides important insight into the power dynamics operating within many coal-mining communities and also reveals how an "outsider stigma" can be applied to certain individuals—even local residents—as a way of discrediting their grievances with the coal industry.

What was it about Communities A and B that made them relatively effective micromobilization contexts? Why were Communities C and D not as effective? And, perhaps most important, why was speaking out against the coal industry censored in Community E?

In the sections that follow, I describe what happened in each of the five communities to block or facilitate the creation of an effective micromobilization context. In each section, I provide a narrative that incorporates observation, interview, and visual data that I collected throughout the Photovoice project. In addition, I also I provide summary data for each community on the total number of Photovoice events each participant attended, how many photographs each participant shared that were critical of the coal industry, how many of the photostories that each participant created and submitted were critical of the coal industry, and how many of those coal-critical photostories participants chose to display in the public Photovoice exhibits. In appendix D these summary data are presented in three different tables for each of the five communities.

Community A

Living in the county with the highest level of coal production in West Virginia means that residents of Community A are constantly reminded of, and affected by, the coal industry. One of the most recent reminders was the discovery that the water in a portion of Community A had become contaminated because of a breach in an underground slurry-injection site. In other parts of Community A, residents have had to contend with mountaintop-removal mining's destruction of beloved creeks, hunting grounds, and ATV trails, as well as structural damage to their homes caused by nearby blasting.

Two activist participants and ten non-activist participants were initially recruited for the Photovoice project in Community A. One additional participant (Aileen) joined the group during the seventh month of the project. Aileen had been interested in participating in the project from the beginning, but because of her work schedule she had been unable to attend the meetings until March. Her sister Arlene (also a Photovoice participant) kept her informed about the project, and when Aileen's schedule opened up, she became a regular participant in the group's meetings and events. Thus, in all, there were thirteen women who participated in some capacity in Community A's Photovoice group. Two of the thirteen—Audrey and Adelle—participated in the project only minimally, each attending only two of the twelve Photovoice events. Though neither Audrey nor Adelle attended any Photovoice events after the fifth month of the project, they never formally dropped out of the group. In fact, a few of the other participants from Community A jointly created photostories with Audrey and Adelle so that their work could be represented in the Photovoice exhibits.

Of the twelve Photovoice events that participants in Community A could have attended, eight were local reflection meetings, two were regional Photovoice meetings, one was the local Photovoice exhibit/presentation, and one was the regional Photovoice exhibit in Charleston. Table D.1 in appendix D lists all the Photovoice participants in Community A and the events they attended during the project.

Local reflection meetings in Community A had an average of seven participants in attendance (a 55 percent attendance rate). Nine (69 percent) of the participants in Community A attended at least half of the local reflection meetings, and eight (62 percent) attended at least half of the Photovoice events (including local reflection meetings, regional meetings, and exhibits).

As was noted in chapter 8, during each local reflection meeting after the initial orientation, participants were invited to share the photographs they had taken since the previous meeting. I brought my laptop computer, a multimedia projector, and a color laser printer to each meeting. Participants gave me the memory cards from their digital cameras, I downloaded their photographs onto my computer, and then I projected their images on a wall so that everyone could view them. Participants took turns scrolling through their photos, describing what they had photographed, why, and the significance of the images. The other participants were invited to ask questions, make comments, and participate in discussions around topics pertaining to the images and stories shared by group members. I served as a facilitator, asking questions and encouraging those who were sharing photos to provide more information about the places, scenes, people, and objects they had photographed. After each participant presented her photographs, I printed as many as fifteen of the images so that the participant could write narratives to accompany her photos. Table D.2 gives the total number of photographs Community A participants shared in each reflection meeting and how many of those images were presented as criticisms of or complaints about the coal industry.

Criticism of the Coal Industry as a Social Norm in Community A

Reflection meetings in Community A were very active, most lasting more than two hours. At the first reflection meeting (Meeting 2), five of the ten individuals in attendance shared at least one photograph that was critical of the coal industry. I purposely organized the meeting so that Alice and Agnes, the two activist participants, would present their images toward the end of the meeting, so as not to influence what the non-activist participants would share. However, I was surprised to see that three of the non-activist participants presented photographs that specifically identified problems with the coal industry. For instance, after sharing two photographs of recreational opportunities on a river in their area, Adelle, a non-activist participant, shared a photograph of a road on a mountaintop-removal site close to her home. (It is presented here as figure 9.3.) She described the photograph as follows:

> This one is a picture from across the river from where [Arlene] and I live—the mountaintop removal. When they blast and stuff. ... When I open up the doors to my cabinets to get a plate, I have to hold my hand up [as I open the doors] because they'll come out and drop down on the floor and break. The pictures will come off the walls. I mean, it's really, really bad. If you're outside, they do a siren so you know it's coming, but if you're inside, you can't hear the siren.

Adelle also revealed that large cracks had appeared in the walls of her house. During the same meeting, Adelle's aunt (and neighbor) Arlene, also a non-activist participant, showed a similar photograph of the

Figure 9.3
A coal-critical photograph shared by a non-activist participant in Community A.

mountaintop-removal mine in the area where she and Adelle lived. "Wild, wonderful West Virginia—with mountaintop removal, it's no longer going to be that," Arlene asserted. "I *love* the 'reclamation'—reclaim is supposed to be put back the same way, right? That phrase don't hold a drop of water for me."

During that first reflection meeting, the two activist participants, Alice and Agnes, also talked about many of their photographs in ways that were critical of the coal industry. For example, Agnes showed a picture of a pink honeysuckle bush that she had recently "rescued" from a mountain that was about to be strip mined. Pointing to an older photograph that she had taken of a scenic stream and fishing hole, Agnes reported that she could no longer visit this favorite spot because the access had been blocked by a mining operation. She talked of the many other special places in the mountains that residents could no longer visit because coal operations had either obstructed access to them or destroyed them. Alice, the other activist participant, continued this theme, sharing two photos of contaminated water in the water tanks of her family members' and neighbors' toilets, remarking:

Figure 9.4
A photograph of water contamination shared by Alice in Community A.

This happens to be the back of my son's commode. And you know, you're not supposed to find anything in the back of the commode other than bare water. There's not supposed to be anything back there ... so there's something causing this. There's something causing it.

At the time of the first reflection meeting, Alice was working with environmental justice organizations and a few local residents to advocate for the delivery of clean drinking water to residents of her area. They were also working to have water testing conducted that would provide scientific evidence that the black substance contaminating the well water was coal slurry that leached out of an underground impoundment close to their homes. After seeing Alice's photographs, Amanda, who lived in the same hollow as Alice, asked, "Why is it black? I was getting something black in mine." Adah interjected: "Well, it could be coal, manganese, or a black iron-type thing—manganese is a black iron." Alice responded: "They're finding out. ... We don't have a print-out on it yet, but we're working on it." Others in the group began to ask questions and share stories about the discolored water that they had seen in the back of their toilets and in their sinks, and they began to express concern about how the contaminated water might be affecting people's health.

Of the photographs shared at the first reflection meeting, 24 percent raised questions about or expressed grievances with the coal industry. It is important to note that a number of the group members who did not present photos that were critical of the coal industry made comments and expressed frustrations and fears associated with coal-mining practices when other participants shared coal-critical photos. This meeting set the tone for the remainder of the Photovoice meetings. At every local Photovoice meeting in Community A, at least one person provided a criticism of or a question about some aspect of the coal industry through one or more images. These Photovoice meetings seem to have provided a safe space for voicing concerns, frustrations, and anger about the coal industry's practices in the area.

The influence of this regular public criticism of the coal industry can be seen in the photostories that participants submitted to me in January of 2009, the fifth month of the project. As table D.3 in appendix D shows, ten of the thirteen participants created photostories that were explicitly critical of the coal industry. The columns headed "Photostories created" show the total number of photostories that each participant submitted to me, the number of those photostories that were explicitly critical of the coal industry, and the number of photostories that were vaguely critical of the coal industry (i.e., they didn't specifically name "coal" as the culprit, but such a conclusion could be drawn). Figure 9.5 is an example of a photostory from Community A that was explicitly critical of the coal industry; figure 9.6 is an example of a photostory from Community A that was vaguely critical of the coal industry.

Interestingly, of the coal-critical photostories the women submitted to me, a number were created using photographs that were not initially presented to the Photovoice group as being about the coal industry at all. In fact, two of the participants who created such photostories did not discuss problems with the coal industry in connection to *any* of the photographs they shared during the reflection meetings. However, when they submitted photostories to me, the narratives that accompanied a few of their photographs were quite critical of the industry.

"Heartbreak"

"Oh these West Virginia Hills, How majestic and how grand."
It breaks my heart to see what mountaintop removal mining is doing to our mountains. I would like to see laws made and enforced to save our hills and their beauty. Reclaiming is not putting back 100-year-old trees.

Figure 9.5
A photostory from Community A that is explicitly critical of the coal industry.

Figure 9.7 provides an example of a photostory that was infused with a criticism of the coal industry after the image had been presented differently at a reflection meeting. During Meeting 3, Annette scrolled through a series of photographs of the scenery close to her home. Coming to the photo shown here as figure 9.7, she remarked: "That's in [Community A] there, when you first start out of the holler. That was early morning. [My husband] was having to take me out that morning because we had appointments in Charleston and Huntington. ... I saw that and said, 'Pull over! Pull over!'" The room erupted in compliments about Annette's photographic

"In Need of Protection"

Creeks are great and should be protected from pollutants.
Splashing. Fishing. Hiking. Hunting crawdads, minnows, and lizards.
How many memories do you have there?

Figure 9.6
A photostory from Community A that is vaguely critical of the coal industry.

eye and comments about how beautiful the mountains are in the fall, especially in the morning. During the reflection meeting, Annette had presented this photograph of a fog-enshrouded mountain as simply one of the many images of beauty in the area. However, the narrative that Annette later wrote to accompany this image (shown here as figure 9.7) turned out to be a sharp criticism of mountaintop-removal mining. Before reading that photostory and a similar one that Annette submitted, I had not heard Annette speak negatively about the coal industry. In fact, I had never heard her talk about the coal industry at all, even while others in the group were talking about water contamination and mountaintop-removal mining. The fact that some of the participants, including Annette, were more critical of the coal industry in their photostories than they were when they discussed

"Early Morning"

A thin fog is slowly rising from the mountain in this early morning picture. With the coal industry's continued devastation of the hills and mountains in our area, picturesque views are small blessings that are few and far between.

Figure 9.7
A coal-critical photostory with an image that wasn't initially presented as a critique of the coal industry.

their photographs during earlier reflection meetings indicates that a process of socialization may have been taking place among the group members, and that it may have become a social norm to express grievances about the coal industry within the group.

During Meeting 7, after making copies for myself, I gave the Photovoice participants back all the photostories they had submitted to me and asked them to each select ten photostories they would like to have included in the local Photovoice exhibit. I also asked each of them to choose three photostories to be displayed in the regional Photovoice exhibit in Charleston. As table D.3 shows, of the 99 photostories that were selected for inclusion in the local exhibit, eighteen (18 percent) were explicitly critical of the coal industry and five (5 percent) were vaguely critical of the coal industry. Furthermore, nine of the thirteen participants (69 percent) selected at least one coal-critical photostory for inclusion in the local exhibit. That such a high percentage of group members selected at least one photostory that expressed concerns (and in some cases anger) at coal industry practices suggests that the Photovoice group setting was an effective micromobilization context for facilitating the micro-level processes of cognitive liberation and solidarity building among participants.

Despite the fact that so many individuals in Community A chose to publicly acknowledge coal-related problems in their community by selecting coal-critical photostories for the local and regional exhibits, most of the non-activist women—even those who created and displayed photostories that criticized the coal industry—did not become involved in the environmental justice movement. Identifying with others in the Photovoice group who were critical of the coal industry does not seem to have been predictive of identifying with participants in the environmental justice movement who were taking action against destructive coal industry practices. This was especially interesting to me because water contamination had become severe in part of Community A. As noted above, one of the activist participants was even holding organizing meetings in her home for a group that had been formed to spread awareness about the water contamination and to raise money for an alternate water supply. Thus, there were ample opportunities for the Photovoice participants to become involved in taking action on behalf of the water issue in some way, but most did not.

In a follow-up interview I conducted with Adah after the project had ended, I asked her to reflect on why she thought people in the Photovoice group had been so reluctant to move from being critical of the coal industry to taking action against its destructive practices. She responded:

> There's been a really big push-back locally, very strong against the EPA … very vocal, sometimes very narrow-minded in that … if your opinion differs, there's something wrong with you, you're a horrible person, you're against coal. And when somebody says "You're against coal," what they mean is "You're against me." That's what they mean. They take it very, very personal.

In this response, Adah describes the implications of the region's economic identity being inextricably linked with coal production. As Bell and York

(2010) argue, the identities of many coalfield residents (especially men) are tied to coal mining, whether or not they actually work for the industry.

Rebecca Scott's 2010 book *Removing Mountains* lends additional insight into Adah's comments. Scott argues that the way Appalachia has been "othered" in the national consciousness as a place where the people, the landscape, and the culture are separate and different from those of mainstream America explains why so many coalfield residents express ambivalence about, or even support, destructive practices such as mountaintop-removal mining. Scott argues that Appalachian people feel that they must prove their national belonging, and that the environmental and social costs of mining coal appear to "constitute the terms for Appalachia's membership in the American nation" (p. 168). In addition, she notes, coal mining is connected to images of masculinity and whiteness, both of which are attributes of "unmarked American citizenship" (p. 171). Thus, by supporting mountaintop-removal mining, and the coal industry more generally, coalfield citizens attempt to shed their status as "others." This explains why any perceived threat to the coal industry could be construed as a threat against one's own person. As Adah further explained to me in our interview, "a lot of it is defensive ... because we are put down a lot. Southern West Virginia, Appalachian people, there is still that negative image."

However, it is important to note that there are many coalfield residents who do *not* support mountaintop-removal mining and other industry practices. "This might seem a little contradictory," Adah commented, "but there *are* a large number of people who are willing to say 'I'm not against coal, but I'm against some of the practices that they're doing now.'" This insight helps to explain why some Photovoice participants in Community A were willing to express criticism of the coal industry in their publicly displayed photostories but weren't willing to take the extra step to become associated with one of the environmental justice groups working in the area. In Community A, there were concrete, well-documented coal-industry-related problems that were affecting the health and safety of local residents. Through photographing and displaying these problems, the Photovoice women were participating in what Mary Anglin (2002, p. 123) calls "dissenting practices," a form of resistance that is less political than traditional social-movement activism but that still challenges the power structure in subtle ways through smaller-scale, more individual actions. However, most of the participants in Community A didn't feel comfortable formalizing their resistance and dissent by becoming affiliated with one of the environmental justice groups, perhaps for fear of acquiring the label of being "against coal."

Though most of the Photovoice participants in Community A did not become formally involved with environmental justice groups, there were three from this group who, for a brief time, did become involved in activist endeavors. The stories of their involvement in the environmental justice movement are told in chapter 10.

Community B

Like Community A, Community B is also located in the top coal-producing county in West Virginia. It, however, is in a far more remote and depopulated portion of the county, an area where the coal industry's oppressive presence is felt all around. Abandoned coal tipples, a burnt-out union hall, boarded-up buildings, and denuded mountaintops are just a part of the landscape. The area had experienced severe flooding a few years before the Photovoice project began, but many in the community were not aware (or did not believe) that there was a connection between the flooding and the increased mountaintop-removal mining taking place in the area.

In Community B, two activists and three non-activists agreed to participate in the Photovoice project. Though this group proved to be the most difficult for recruiting participants, it ended up having the highest retention rate of all the groups. All five of the women in Community B who signed up to participate in the project remained involved for the entire eight months. This Photovoice group also had the highest attendance rate of the five. As table D.4 in appendix D shows, everyone in the group attended more than half of the local reflection meetings and more than two thirds of the Photovoice events.

From the first meeting onward, there was a great deal of discussion about irresponsible mining practices and the injustices resulting from the coal industry's power in their community. As table D.5 shows, at the first reflection meeting three of the five participants shared photographs representing problems caused by the coal industry and their frustrations with and disapproval of the industry. Betty (one of the activist participants) shared photos of a coal truck crossing the center line of a road, forcing an oncoming vehicle toward the side. Belinda (the second activist participant) shared photos of abandoned and dilapidated coal tipples and of mountaintop-removal mining sites that were visible from one of the roads she regularly traveled. Bonnie (a non-activist participant) shared photos of mountaintop-removal mines and sludge impoundments that she found while riding her ATV in the mountains behind her home. Throughout the course of the project, participants in Community B frequently shared coal-critical photographs and engaged in lengthy discussions about the problems associated with irresponsible mining practices, dangerous coal trucks, and the mine fire that had been burning for many years through a coal seam in a nearby mountain. As calculated from table D.5, among the Photovoice meetings in Community B where photos were shared (a total of six meetings), an average of 30 photographs per meeting were shown that were critical of the coal industry. Thus, like Community A, it became a social norm Community B to take a critical stance with regard to coal-industry practices during the reflection meetings.

Awakening to the Destruction Caused by the Coal Industry

Even though Betty had been an environmental justice activist since 2003, her daughter Bonnie, one of the non-activist participants in the group, had never been interested in the environmental justice movement. Having been an underground coal miner for almost ten years in the 1970s and the 1980s, Bonnie still felt loyal to the industry. When her mother tried to talk with her about the problems that mountaintop-removal mining was causing in their community, Bonnie's typical response had been "Mom, they've gotta get the coal somehow!" Bonnie told me, however, that her participation in the Photovoice project had caused her to "wake up to this community and what's going on in it."

At the beginning of the project, Bonnie searched for images to photograph. Riding her ATV to the ridgetops, she began to see the familiar landscape with different eyes, observing devastation she hadn't noticed before. She photographed slurry impoundments, barren landscapes, felled trees left to waste, and mountains being violently blown apart. Over the course of the Photovoice project, Bonnie became more political, eventually participating in some events organized by the environmental justice groups in the area and even attending a Sludge Safety Project "lobby day" at the West

Figure 9.8
A photograph, shared by Bonnie, depicting mountaintop-removal mining in Community B.

Virginia state capitol to talk to legislators about water contamination in her community. Her story is detailed further in chapter 10.

Bonnie's awakening to the extent of the mountains' destruction in her community also affected Barbara and Brandy, the other two non-activist participants in Community B. Like Bonnie, they had been largely unaware of the extent of mountaintop-removal mining and the severity of its impacts on their community. Bonnie's ATV (and her daring) afforded her access to mining sites that weren't visible from roads and population centers. The images that Bonnie shared at reflection meetings, such as those shown here in figures 9.8 and 9.9, helped Barbara and Brandy begin to understand how vast the mining operations are, and to recognize connections between the expansion of mountaintop-removal mining and the increased flooding and landslides their community had experienced in recent years.

As noted above, some of the same processes of socialization that occurred in Community A also seem to have taken place in Community B. As table D.5 shows, each Photovoice participant in Community B shared multiple coal-critical photographs and engaged in discussions about the environmental, health, and safety problems the coal industry was causing in their area. Many coal-critical photographs were shared (an average of 30 per reflection meeting, as already noted), often by multiple participants. And, as table D.6 shows, a very high percentage of photostories selected for the local and regional exhibits depicted problems associated with the coal industry. In fact, 46 percent of the photostories included in the local exhibit and 50 percent of the photostories included in the regional exhibit were

Figure 9.9
A photograph, shared by Bonnie, depicting mountaintop-removal mining in Community B

explicitly critical of the coal industry. (See figures 9.10 and 9.11 for examples of explicitly coal-critical photostories that participants selected to include in the exhibits.)

Brandy's Evolving Critique of the Coal Industry

Brandy, unlike Bonnie, did not become involved with the environmental justice movement during the project. However, she did become increasingly more aware of the coal industry's negative effects on the region, and she became more willing to acknowledge those effects publicly over the course of the project. During the first round of picture taking, the subject matter of Brandy's photographs was not focused on the coal industry at all. At our first reflection meeting, Brandy shared a photo she had taken of a sunflower that her husband and young son planted. She then presented a photo of a still-life scene depicting two ripening homegrown tomatoes, a squash, and a jar of home-canned tomatoes. The final set of photos revealed

"Death and Destruction"

Death and destruction in central Boone County. About three quarters of a mile from Frasure Creek #7 strip mine, a head stone was spray-painted on a rock cliff by someone in the Van area. Why is it that people in the communities realize the destruction, but the government does not?

Figure 9.10

A coal-critical photostory that was included in the local Photovoice exhibit in Community B.

"Loyalties"

Some people proudly display stickers on their vehicles for coal, others display "I Love Mountains" stickers because they are trying to stop mountaintop removal coal mining. They feel it is destroying the state of West Virginia, their communities, and their families. Which do you love the most – your beautiful mountains or the coal under them? I say go green, and keep our beautiful mountains.

Figure 9.11
A coal-critical photostory that was included in the local Photovoice exhibit in Community B.

two pairs of athletic shoes with the laces tied together dangling over a telephone line above a house close to her church. Brandy photographed the last scene, she said, because she had heard that shoes over a telephone or power line meant that drugs were being sold in the house below the shoes, and she felt that drugs were a big problem in her community.

Although Brandy did not photograph any scenes that were critical of the coal industry during that first round of picture taking, Betty, Belinda, and Bonnie did, and they shared those photographs at the first reflection meeting. Images of mountaintop-removal mining sites that were visible from old logging roads, abandoned coal structures that had been left behind as eyesores for the community, a coal truck drifting into the lane of an oncoming vehicle, a mine-crack in the mountain, and a valley fill dominated the visual space of that first meeting. Betty, an activist participant who freely expressed her negative opinions of coal mining, spent a large portion of the meeting talking about the devastation that the coal industry had caused to her home and her family, sharing her belief that the coal industry had contaminated the water in her community and caused her husband to develop pancreatic cancer, from which he had died.

At the second meeting, there were only two Photovoice women in attendance—Brandy and Bonnie. As with the first meeting, Brandy shared numerous photographs about strengths or beauty in her community: her son in front of a cherry tree, beloved mountains in front of her house, a church she thought was pretty, and various scenes of beauty from the Bullet Mountain[2] area. The scenes of community problems she photographed included piles of litter and graffiti at an overlook on Bullet Mountain, a power station from which copper wire had recently been stolen, downed trees on a mountainside, and a few areas around the coal facilities close to her home that she also thought looked bad ("I just think they should at least make it look halfway decent," she explained). Through this last set of photographs, Brandy began to hint at some mild criticism of the coal companies.

As she had at the first, Bonnie shared a number of striking photographs of destructive coal-industry practices at this second meeting. Once again, most of her images were ones that she had captured while riding her ATV in remote areas of the mountains; thus, these were images that most people living in the area had never seen. Bonnie showed photos of active mountaintop-removal mines, sludge ponds, and land that had supposedly been "reclaimed" by the coal industry but that still looked desolate and damaged.

Brandy wasn't present at the third meeting (in December), but she sent some photographs with Barbara, another non-activist participant. The photographs that she submitted for this round of picture-taking included scenes of the first snow of the season, her son and her husband filling a bird feeder, and her son playing at a park located along the river that flows through the community.

Brandy did attend the fourth reflection meeting (which took place in January), and she brought some new photographs. Many of her photos showed the flooding that had occurred earlier that month. Brandy expressed a feeling that mountaintop-removal mining was contributing to the increased flooding she had seen in the area in recent years. Some of the other women concurred with this, and a discussion of it ensued. This was the first time that Brandy had initiated an explicit discussion of problems linked to coal mining. After all the participants had shared photographs, I asked the women to prepare their photostories to turn in to me, because this meeting marked the halfway point in the project. The women spent some time toward the end of the meeting writing and/or finalizing narratives to accompany the photos they had taken during the first half of the project, and they submitted those photostories to me before we ended the meeting.

Brandy's photostories in particular were interesting because, as was the case with some of the participants in Community A, a few of the narratives she wrote differed quite a bit from the way she had presented the accompanying photographs during the Photovoice meetings. The most obvious example is the narrative Brandy wrote for a photograph she had taken from the top of Bullet Mountain. During the second meeting, when she shared these photos, Brandy did not mention mountaintop-removal mining. In fact, she did not mention coal-mining practices at all until the fourth meeting, during which she discussed her photos of the flooding. In the second meeting, as we scrolled through the photos she had taken from the top of Bullet Mountain, she smiled and said "It's so pretty up there. Just wait until you see the winter pictures when it snows! It is just *so* beautiful when it sticks to the trees." She didn't said anything negative about the Bullet Mountain scenes, except to express her disgust with the litter and graffiti at the overlook and to say that she wished locals would have more pride in and respect for the beautiful places in their community. However, when she turned in her photostories in January, the narrative she had written to accompany the Bullet Mountain image clearly articulated disapproval of mountaintop-removal mining, which, her photostory laments, is "slowly taking these mountains away."

In addition to the photostory shown in figure 9.12, Brandy also submitted one other photostory that was explicitly critical of the coal industry (figure 9.13) and one that was vaguely critical. Interestingly, she selected all

"Mountains Aplenty"

West Virginia, the "Mountain State," is full of beautiful mountains. But mountaintop removal mining is slowly taking these mountains away.

Figure 9.12
A coal-critical photostory created by Brandy in Community B.

three of these photostories for public display in the local Photovoice exhibit.

Taking Action

During the Photovoice project, Community B became notable for the increasing political engagement of its participants. Also notable, however, are the choices various participants made about what problems to focus their advocacy on, and how to frame those problems, especially in relation to the coal industry.

As has already been noted, we held a regional Photovoice meeting in January, about halfway through the project. I created a PowerPoint presentation that included photostories from all the women in all five communities. Through seeing one another's photostories and through participating in group discussions, many of the participants were awakened to the fact that most of the problems in their own communities—including litter,

"Flooding"

High water is a major concern for local residents. Mountaintop removal and logging cause more water run-off from the mountains when it rains. That, in turn, causes flooding.

Figure 9.13
A coal-critical photostory by Brandy in Community B.

drugs, water contamination, and mountaintop-removal mining—were also problems the other Photovoice communities were experiencing. A representative from one of the local environmental justice organizations gave a brief presentation about the work her group was doing, and a number of the participants asked questions of her. The meeting seemed to be very energizing for many of the Photovoice participants.

As was briefly described in chapter 8, during the round of meetings in February, which took place a few weeks after the regional meeting, I led the women in each Photovoice group through a process of prioritizing the major problems in their communities. I provided each of them with a handout that included a list of eleven or twelve problems about which the group members had created photostories. I asked each participant to rank these problems, the ranking of 1 representing the biggest problem. I also provided spaces for the participants to add and rank other problems that weren't on the list. I then asked them to circle the problems they ranked first, second, and third. After collecting all their sheets, I tallied up their responses on a flip chart.

In Community B, the three problems that the participants ranked as the most significant were "Irresponsible Mining," "Flooding," and "Poor Road Conditions." I wrote these problems on a flip chart, and we began our discussion with the problem "Irresponsible Mining." I asked the group to talk about that problem further, specifically its causes. Activist participant Betty immediately asserted:

> [It's] because it's a few cents cheaper to mine [this way], to tear our mountains down. On the ton, it's only a few cents [cheaper], and to me, that's ridiculous to tear our mountains down and cause all this destruction to the communities and the people. ... And we are paying the taxes on this, on the roads, and all this stuff. The mining [industry] ... they are getting away with hardly paying anything. So, we're not, I mean, where is the money that is supposed to be coming into this community to restore all of this stuff? It's not coming. What are they doing with it?

To encourage others from the group to speak, I looked at Brandy and asked her if she had anything to say. She shook her head and said "No." I then looked at Barbara; she shook her head, indicating No, and then said "I don't really know a lot about that." Betty again spoke up:

> They [Brandy and Barbara] didn't attend the meetings we had down here to try to teach people in the communities [about mountaintop-removal mining]. I don't really think a lot of people understood what we were trying to do. We were just trying to make people aware of what was happening here to the people. And what really gets me aggravated is that people don't take any interest. There wasn't a dozen people hardly that would come [to those meetings]. You know, everybody says they love living here, they love the mountains, they love their communities, and if they go someplace else and they come back, how they're always so glad to be home, but yet they won't stand up for their community. You know, if the people would gather together, they couldn't do it this way. They couldn't. If everybody that lived in these hollows, we would choose one day, or the whole state, to have everybody descend on that capitol over there, on [Governor] Joe Manchin—because he is nothing but a Coal you-know-what. ... We have roots here. We growed up here. We love it here. I've been to New York, I've been to Florida, I've been out West ... . But I like it here better than everywhere else I've been. ... I want them out of here. I want them to leave me alone. They ain't got enough money to pay me for what they've done to

me. 'Cause they have destroyed my health. ... People in our communities are all dying of cancer, and it's all because—look how polluted, look at what we have to put up with. ... You've got blasting behind you, you've got smoke in front of you [from underground mine fires], you know, it's just something all day long to irritate you. Really. And then you've got all these impoundments around you with all those chemicals that they put in that. On these hot days, those chemicals rise up, and it goes all in the air here, and the chemicals from the blasting, it comes over these hills here and lands on our houses and our cars and stuff. ... And the water. The first thing they destroyed in our community here was the water. They had to close this [community water] plant down here. Everybody I know of [has] had their gall bladder removed. And the lawyer told me that what killed my husband was the water here. He said, "I know it's what killed your husband." So how can you like anything that does so much destruction? It is, it's irresponsible. It's all irresponsible.

Neither Brandy nor Barbara spoke during or after Betty's vehement comments about the harms the coal industry was causing. Recognizing that this topic was not generating the group discussion I had hoped for, I acknowledged the importance of Betty's contribution and thanked her for sharing how she felt about the coal industry. Then I moved down the list we had generated, saying: "Another top priority problem you all identified was poor road conditions. Can you tell me about that? What are the main problems with the roads?" As soon as I had introduced the new topic, both Barbara and Brandy visibly perked up. Barbara declared:

Potholes. Potholes big enough to bury a car in. ... They'll come along and patch [the potholes] and before you know it, it's already out and worse than what it was before. But they don't patch them that often, I'll tell you, honey, they don't patch them that often. ... I don't understand. I don't understand—if you live in a place where you pay taxes, then you have a right to have some decent roads to ride on. I think we need somebody representing us that's going to get us some good roads.

"If I'm not mistaken," Brandy then interjected, "anybody ... . Can anybody just introduce a bill in the legislature?" I told her that someone other than a legislator can write a bill, but that a legislator has to be willing to sponsor it and introduce it. Brandy continued enthusiastically:

OK. Here's what I think we should do. I think we should introduce a bill, I think we're not going to have a problem finding someone willing to sponsor it. ... I don't know how to word it, we'll need to figure out a way to word it, but the severance tax that's going out of this county. ... We should introduce a bill that we should get so much of a percent of that severance tax in [our] county for roads. ... I realize that it will have to go to the State Roads, because the State Roads is the ones that are responsible, but, I mean we'll have to figure out a way to word it to where ...

a certain percent will go to the State Road Department, just for the repair of these roads in [our] county.

Brandy's idea had been inspired by discussions that had taken place at our Regional Photovoice Meeting two weeks earlier. The environmental justice organizer who had attended that meeting had said that revenues from the coal severance tax do not return directly to the communities from which the coal is mined. Instead, it goes into a general fund that is divided among all the counties in West Virginia (even those that do not produce coal), and each county decides how to use its portion of the funds. Because the communities with the most coal mining tend to be unincorporated towns, they rarely see any of the revenues from the coal severance tax. This injustice was a surprise to many of the Photovoice participants, but the weight of it hit particularly hard in Community B.

After Brandy had shared her idea of working on a bill calling for a portion of the coal severance tax revenue to be designated for road repairs in the unincorporated towns where coal is being mined, Barbara expressed her agreement, exclaiming:

> You know, you think about all the severance tax from all this coal in [our] county, this coal, and it's supposed to go for roads—and it's not! We're not getting it. ... People's getting busted tires and they're getting all tore up, everything's happening on account of the roads. There's no way of missing [the potholes]. If you've got another vehicle coming [the other way], you're going to have to hit potholes.

After some discussion, Barbara eagerly asked "Can we get an appointment to go and just, just talk to [a legislator]? Let's make a difference—I'm ready!"

The timing of Brandy's and Barbara's passionate commitment to improving the roads in their community suggests that they may have been spurred to take action, at least in part, by Betty's reproach of their absence at community meetings held to educate and organize residents to take a stand against problems caused by mountaintop-removal mining. Betty's words were quite stinging, particularly her statement that "people don't take any interest" and "won't stand up for their community." Soon after Betty's admonishment, Brandy and Barbara proposed that members of the Photovoice group lobby their legislators about the road conditions in their community. There seemed to be a great deal of enthusiasm for that idea, so I printed out contact information for the participants' state senators and delegates. Barbara volunteered to call and make appointments for meetings at the West Virginia State Capitol in Charleston. Next, the women discussed who would be responsible for photographing various roadways in order to create a series of photostories about the poor road conditions. By the next meeting, the participants had created five photostories about the roads (see figure 9.14 for an example), and Barbara and Brandy had taken video footage of driving conditions along the cracking, potholed highways. Barbara called the state capitol and was surprised at how easily she was able to schedule appointments with two representatives (one senator and one delegate).

The day of the appointments, I met Barbara, Brandy, and Brandy's 3-year old son at the state capitol building in Charleston, and we went to their legislators' offices. The photostories, the video footage, and Barbara and Brandy's vivid descriptions seemed to make a profound impression on the two policy makers. Both legislators promised the women that they would see what they could do to have the roads in Community B moved up on the list of repaving projects. (The roads there had not been fully repaved in more than 25 years.) During our visit, both legislators made phone calls to the Department of Highways to request that the roads be patched as a temporary fix. Later that same day, the Department of Highways was in Community B patching the roads that Brandy and Barbara had complained about. (One of the women in their Photovoice group even happened upon the repair work while it was taking place and snapped a picture!) In the following months, Barbara kept in regular contact with her legislators, checking on the progress being made toward full repaving of the roads. Although Brandy and Barbara didn't pursue their original idea of proposing a bill that would require a certain percentage of revenues from the coal severance tax to be earmarked for roads in their community, they seemed satisfied with the outcome of the meetings.

Bonnie, a non-activist participant, also lobbied at the state capitol, but on a different day than Barbara and Brandy. Bonnie lobbied alongside environmental justice activists in Charleston, whereas Barbara and Brandy chose not to lobby with the environmental justice groups, even though they were given an opportunity to do so. The pair seemed to want to be viewed as independent from the activists who were there. Furthermore, during their discussions with their legislators, Barbara and Brandy did not speak critically of the coal industry. When they did mention the coal industry, it was in reference to the revenues from the coal severance tax that their community was not receiving—something that was, they said, not the fault

"Hazard for Critical Care Transport"

Road conditions are a critical aspect of transporting a patient by ambulance to the nearest hospital. If the road is full of potholes, then it is extremely difficult for a paramedic to start an IV line or to intubate (provide an airway by putting in a tube) on a critical patient. These procedures will sometimes save a person's life, or if not done, can mean death for a critical patient. The roads in our area are full of potholes like these, especially along Route 26 and Route 85 on our end of Boone County. We desperately need to have the roads re-paved, not just patched.

Figure 9.14
A photostory about poor road conditions in Community B.

of the coal industry, but the fault of state and county officials who weren't allocating funds to their community for road improvements. On the other hand, Bonnie went to the capitol specifically to lobby her legislators about the problems the coal industry was causing in her community, and the water contamination was something that she was particularly eager to discuss. She aligned herself with the environmental justice groups there that day, and introduced herself as being part of their environmental-lobbying effort. Thus, I maintain that Brandy and Barbara's advocacy was socially "safer" than Bonnie's, because they were not challenging the power of the coal industry through their efforts, while Bonnie was. (Bonnie's environmental justice advocacy is recounted in more detail in chapter 10.)

It was clear that Brandy and Barbara had a deep desire to take action on behalf of their community. But although they (especially Brandy) found fault with the coal industry and created photostories that were critical of its practices, they didn't seem to feel comfortable being associated with the environmental justice movement per se. In a follow-up interview, Barbara confirmed this assessment when I asked her if she would like me to put her in touch with any of the environmental justice group members she had met. She hesitated for a moment, then said: "Well, I don't mind them contacting me, honey. You know. I, I—I just don't like to get into a lot of the mountaintop-removal stuff. ... As far as, you know, like working with the legislature about the community and stuff, then yes." It is clear from Barbara's reluctance that she wanted to work to improve her community but she didn't want to become an "activist" against mountaintop-removal mining. Brandy and Barbara advocated on behalf of an issue that was caused by—but did not threaten or challenge—the coal industry's power. Thus, the bad roads acted as what I will call a "non-contentious advocacy issue," or an issue that Brandy and Barbara could safely take on to feed their desire to take action while not risking acquiring the label of being "against coal."

Community C

Community C borders the county in which Communities A and B are located. Like Communities A and B, a large amount of out-migration over the past fifty years has left the community with a much smaller population than it once had. Many of the mountains surrounding the community are covered with large mountaintop-removal mining operations, but for the most part these operations are not readily visible to the majority of residents. However, because of a coal load-out facility very close by, there is a large volume of coal-truck traffic moving through Community C on a daily basis. The roads in this community are narrow and winding, and there have been a number of accidents caused by speeding, overweight coal trucks. Although residents of Community C are now on a municipal water line, there is evidence that the groundwater is contaminated with coal slurry from nearby injection sites. Residents are not drinking or bathing in this water, but some still use the water from old wells to water their gardens.

As table D.8 in appendix D shows, during the course of the Photovoice project only ten (2 percent) of the 512 photographs that were shared in Community C during reflection meetings were related to problems the coal industry was causing in the area. Interestingly though, as table D.9 shows, participants in this same group created and submitted fourteen explicitly coal-critical or vaguely coal-critical *photostories* (11 percent of the total). The women selected twelve of these fourteen photostories to appear in the local Photovoice exhibit. Carolyn (the activist participant), Cecilia, Constance, Cora, and Charity were the five individuals who submitted explicitly or vaguely coal-critical photostories. Of the five, the activist participant, Carolyn, created the majority of these photostories. Four of the photostories she submitted were explicitly critical of the coal industry, and two were vaguely critical. None of the non-activist participants from this group expressed an interest in becoming involved with the environmental justice movement. Overall, Community C did not seem to become a successful micromobilization context.

There were a number of dynamics going on within Community C that may have led to its lack of success in becoming a micromobilization context. I believe one of the most significant factors may have been related to activist-participant Carolyn's not sharing coal-critical photographs during any of the reflection meetings. Although Carolyn did discuss her opinions about the problems caused by irresponsible mining practices a number of times during the project, much to my surprise, she did not share any coal-critical photographs during the reflection meetings, and she only shared a very small number of photographs overall during the eight-month project. Despite my having expected her to share photographs that focused on coal industry problems, I did not ask Carolyn why she wasn't photographing the coal industry practices that I knew troubled her, because I wanted the participants (including the activist participants) to have control over what they chose to photograph.

At Meeting 8 (in March), Carolyn apologized for not having taken many photographs during the project, explaining that taking care of her ailing mother-in-law and her developmentally disabled son had made it difficult for her to find time to take photographs. She asked if I might allow her to supplement her photostories with pictures she had taken before the official start of the project. It was not until this point that I realized she had believed participants were not "allowed" to share photographs they had taken before the start date of the project. I told her that, yes, she could definitely supplement her photostories with photographs she had taken before the project began, and I apologized for not having been clearer that there were not any rules about when the photographs had to be taken. Thus, not until Meeting 9 (when we were practicing our presentation for the local exhibit later that week) did the other women in Community C have an opportunity to see Carolyn's striking photographs of the hidden coal-related destruction and pollution in their community. (See figures 9.15, 9.16, and 9.17.) By this point, all the other participants had already submitted their photostories for the exhibits, and the project was nearly over. Had this misunderstanding not occurred, and had Carolyn shared these images earlier in the project, perhaps the Photovoice group in Community C would have become a more effective micromobilization context. But as it was, participants in this group did not become mobilized to take action in the ways that certain participants in Communities A and B did.

Another factor that may have contributed to Community C's lack of micromobilization may have been a limited level of knowledge among participants about the extent or causes of the problems related to coal-industry practices. Though the same was true of most of the non-activist participants in other communities, in Community C it became especially important because so few coal-critical photographs were shared during the reflection meetings. One example from the second meeting demonstrates this lack of recognition of coal-related problems quite clearly. At this meeting, Cathleen shared a series of photographs of slurry impoundments on top of a mountain close to the community (figure 9.18). When Cathleen presented her photographs, she said "That is a sludge pond on top of [a nearby] mountain. ... It was just neat in person. And one of [the ponds] has little

"Our State Looks Like a War-Torn Country"

I grew up in a coal mining community. Both of my grandfathers were coal miners, as well as my Dad and lots of my uncles. I am not against coal mining, but I AM against Mountaintop Removal mining. I recently had the opportunity to fly over Southern West Virginia in a small plane to view the devastation. From the air, our state looks like a war-torn country. If you are just looking from the road below, you only see a very small part of the devastation. Unless you have flown over the mountains, it's hard to realize how bad it really is. It brings tears to your eyes when you see it. There is NO way these mountains can EVER be "reclaimed." Reclamation is a farce.

Figure 9.15

Activist participant Carolyn's photostory about mountaintop-removal mining in Community C.

"Coal Slurry"

The coal industry's wonderful reclamation sites are all they want you to see. THIS is what they don't tell you about!
THIS IS COAL SLURRY IN OUR MOUNTAINS. Notice the animal tracks — what is the effect of this coal waste on the wildlife?

Figure 9.16
Activist participant Carolyn's photostory about coal slurry in Community C.

footprints on it!" Explaining why she had felt compelled to photograph the sludge impoundment, Cathleen said "I just liked it. I thought it was neat! To see it when it goes in and it's all water and nasty looking, but when it dries up, they can re-mine this and get more coal." Carolyn quickly jumped in to correct Cathleen: "No, no, no. They're getting rid of the *waste*." Carolyn went on to describe how the coal companies also inject this toxic waste into abandoned mine shafts, expressing her worry that the one behind her own house might break loose one day and flood her family out of their home. Cathleen seemed taken aback, and perhaps a bit embarrassed, by the idea that the sludge ponds could be filled with something that was toxic. I offered to bring information about the chemicals and heavy metals present

"Toxic Pond?"

Why is the water in this pond this color? What chemicals are in it? Will it seep into our groundwater? Even if the coal company told us something, could we believe them?
TOO MANY QUESTIONS AND NOT ENOUGH ANSWERS!

Figure 9.17
Activist participant Carolyn's photostory about a bright turquoise coal-company pond in Community C.

in coal waste to the next meeting. I did, and unfortunately, that was the last meeting Cathleen attended. She didn't return my phone calls, and she dropped out of the project.

Aside from the exchange about the coal slurry impoundments quoted above, there were very few discussions during the reflection meetings about problems with the coal industry. Most of the photographs focused on other problems, such as litter, or on positive aspects of their community, such as beautiful scenery or interesting historical sites.

The only woman other than activist-participant Carolyn to create photostories that were explicitly critical of the coal industry was Cecelia. Three other participants (Constance, Cora, and Charity) created a few photostories that were vaguely critical of the industry, but these did not overtly indict the industry as the main source of the problems they had photographed. For instance, the one vaguely coal-critical photostory Constance created was about a deadly accident that had happened in Community C

Figure 9.18
Cathleen's photograph of a sludge impoundment in her community.

when a car was struck by a coal truck. The photo showed a smashed car with a blue tarp over the windows to hide the undoubtedly awful scene inside. As was mentioned above, accidents with coal trucks are not uncommon in Community C. Interestingly, however, rather than writing about the dangerous high speeds at which many coal trucks travel along that stretch of road (that I myself witnessed first-hand), Constance wrote that the intersection needed a traffic light. Similarly, Charity's vaguely coal-critical photostory depicted a mountaintop-removal mine site with a series of black sludge ponds. The text simply stated "These are three sludge ponds that the coal mines have made on [a mountain close to our community]." In her narrative, Charity made no normative judgment about whether the ponds were good or bad; they were simply there.

As was noted above, the one non-activist participant who did create photostories that were explicitly critical of the coal industry was Cecelia, who stated she had been one of the first women hired to work in the coal mines. (She was retired at the time of the study.) Cecelia created three coal-critical photostories and one vaguely coal-critical photostory. Like Charity, Cecelia photographed a sludge pond in the area (the same one that Carolyn photographed), but the narrative she wrote for her photostory was clearly critical:

> This is a sludge pond [in our community]. This pond is full of lots of chemicals. These chemicals soak into the ground and can't be washed away. This ground may someday have houses built on it—think about what the kids will be playing on? Or what our water lines will be laying on?"

In another of Cecelia's photostories, one titled, "Fire in the Sky," a bright pink-and-orange sunrise filled the sky above a gently curving silhouette of a mountain. The text below the photo read "This is a picture of God's Art ... this is like a fire in the sky. There is a lot of beauty in West Virginia, but the logging and mining are messing the mountains up."

Despite Cecilia's history as an underground coal miner, when the rare opportunity arose during our reflection meetings, she wasn't shy about discussing the problems she felt the coal industry was causing in West Virginia. I believe Cecelia may have taken the opportunity to become more involved in the environmental justice movement if she had not had a husband with Alzheimer's Disease at home. When I invited her to come to Charleston to lobby as part of the "Clean Water Day" at the legislature, she told me that she couldn't be away from her husband for that long because of his illness. What seemed to be preventing her from becoming more involved in the environmental justice movement was a lack of "biographical availability," which, as I noted previously, is "the absence of personal constraints that may increase the costs and risks of movement participation" (McAdam 1986, p. 70).

There are several reasons why Community C wasn't a successful micromobilization context for coal-related issues, but the primary reason, I believe, was a lack of consciousness among group members about the extent and severity of the problems the coal industry was causing. In Community C the coal industry is a part of life and is present all around. But the tangible, negative effects of the coal industry weren't discussed in the group setting nearly as often as they were in Communities A and B, each of which had two activist participants sharing coal-critical photographs fairly regularly. In all likelihood, this lack of critical discussion stymied the process of cognitive liberation among the non-activist participants in Community C.

Community D

Community D is known for its small family farms, which have been there for generations. Farming makes up a significant portion of the economy in the county where Community D is located. In recent years, however, coal operations have increased significantly in the areas surrounding and including Community D, and so have their impacts. Close to the time when the Photovoice project began, one of the environmental justice groups had begun organizing in Community D in response to some residents' fears of water contamination and the problems they were experiencing from mine blasting in the area.

As tables D.10 and D.11 in appendix D and figure 9.1 in this chapter show, although attendance rates were relatively high at the reflection meetings, of all the groups, Photovoice participants in Community D shared the lowest number of photographs that were critical of the coal industry. Of the 1,179 photos that Community D participants shared during the eight-month project, only three depicted problems with coal-industry practices. Community D also had the smallest proportion of explicitly coal-critical and vaguely coal-critical photostories created by participants. As table D.12 shows, of the 81 photostories that participants submitted to me, only one (shown here as figure 9.19) was explicitly critical of the coal industry, and it was created by the activist participant, Diane.

Three photostories that were vaguely critical of the coal industry were submitted, one of which was also created by Diane. The other two (one of which is shown here as figure 9.20) were created by Dorothy, one of the five non-activist Photovoice participants who became involved in the environmental justice movement during the Photovoice project.

With the exception of Dorothy (an anomalous case, discussed further in chapter 10), Community D was similar to Community C in that it was not, for the most part, a successful micromobilization context for generating action against the injustices of the coal industry's practices in the region. In Community D, as was also the case in Community C, the activist participant did not share many photographs during reflection meetings. Over the course of the project, Diane shared only 21 photographs. In fact, she didn't share the two photographs that she used for her coal-critical photostory (figure 9.20) during any of the Photovoice meetings. She scanned and emailed those images to me, along with a narrative, the week before I sent

"Mine Blowout"

This is the aftermath of highwall mining when coal companies come too close to the other side of the mountain. When the Department of Environmental Protection (DEP) fails to make the coal companies liable to the landowners on the other side of the mountain from where they are mining, things like this can happen and affect the private owners. These pictures show a mine blowout that happened on my property.

Figure 9.19
Activist participant Diane's photostory about a mine blowout in Community D.

the photostory files to the printer for our exhibit. Thus, as in Community C, the fact that there were so few discussions during reflection meetings focusing on the problems with coal industry practices meant that the Photovoice process in Community D did not generally lead to an increased awareness of irresponsible mining practices in the community, or to mobilization around those issues.

More Pressing Concerns

As in Community B, though, Photovoice participants in Community D *did* find other issues about which to take a stand. Many of the participants

"Cloud Shadows"

Watch cloud shadows cross [my] county. The land is ageless.
It could be the 1700s, 1800s, 1900s, or today.
Hopefully it will be tomorrow.

Figure 9.20
A photostory created by non-activist participant Dorothy that is vaguely critical of the coal industry.

strove to create photostories that would draw attention to certain problems in their communities and/or advocated for specific changes. For instance, some of the women took photographs of dangerous areas along their winding roads and wrote narratives about the accidents they had seen or their fears of future accidents. One example is shown here as figure 9.21. Created by Deanna, it shows a large rock hanging over a narrow curve on the main road leading into Community D. "The rock is cracking," Deanna's photostory states, "and it looks like it might fall at any time. ... I drive by this every day, and it scares me to death. ... I fear for my life, for my friends, family, and others I know."

For many of the participants, including Deanna, the Photovoice project was one of the first occasions on which they had been encouraged to think

"Dangerous Cracking Rock Cliff Hanging Over [the Road]"

This is a very dangerous rock cliff overhang..... The rock is cracking and looks like it might fall at any time. The rock cliff hangs over the road, and if it were to fall while someone was driving by, they would be killed. There is also a phone line directly under the rock. I drive by this every day, and it scares me to death. I watch it every day, just wondering when it is going to fall. I fear for my life, for my friends, family, and others I know. I have called about this rock before, but State Roads says it is the phone company's responsibility, and the phone company says it is State Roads' responsibility. So no one is doing anything about this dangerous rock overhang. I worry that it will take someone getting killed before something is done.

Figure 9.21
Deanna's photostory about a dangerous rock overhang in Community D.

of themselves as change agents within their communities. This personal transformation in the way that the women saw themselves and what they believed they were capable of accomplishing was particularly pronounced in Community D, despite the fact that it didn't become a successful micromobilization context with regard to irresponsible coal-industry practices. Deanna was perhaps the most deeply affected by the experience of being listened to and being told that her ideas mattered. At the start of this project, Deanna was an extremely shy individual who became paralyzed with fear at the thought of public speaking. In fact, during our first reflection meeting, she asked if her friend Dawn could present her photographs for her so that she would not have to speak in front of the small group of Photovoice women, most of whom she already knew. Through the eight-month project, however, Deanna gained confidence and lost some of her fear of speaking in public. It was still a challenge for her, but by the time we held the community exhibit at the end of the project Deanna had gained enough confidence to read her photostories herself during the public presentation. Her deep concern about the rock overhang gave her the courage to talk to a state legislator at the community exhibit and ask him if there was anything he could do to have the rock removed. During our post-project interview, I learned that Deanna had continued to spread the word about the dangerous cliff after the project had ended. Less than a year later, money was appropriated to fix the problem, and the rock was removed.

In our interview, Deanna described the increased feelings of efficacy she gained from sharing her photostories with community leaders and the general public: "That was *somethin'*—made me feel like I was on top of the world! Like I could make a difference. 'Cause I didn't think I could do it, because I'm not a talker." The experience of participating in Photovoice made Deanna much more engaged in her community than she had been and helped give her the confidence to advocate for positive change.

One of the biggest problems that Photovoice participants in Community D (and in most of the other communities) discussed during reflection sessions was the huge amount of trash littering their roadsides and creek banks. Five of the seven participants in Community D created photostories depicting the trash problem and chose those photostories for the Photovoice exhibits. (For an example, see figure 9.22.) As the litter problem emerged as a theme within Community D and the other communities, I told the women about a bill that was being considered in the West Virginia

"Trash, Trash Everywhere"

I recently took a drive with my family in the mountains and came upon this unsightly mess! Someone or a group of people have been using this place as a dumping ground to dispose of their trash and unwanted items. It makes me angry that someone would do this — why not haul your trash to a dump? Is it worth saving money if you have to look at this eyesore in return? I think not. The county even offers a free dump day that people could take advantage of getting rid of this stuff! I wish there would be stricter patrolling or policing of these areas so nature is not destroyed like this!

Figure 9.22

Dixie's photostory about an illegal trash dump in Community D.

legislature (for the seventh year in a row) that, if passed, would place a three-cent deposit on the container of every beverage sold in the state. I gave the women the contact information for their state legislators and suggested that they send some of their photostories about the litter problem to these representatives with a note about how the bottle-deposit law might help clean up their communities. There was a great deal of enthusiasm for this idea, and a number of the women from Community D (and some from other Photovoice groups as well) sent their photostories to their state legislators. (See figures 9.23 and 9.24 for examples.) Many of the women were surprised by the positive reactions they received. For instance, when Deidre received a return phone call from a legislator about the photostory she sent (figure 9.24), she was amazed. Although the bottle-deposit bill didn't pass during the 2009 legislative session, the experience of being listened to had an empowering effect on Deidre (and on many of the other women). "[A bottle-deposit law] hasn't happened yet," Deidre told me in our post-project interview, "but [being listened to] made me think that it was possible, you know? A lot of times whenever [I] get a big dream or idea in [my] head, I've never really thought real positive about it. It gave me a positive outlook on it anyway, you know, instead of being such a downer."

Other issues the Photovoice participants in Community D drew attention to through their photostories included over-spraying of herbicides along the roads (which had led to the killing of one Photovoice participants' fruit trees and grape vines), graffiti, and crime.

Even though Community D didn't become a successful micromobilization context for taking action against the injustices of the coal industry, the participants from that community were by no means passive, and they did advocate on behalf of other issues. As in Community C, most of the Photovoice participants in Community D had not yet been directly affected by irresponsible mining practices. Because the activist participant, Diane, did not share many coal-critical photographs during the reflection meetings, most of the Photovoice participants were not hearing about the negative side of coal mining. They were simply hearing that the coal industry was providing jobs in their community, and so they were generally supportive of it (with the exception of Dorothy). However, these Photovoice participants *did* want to take action on behalf of their community, so they focused on other problems that seemed more pressing and more directly pertinent to their lives.

"Please Pass the Bottle Bill!"

This picture was taken of [our] creek after a rain. As you can see, trash piles up against our bridges almost anytime it rains. Look at all those bottles! The biggest part of the trash we see piled up by our bridges is pop bottles and water bottles. This is really nasty to look at, and all this trash is also very hard on the wildlife in our area. If we had a bottle deposit in our state, a lot of this wouldn't be here. I would really like to see our state pass the Bottle Bill this year.

Figure 9.23
Deanna's photostory advocating for a bottle deposit in West Virginia.

"A Bottle Deposit Could Provide Fundraising Opportunities"

In almost every place along the roads where I see litter, bottles and cans make up the majority of the trash. If we had a 10 cent deposit on all beverage containers, what you see in this one picture would be worth 50 cents for someone who picked this littler up and recycled it. Think of this —whenever you are doing something with your church or another group and want to raise money, all you would have to do would be to take your youth group, go out to any area along the road, and pick up bottles and cans to turn in. After doing that for just one afternoon, I bet you would have four or five truckloads of bottles to turn in for money. This would be an easy fundraiser and it would teach kids that instead of throwing their bottles and cans out of the car window, they should recycle.

Figure 9.24
Deidre's photostory advocating for a bottle deposit in West Virginia.

Community E

The story of the Photovoice project in Community E is very different from the stories of the previous four communities. What took place over the course of the eight-month project in Community E provides a clear picture of how local power structures can influence local residents' willingness to speak out against environmental injustices.

Eve was the local activist I recruited to participate in Community E's Photovoice group. At the start of the project, Eve had been participating in the environmental justice movement for only about a year. Her involvement had begun when she had learned that a coal company had applied for a permit to begin a mountaintop-removal mining operation on the mountain behind her home. Eve had been working to organize her neighbors against this permit, with limited success. Since initiating her involvement in environmental justice activism, Eve had also become very engaged in efforts to promote the development of a wind farm in her county as a source of "green jobs" for local residents. She and her husband, a retired underground coal miner, were hoping that a wind turbine could be placed on their land as a demonstration site. As I would learn during the course of the Photovoice project, Eve's participation in environmental justice organizations had not been well received by certain powerful individuals in her community.

I recruited ten non-activist participants for the Photovoice project in Community E through a church network. Although Eve wasn't a member of any church congregation, she helped me make contact with the pastor of one of the largest churches in the community. I presented the Photovoice project to a group of church members before a meeting of the church council, and they helped recruit other women to the project. Though only six participants attended the Photovoice orientation, because another community event was being held that evening, all eleven of the participants attended the first reflection meeting. They seemed enthusiastic about the project and committed to participating in it.

The First Reflection Meeting

Eight of the eleven Photovoice participants who attended the first reflection meeting shared photographs they had taken. Some of the photos depicted problems in the community, such as closed businesses, defunct recreational facilities, and hazardous road conditions. Some of the participants talked about their ideas for change, such as creating a walking track on a piece of overgrown property and reopening a campground and a pool that had once been important regional assets. Many participants also shared photographs illustrating the strengths and assets of their community. Images of local businesses, beautiful scenery, and important cultural traditions, such as digging ginseng and enjoying the outdoors, appeared throughout the two-hour meeting. In all, participants shared 181 photographs during the first reflection meeting, more than were shared in any of the other Photovoice groups that week. All signs indicated that this would be an engaged and dedicated Photovoice group.

Eve was the sixth participant to share her photographs. Until she presented her photos, no other participant had mentioned the coal industry or problems with its practices. As Eve sat down and handed me the memory card from her camera, she said to me quietly, with some trepidation, "I hope that no one gets offended by my pictures." As table D.14 in appendix D shows, 22 of the 39 photographs Eve shared during that meeting were critical of the coal industry. Below I provide the transcript of a portion of Eve's 14 minutes of photo sharing. The photographs she shared (shown here as figures 9.21–9.35) are interspersed with the text of her presentation.

Eve:

This is the sign as you're leaving Kentucky and heading into West Virginia. "Welcome to wild and wonderful West Virginia" … . I like this sign because it shows the beautiful part of West Virginia that's really nice, that people should take pride in.

Emily:

I like the new [slogan]. I didn't like the old one![3]

[The room erupts with agreement.]

Eve:

Oh, yeah, everybody was so upset over that. I'm glad they changed it [back].

[Eve flips through two more pictures of the same sign, and there are a few other comments from around the room about how glad they are that the "Wild and Wonderful" slogan is back].

Figure 9.25
Eve's photograph of a "Welcome to West Virginia" sign.

Eve:

And this is just a picture I took that I thought just showed how beautiful West Virginia is, especially in the fall with the colors and stuff.

Eve:

And ... um ... this is, um, a billboard showing, um, that people are beginning to wonder about mountaintop removal. Because if they keep taking the tops of the mountains off, we're not going to have any mountains anymore.

SB:

So, what does it say on the sign there?

Eve:

Um, "Mine coal responsibly"—"Be a true hero to the mountains, mine coal responsibly." And the picture says to mine coal underground. That would put more people to work, plus preserve what we have already. I just thought that was a neat sign.

Edna:

Is that in Kentucky?

Eve:

No, that one is ... on 119 [in West Virginia] ...

Figure 9.26
Eve's first photo of fall leaves.

Figure 9.27
Eve's photo of a "Mine Coal Responsibly" billboard.

[Eve shows another photograph of the same sign from another angle]
[SILENCE]

Eve:

This one also, "Keep West Virginia wild and wonderful; be a friend to the mountains; mine coal underground." So, you know, people's starting, I think, to realize what we have to lose from just being so destructive to the earth in general.

[SILENCE]

Figure 9.28
Eve's photo of a "Mine Coal Underground" billboard.

SB:

Where is that sign?

Eve:

That sign is at [a gas station] on 119.

[SILENCE]

Eve:

And this is a picture of a mountaintop-removal site. That's on 119. To me this shows what devastation it is. Plus, it increases floods and hurts people's water ...

[SILENCE]

Eve:

And this is the same [mine], and that's showing the railroad tracks, too. And I just thought that was sorta sad because there wasn't any coal on the railroad cars. They're all on the coal trucks, which makes it more dangerous on the

Figure 9.29
Eve's first photo of a mountaintop-removal mine.

roads. Because I think most everyone has been touched by some sort of accident that's happened with the coal trucks.

[SILENCE]

Eve:

I just thought that was sad, you know, running a coal train without nothing on it.

[SILENCE]

Eve:

This next picture of the coal train, it's got UPS trucks on it and not coal cars for the same reason.

[SILENCE]

Eve:

And that's just a different shot of the mountaintop-removal mines.

Figure 9.30
Eve's photo of an empty coal train.

SB:

Is that the same one?

Eve:

Yeah, the same one. It shows the valley fills coming down.

[SILENCE]

Eve:

And there's one that's just started. The mountaintop. That's also on 119.

[SILENCE]

Eve:

Same one. That's the one that's just being started.

[Eve shows three more pictures of the same mountaintop-removal mine]
[SILENCE]

Eve:

And I just seen all kinds of plastic bags and garbage waving around.

Figure 9.31
Eve's photo of a "coal train" hauling UPS cars instead of coal cars.

Eve:

And, uh, … [getting rid of litter] is what we all think would make our community better, you know, that was one [idea] I think we all shared was to clean up what we have.

[There is some limited discussion among other group members about plastic-bag litter, where people can buy reusable bags, and why so few people use reusable bags.]

Eve:

And the reason I took a picture of this CONSOL Energy [coal company] sign is there's a mountaintop-removal mine that they've proposed down in [a nearby town].

Eve:

It will be about 300 acres. … I think that's going to be pretty devastating to … have all those hills gone, plus the devastation it could have to residents that live

Figure 9.32
Eve's photo of a mountaintop-removal mine from a different angle.

there, you know, that have to rely on that [well] water, and there will be more floods.

[SILENCE]

Eve:

And here's some other pictures of that CONSOL [mine sign]

[Eve shows two more similar photographs]
[SILENCE]

Eve:

And that's a picture of the mountain where the mountaintop site is supposed to go. All across that. And you know, with the environment being so bad with air pollution and all that …

[SILENCE]
[Eve shows two more photographs of the proposed mountaintop-removal mine site.]

Figure 9.33
Eve's photo of a recently started mountaintop-removal mine.

Eve:

That's still some more of the mountainside.

[SILENCE]
[Eve shows two more pictures of road-side litter].

Eve:

And that's more garbage

[SILENCE]
[Eve shows a photograph she took in her yard].

Eve:

That's my pretty yard.

[SILENCE]

SB:

That's really nice light. Was that in the evening?

Figure 9.34
Eve's first photo of plastic-bag litter on the highway.

Eve:

Uh-huh. That's my walnut trees.

[SILENCE]

Eve:

And that is wild ginseng berries ...

Eve:

I've always planted [ginseng] after finding it [in the mountains], and that's the biggest one I've had so far. It was a double four-prong [root]. I just think it looks so neat to see the berries there and stuff. And what I do then is to take the berries off of that and plant them.

Elaine:

So you plant the berries?

Eve:

Uh-huh, yeah, and it takes years for it to come up, you know, and I never dig mine [up] or anything.

Figure 9.35
Eve's first photo of a coal company's sign.

[Group members ask a few more questions about the ginseng and the hosta plant in the picture.]

Eve:

And [this is] just showing, I think it would be great if we could get some [wind turbine] factories …

Eve:

We're always saying "Well, no one wants to bring factories here." Um, I think we do have room for factories, but nobody's jumped on the bandwagon yet about, um, building some solar panels or wind turbines or something. Because once the coal is gone, we're going to have to do something.

Emily [nodding head in agreement]:

Right.

Eve:

There's not going to be anything left here.

[SILENCE]

Figure 9.36
Eve's photo of a future mine site.

SB:

Do you know anything about the proposed wind farm that some people are trying to get built on a mountain that is permitted for mountaintop-removal mining in [another county]?

Eve:

Yes, I think they even had all the backing to proceed with the wind farm, and then all at once Massey, the coal company, you know, got their permit, and they're not going to let them apply for the wind farm. And it was proven that [the wind farm] would have put more people to work than that mine site would. … You know, making jobs and the energy that would last. And right now they just sorta got tied up in courts.

[SILENCE]

Eve:

That's another picture.

[Eve shows another picture of the pro-wind yard sign]
[SILENCE]

Figure 9.37
Eve's photo of ginseng berries.

Eve:

That's just another shot of the woods.

[Eve shows a photograph of the woods on her property; there are a few comments within the group about how pretty the autumn leaves are.]

Eve:

And this is another reason I took a picture of the CONSOL sign, because last year CONSOL was fined $400,000 for water violations that they've done to people. And if they had been fined the proper amount, it would have been millions. That just shows, you know, how that they do people bad, and I think, you know, people do need to hold them accountable once they get involved in the mining process. There have been communities that has put down things that they have wanted the coal company held to do. If you make that public enough, they will do it.

SB:

So, what were the violations?

Figure 9.38
Eve's pro-wind-power yard sign.

Eve:

With that it was with the valley fills. People's water was becoming contaminated with selenium and just all kinds of heavy metals, uh, private wells was sunk ... from the blasting ...

[SILENCE]

Eve:

I tried to take a picture where you could read it all, but it didn't turn out.

[Eve shows another picture of the text of the violations].
[SILENCE]
[Eve's final photographs are pictures of her own reusable bags and paper bags. After some further discussion about bags, Eve concludes her sharing of photos.]
***

What was striking about Eve's photo sharing was how frequently the room became completely silent, particularly while she was discussing her

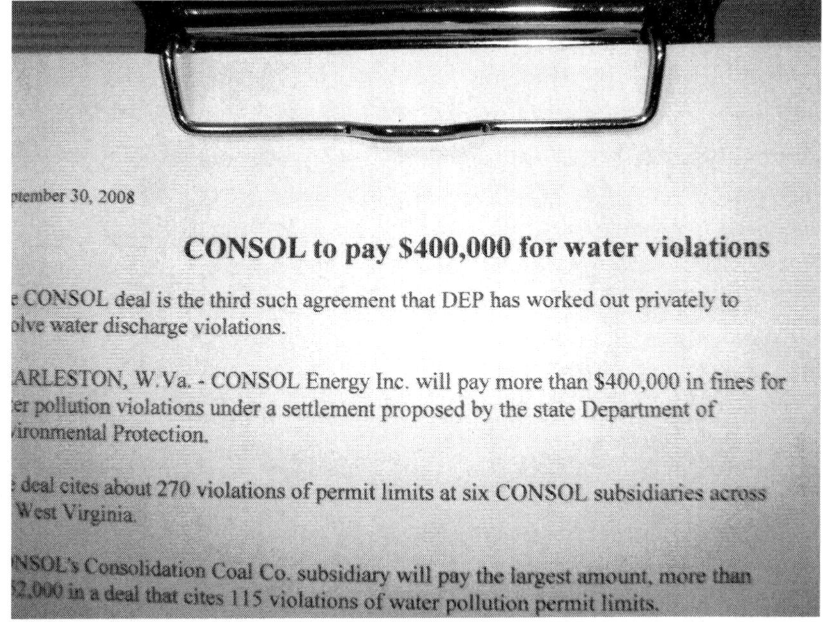

ptember 30, 2008

CONSOL to pay $400,000 for water violations

e CONSOL deal is the third such agreement that DEP has worked out privately to olve water discharge violations.

ARLESTON, W.Va. - CONSOL Energy Inc. will pay more than $400,000 in fines for er pollution violations under a settlement proposed by the state Department of ironmental Protection.

deal cites about 270 violations of permit limits at six CONSOL subsidiaries across West Virginia.

NSOL's Consolidation Coal Co. subsidiary will pay the largest amount, more than 2,000 in a deal that cites 115 violations of water pollution permit limits.

Figure 9.39
Eve's photo of a report on CONSOL's water violations.

opinions about the coal industry's practices. The frequent moments of silence that occurred during Eve's photo sharing were not characteristic of other participants' photo sharing. During all the previous participants' photo sharing, group members offered frequent comments on the images, and a number of extended discussions took place around certain issues sparked by the photographs (e.g., re-opening the closed campground and pool). Interestingly, almost all the instances in which group members commented on, asked questions about, or discussed Eve's photographs occurred when she presented a photograph that wasn't related to coal (e.g., plastic bag litter or ginseng berries). After almost every coal-related photograph she presented, there was a noticeable silence. To this observer, the silence was uncomfortable, particularly because it contrasted so much with the lively discussions and comments the other Photovoice women elicited with their photographs.

Only one other participant presented a photograph that was critical of the coal industry during the meeting. Emily, who shared her photos immediately after Eve, included one photograph of a roadside memorial for an

18-year-old boy who had been killed by a coal truck in 1998. She commented that she had taken the picture because she felt that his death was "something that was important." However, Emily didn't offer any further reflections at that time on the danger of coal trucks in Community E. Emily also was the only person I observed making an outward, if subtle, sign of agreement with Eve's comments. This was particularly noticeable when Eve expressed her desire to see wind power and wind-turbine manufacturing developed in the region, stating "Once the coal is gone, we're going to have to do something." In response to that comment, Emily nodded her head and said "Right." This small signal of agreement was the only one I saw directed toward Eve's coal-related comments that entire evening.

I wasn't sure what to make of this first meeting in Community E. Should I interpret the palpable discomfort among many of the participants as an indication that the group didn't agree with Eve that there were problems in the community related to coal mining? Or did they feel uncomfortable acknowledging the problems in a public setting?

Fallout from the First Reflection Meeting

After the first set of reflection meetings had taken place in the five communities, I flew to Oregon for a visit during the two-week period between reflection meeting weeks. I was planning to return on Saturday, October 18, in time for the next week-long series of reflection meetings, which were scheduled to begin on Monday, October 20. However, instead of going to the airport the morning of October 18, I went to the emergency room with acute appendicitis. Later that day, I had emergency surgery. Sunday morning, while recovering in a hospital bed, I began calling the members of the Photovoice groups to explain the situation and to cancel the next week's meetings.

Coincidentally, before I had starting making my phone calls to Community E participants, Emily called me. Emily had no idea that I had just undergone unexpected surgery. Her purpose in calling was to talk with me about a crisis that had emerged—a crisis that centered on me—during the two weeks since the first reflection meeting. "Shannon," she said, "I have been defending you for the past two weeks. All these rumors are going around about you here." I was taken aback—what "rumors" could there be about me in a town where I knew almost no one and had spent very little time? Emily proceeded to tell me that some people in the community believed that I was staying at Eve's house, and some claimed to have seen me walking around the community over the past week, knocking on people's doors and asking them to sign a petition to stop mountaintop-removal mining. According to the rumors, I was also offering to pay people in the community to take me to mountaintop-removal mining sites so that I could photograph the operations.

"You know how some communities have the Rockefellers or the Kennedys?" Emily asked. "Well, we have the Jackson[4] family. They are really rich and are connected to a bunch of the mines in this area." (Later I learned that the Jackson family owns a logging operation and that they contract with a number of coal companies to clear the land before surface mining takes place.) Members of the Jackson family belonged to the church where I recruited Photovoice participants, and they apparently held a great deal of power within the congregation and the wider community. According to Emily, someone from the Jackson family had seen a non-local woman with a camera staying at Eve's house, and he had assumed it was me. He had confronted the pastor of the church, and had expressed his concerns over the Photovoice group in light of Eve's ties to the project and her recent outspokenness against the coal industry. The pastor had then called Emily to ask her what she knew about me, my connection to Eve, and my intentions for the Photovoice project.

Apparently, I had been mistaken for a young photographer from an art school in Boston who had been an intern with an environmental justice organization in the area the summer before. She had returned for a brief visit while I was in Oregon. Though I believe she is the person for whom I was mistaken, I am doubtful that the rumors that she was knocking on doors with a petition to stop mountaintop removal mining and paying people to take her to mining sites were true. However, I do know that she stayed at Eve's house during the time of her visit. The coincidence of there being another non-local woman with a camera associated with Eve was enough to initiate the rumors. Eve's photographs and comments about the coal industry at the first meeting had already caused some discomfort among the Photovoice women in attendance at that session, so adding this case of mistaken identity was enough to mark the Photovoice project—and me—as suspect.

Emily told me that when the pastor had called her she had "defended" me, assuring him that I was in Oregon and that the woman staying at Eve's house could not be me. I confirmed that I had, in fact, been in Oregon the entire time and that I would not be returning to West Virginia for at least another week because of my unexpected surgery.

I was dismayed by the emerging mistrust and suspicion in Community E. I had wanted to create a project that would empower the participants and the communities in which I was conducting research, not one that would cause conflict in those communities. I hadn't prepared myself for the possibility that the Photovoice project might be viewed as a threat to certain people in the community. Under the circumstances, I felt that it was important for me to divulge my own environmental views to Emily. "I have to be honest with you," I said. "I am against mountaintop-removal mining. But I'm not trying to push that agenda on the group. What you all decide to photograph and what you decide to write about your photographs is up to you." I told her that what came of this project was the participants' decision, not mine, and that I wanted the project to make the Photovoice participants proud. Emily responded: "I hate what they're doing to my mountains." But on the other hand, she told me, she saw that mining was an important employment opportunity for many people in her community and that very few jobs in the area paid as well as coal mining.

After my phone call with Emily ended, I telephoned the pastor to give him an opportunity to ask me about the project directly. The pastor told me that he had some concerns about Eve's involvement in the project and asked whether she was being paid to participate in the project. I told him that I wasn't paying Eve, or anyone else, to participate. We talked briefly about Eve's outspoken views against mountaintop-removal mining and her environmental activism. He explained that he was in a delicate position and that he had to "toe a line" because so many people in the community support the coal industry and depend on it for jobs. As a pastor, he told me, he could not "get political." Despite his concerns, though, he agreed that Eve should remain in the project. He added that Eve and her husband sometimes attended his church. After my conversations with the pastor and with Emily, I was beginning to see how the local elite's power constrained community members' willingness to speak freely about the coal industry's practices.

After the Controversy

The second reflection meeting took place during the first week in November. As table D.13 in appendix D shows, whereas eleven people had attended the first reflection meeting, only three attended the second

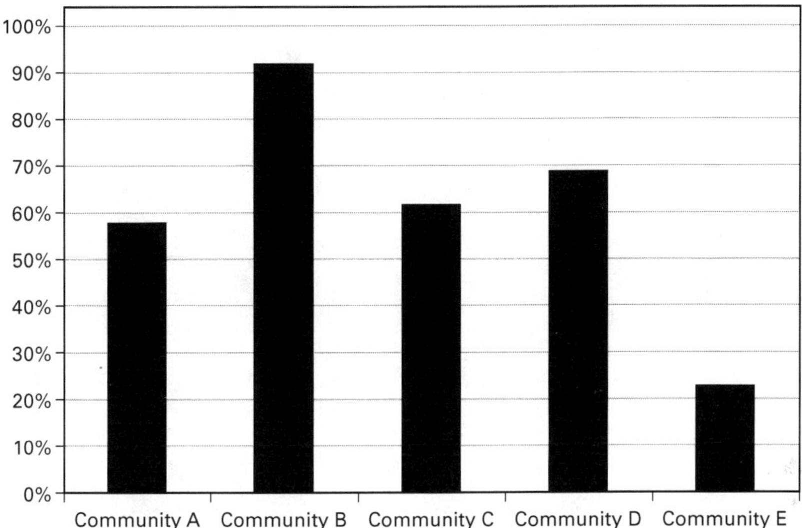

Figure 9.40
Median attendance rates at Photovoice events by community. (Calculations include participants who dropped out at some point during the project.)

reflection meeting, a decrease of 73 percent. Though every Photovoice group except for the group in Community D saw a decrease in attendance between these two meetings, none of the other decreases was as sharp as that in Community E. As figure 9.40 shows, at 23 percent, Community E also had the lowest median rate of participation in Photovoice events during the project.

Only Emily, Elaine, and Ethel attended the second reflection meeting. Eve didn't attend; in fact, she dropped out of the project entirely, despite my multiple attempts to convince her to continue participating. She told me that she felt like she was too unpopular in the community because of her outspokenness about mountaintop-removal mining, and she worried that her involvement would hinder the success of the Photovoice project, which she thought was something the community really needed. Eve did attend the local Photovoice exhibit we held at the community's middle school at the end of the project in April, but she didn't submit any photostories for inclusion in the display. She continued to speak out about mountaintop-removal mining, and in the months after leaving the project, she began to take on a more active leadership role in the environmental justice organizations working to end irresponsible coal-mining practices.

Figure 9.41
Emily's photograph of a pond filled with a substance smelling like diesel fuel.

Much to my surprise, and despite the indications that discussing coal-related problems was a taboo subject in Community E, Emily presented nine photographs that were critical of the coal industry during the second reflection meeting. The first, shown here as figure 9.41, was a photo of a small pond on top of a mountain close to Emily's home. Her husband's dog had fallen into the pond one night while hunting for raccoons. Emily reported that the pond was filled with a substance that smelled like diesel fuel. Emily's husband had had to wade into the pond to rescue his dog when it was unable to climb out. According to Emily, they both came home that night "reeking of diesel fuel." Emily asserted that the unmarked pond could be hazardous to many more than just the people who may come across it while hunting or exploring in the mountains. "When that pond fills up, what happens with it?" she asked. "It goes right down into our creek."

Emily also took four photographs of another coal-industry pond in the same area. Much larger than the one mentioned in the preceding paragraph, this "sludge pond" was black and had a strange substance floating

Figure 9.42
Emily's photograph of a "sludge pond" in Community E.

on the water's surface that Emily said didn't look like plant life. (See figure 9.42.) She expressed worry about what was contained in this strange impoundment.

During her photo sharing, Emily also talked about a series of four photographs she took of an abandoned coal tipple in her community. Referring to the structure shown in figure 9.43, she stated:

> There's no mines up there anymore, and they just left that. ... That could rust and fall. And I mean, this [road] is the way to people's houses! ... But they just leave this. I mean, you know, they have a mine, and they put all this money into all this, and then they just leave it [when they are finished]. Why not take it with them? I don't see why they couldn't take it and use it. Recycle it.

In contrast with the first reflection meeting, at which there had been little response to Eve when she had shared coal-critical photographs, in the second meeting members of the Photovoice group did engage in some discussion of the coal-related photographs that Emily had shared. However, Emily's photos were not as controversial as Eve's (or as numerous), and she didn't specifically mention mountaintop-removal mining. It is also possible that Emily's status as a member of the church, and the fact that she had never been associated with one of the environmental justice organizations

Figure 9.43
Emily's photograph of an abandoned coal tipple in Community E.

or involved in environmental activism, may have led the women to be more accepting of her questions about and criticisms of the coal industry.

The only other reflection meeting at which any participant discussed problems related to the coal industry was at the third reflection meeting, which was in December. (See table D.14.) Elise shared four photographs she had taken of the polluted creek that runs through Community E. Referring to the one reproduced here as figure 9.44, Elise explained:

> Now, this picture right here, this is in the creek ... . The orange that is on top of the water is actually like a gas or an oil or something that has, I don't know, has contaminated it. ... That was after that storm we had.

Emily excitedly interjected, telling Elise about the photos she had shared during the previous Photovoice meeting, which Elise had not attended:

> I had a picture the last time and it was up here on [the mountain]. ... Me and [my husband] rode up to this pond, and it was just like there was gas in there. And, I didn't know why I was taking the picture, I just snapped it. Well, then that night, [my husband's] dog got caught in it. And there's oil and all kinds of gas [in the pond], and his dog got in it. ... You go around through there and you don't know

Figure 9.44
Elise's photograph of a polluted stream in Community E.

it's there, and if you're on a four-wheeler, you could run right into it. ... We had all that water and stuff, you know, we had all that rain. That's just right there, it could've overflowed and come right down off of the hill here [into the creek]. ... And that's probably not the only one. They're probably all the way back up through there.

Elise replied:

I was just telling Shannon that there was a mine up [on that mountain]. Remember when they brought in all that water because the mines sunk the wells? You know, the mines where they do the blasting and stuff like that? And I just wondered if some kind of chemical was actually going into the creek. ... There's all kinds of sludge ponds up there ... and that's what's in the water, I think.

This exchange started a conversation about water contamination in the community. Edna shared a story about how, years back, her water had turned orange, and she had decided not to wash her clothes in it anymore. Edna and her husband have municipal water now, but she never found out why her well water was orange.

I was very surprised by the statements that were made during this meeting—particularly by Elise, who boldly told us that she believed the orange substance in the creeks was from coal-mining activity on the mountains in the community. However, this was the last meeting at which anyone in Community E shared any coal-related photographs.

De-Politicizing Concerns

As I noted in my description of Community B, during the sixth meeting of each Photovoice group I led the participants through a process of prioritizing the concerns and ideas for change that had emerged during the previous five months of reflection sessions. For each problem, I planned to lead the group through a discussion of three questions: Why is this problem happening? What would be some solutions to address this problem? Whom do we need to involve?

In Community E, one problem that ranked highly among the participants was "dangerous roads and bridges." During a discussion about the causes of the dangerous roadways, Emily attempted three times to suggest "coal trucks" as a reason for this problem. Each time she began to make this suggestion, however, she was cut off or dismissed by the other three women in attendance at the meeting. Below is an excerpt from the discussion. A dash at the end of a line indicates that the person talking was cut off by another participant.

SB:

So, one of the issues that got the most votes was dangerous roads and bridges. So, first, why do you think this problem is happening?

Emily:

Coal trucks.

Elaine:

I don't think it's due to the coal trucks. I think there's just not enough population in the area.

Emily:

Well, that's true.

Elaine:

We don't really count.

Emily:

And—

Edna:

I think that was what was available—those bridges, I mean, that was what was here. And actually –

Emily:

So, to save money, they just maintain what they have—

Edna:

Yeah.

Emily:

But I think coal trucks have—

Edna:

I think our road actually went up [motioning out the window with her hands]. … That was the old railroad bed, and that's the one we gave back to the county to use as a road because the railroad stopped using it. … The road that goes up by my house, that's the main road in and out of here.

SB:

You were trying to say something, Emily.

Emily:

That's what I'm saying, right there where that, where the garage, railroad garage is, that's where that main road ends that way—

Eloise:

We don't have anybody to speak up for us.

Elaine:

True. It's time to replace those bridges, you know, but instead they just go on doing what they have to do.

SB:

Emily, you were starting to say something, something about coal trucks.

Emily:

Yeah, I mean, we do have a lot of coal trucks coming up and down through here, and I think that's got to do with –

Eloise:

But these coal trucks pay an extra tax, a road tax.

Elaine:

Exactly.

Eloise:

We're just not as populated as other areas. ...

Edna:

Now the coal trucks ... . Actually these bridges have always been bad—before we ever had coal trucks running this road.

Elaine:

I don't think our roads have ever been maintained.

Emily:

Now, I'm not from here, so—

Edna:

They've always been like they are right now

Elaine:

And it's like, in a lot of areas where Massey mines, Massey puts a lot of money back into the community

Edna:

Exactly.

Elaine:

See, we don't have that [going on] in this area.

It was quite clear to me, as an observer and a facilitator, that Emily was being silenced by the other women in the group every time she tried to bring up the issue of coal trucks' contribution to the danger on roads and bridges in the area. (Recall that in the first reflection meeting Emily had shared a photograph of a roadside memorial for an 18-year-old boy who had been killed by a coal truck.) It was apparent from the interactions during this later meeting that the other participants did not feel that coal trucks should be cited as part of the road problems in their community. Also of interest in the interaction reproduced above is Elaine's suggestion that that if Massey Energy had mining operations in their community they might not have so many problems with dilapidated bridges and roads: "In a lot of areas where Massey mines, Massey puts a lot of money back into the community." This comment, in conjunction with the silencing of Emily's concerns about coal trucks, contrasts significantly with the discussions that had taken place in the December reflection meeting two months earlier, in which Elise and Emily had openly expressed concerns about the effects of mining operations on the creeks and water supply.

The change in tone may have been, in part, a reaction to some of the discussions that had taken place two weeks earlier at the regional Photovoice meeting, which Emily, Elise, and Edna had attended. At that meeting, a number of women from other Photovoice groups (especially Communities A and B) had criticized the coal industry vocally (some quite angrily) for health and other quality-of-life problems that they were experiencing in their communities. The commentary about coal-related problems had dominated the regional meeting at some points so completely that the other issues and ideas depicted in the photostories could not be discussed. As a result, in a number of instances, I had had to redirect the conversation so that these other subjects could also receive some attention in the meeting. It is possible that some of the coal-defensive statements made in Community E during Meeting 6 could have stemmed from the women's discomfort with the coal-critical tone of some of the other participants at the regional meeting. Whatever the cause, from the interactions that took place during Meeting 6 and my observations during the next meeting, it was clear to me that some of the participants were beginning to feel uncomfortable with the expression of *any* criticism of the coal industry during the reflection meetings.

In addition to the interactions at meetings, some of the decisions about and negotiations over the photostories that Community E participants created and selected for inclusion in the exhibits provided important insight into the struggles taking place regarding the perceived appropriateness of criticizing the coal industry. Before the local Photovoice meeting in January, I had asked all the women to select ten or more photostories for inclusion in a presentation at the regional meeting on January 24. Most of the women in the group submitted many more than ten photostories. As table D.15 shows, Emily submitted sixteen photostories to me, two of which were explicitly critical of the coal industry and two of which were vaguely critical of it. Elise also submitted a photostory that was vaguely critical of the industry. A month after the regional meeting, at Meeting 7, I asked the participants to choose the ten photostories they wanted to have included in the local Photovoice exhibit in their community, and also to select the three that they wanted to be part of the regional exhibit in Charleston.

"Community Informed"

This is an industry-made pond on a mountain in our area. What is this settling on the water? The community should be informed of what is kept in this pond and whether or not the contents are toxic.

Figure 9.45
Emily's photostory about an "industry-made pond" in Community E.

During this prioritization process, Emily and Elise decided to modify their coal-related photostories. The new versions of these photostories included narratives that were either more ambiguous about the causes of the coal-related problems, or that reframed the problems slightly so that the coal industry was no longer the focal point.

Emily's photostory "Community Informed" (shown here as figure 9.45) had originally referred to the pond in the picture as a "coal sludge pond," which is how she talked about this body of water during the reflection meeting at which she had first shared the photo. During Meeting 7, however, Emily told me that she wanted to change "coal sludge pond" to "industry-made pond" so that she wasn't specifically naming the *coal* industry as the creator of the impoundment. In addition, she altered the narrative of this photostory and the narrative of the photostory shown in figure 9.46 so that the locations of the ponds were not disclosed, as they had been in the original narratives. Emily told me that her husband had

"Danger"

This is a man-made pond on top of a mountain in our area. Coming up on the pond it smells like diesel fuel. What happens when this fills up with rain water? It overflows into our creeks. It has no fence surrounding it and no warning signs. This is also dangerous to anyone who is either hunting or exploring in the area. My husband's dog fell in this pond and had to be pulled out. He reeked of diesel fuel.

Figure 9.46
Emily's photostory about a "man-made pond" in Community E

expressed concern that she was "stirring up trouble" by making these photostories, and that his concern was the reason she wanted to remove the location of the ponds and her references to the coal industry.

Emily submitted two other photostories related to the coal industry. The subject of the first was a young man who had been killed by a coal truck in an incident Emily had discussed during the first reflection meeting. Interestingly, Emily chose to word the accompanying narrative so that its focus was on "remembrance" of the young man rather than on the dangers associated with speeding, overweight coal trucks. The second of these photostories remained explicitly critical of the coal industry in its depiction of abandoned coal-mining structures in the community, which Emily believed to be a hazard as well as an eyesore. However, when Emily selected the ten photostories to include in the local exhibit, this photostory was not among them.

Elise was the only other participant in Community E to submit a photostory that was vaguely critical of the coal industry. As described above, at the December meeting, Elise had shared a photo of an orange substance in the creek by her home, and her photostory had focused entirely on her worries about water contamination. However, by the time of the February meeting, Elise had modified her photostory so that her concern about the orange water contamination was not the sole focus. To this photostory she added a second photograph of litter in a stream and incorporated "trash and debris" as another problem affecting the waterways. (See figure 9.47.) By doing this, Elise was able to deflect some of the focus of the photostory onto citizen-caused stream pollution, thereby diluting her critique of the coal industry.

The changes in the content of Emily's and Elise's coal-critical photostories indicate that some struggles were taking place within and among the Photovoice women, and perhaps in the larger community, over how acceptable it was to speak negatively about the coal industry. My follow-up interview with Emily four months after the end of the project provides further evidence supporting this interpretation of my observations. I asked Emily if she had any ideas about why so many people in her community had dropped out of the project and why so many of the remaining participants seemed to want the project to end more quickly. (Elaine once told me that she thought people were feeling that the project was "dragging on for too long." In contrast, the other four Photovoice groups expressed regret at seeing the project end.) Struggling to articulate her impression of what had happened without implicating anyone in particular, Emily replied:

> A lot of them I think had, I don't know, we kinda got, I think a bad thing with—I felt that people was trying to—I mean, *I* don't feel that—but I think that [other] people thought that we were trying to put the coal mines down. You know what I'm saying? And, I, that's what I feel. I feel it was just—to me, the, it, I don't know. I felt that I could voice my opinion, but then it felt like, well, if you do voice your opinion [about coal], somebody's going to get hurt and whine about it. You know what I'm saying?

"Troubled Streams"

Whether trash, debris, or chemicals, it all is a potential hazard for our community. Trash and debris bocks the streams and creeks, which causes the waters to back up and eventually flood the nearby homes and property. This rusty greasy film was found on top of the water in a stream located at [Rhoda] Creek Road. Our children play in these creeks—is there something in the water that could make them ill?

Figure 9.47
Elise's photostory about polluted streams in Community E.

It seems that at the end of this remark Emily was struggling to express a feeling that she needed to censor her opinions about the problematic practices of the coal industry so as not to upset anyone in her community.

Emily and Elise's modified photostories, the silencing of Emily's comments about coal trucks, the high attrition rate and low levels of attendance at the reflection meetings, Eve's worry that her participation in the group could "cause problems" for the project, and the rumors that spread through the community about my "intentions" for the Photovoice group all point to the power that the local elites held to stifle community expressions of disapproval toward the practices of the coal industry. The powerful social control that was taking place within Community E seemed to have been strongly enforced through the threat of an "outsider stigma" imposed on those who stepped over certain boundaries. Whereas I was clearly an outsider from the beginning because I was a non-local, it seemed that even locals—such as Eve—could acquire this outsider stigma by speaking out too vocally against the coal industry. During an interview I conducted with Emily four years after the project ended, she confirmed this supposition, telling me that the community had "shunned" Eve because of her continued activism in the environmental justice groups. As Emily told me twice during our follow-up interview, "If you talk about the bad things that's happened [because of coal mining] ... everybody's like, 'Oh, you're against coal.'" And, as Adah from Community A revealed, "When somebody says, 'You're against coal,' what they mean is, 'You're against me.'" Once you're labeled as an outsider in that way, Adah told me, "that doesn't go away."

I would argue that Emily's and Elise's re-negotiations and re-working of photostories were attempts to stay within what they perceived to be the boundaries of insider-ness in Community E. Being an insider in that community—and remaining an insider—depended on not threatening the profits and power of the local elite. The power of the Jackson family was deeply entwined with the power of the coal industry; thus, a threat to the industry's profits (e.g., through stricter enforcement of environmental regulations or through a diversification in the energy economy) would also be a threat to the Jackson family's profits.

Successes on Non-Contentious Advocacy Issues

Although significant tensions emerged around the topic of coal-industry-created problems within Community E, there were also many instances of intellectual synergy and enthusiastic agreement among the Photovoice participants in this community during the course of the eight-month project. The women shared images of beauty from their community, wonderful cultural traditions, and strengths that they felt typified the people who lived there. They also shared photos depicting some of the problems that troubled them, including drugs, abandoned buildings, and dangerous roads. The members of Community E who stayed involved with the project seemed to deeply *want* the Photovoice process to work to bring about positive changes in their community. Thus, although it became clear during the eight-month project that advocating for changes in the coal industry's practices wasn't acceptable, they (like Brandy and Barbara in Community B) did focus—quite enthusiastically—on what I identified earlier in this chapter as *non-contentious advocacy issues* through their photostories and the public presentation we organized.

When I interviewed Emily and Elaine four years after the project's end, they told me about a number of improvements that had taken place in Community E in the intervening years. Many of these improvements had addressed the problems and ideas on which the Photovoice group members' publicly displayed photostories had focused. In particular, a community park whose beloved pool had been closed for a number of years had been rejuvenated with new playground equipment, a walking club, movie nights, holiday events, and the renovation and re-opening of the pool. Elaine also told me that two of the dangerous bridges about which she had created photostories had been replaced. Both Elaine and Emily seemed to feel that Community E was improving and was receiving a bit more attention from the politicians than it had been four years earlier. When I asked them if they thought the Photovoice project had anything to do with the improvements, they seemed to cautiously believe it had. "I mean," Elaine said, "the pictures were on display in Charleston, and at the school." (They also had been published in the local newspaper.) Furthermore, a few state legislators had attended the exhibits and the final regional Photovoice meeting, even buying copies of the book we had created to showcase the photostories that had been displayed in Charleston.

Despite the tensions that emerged during the project in Community E, the overall experience seemed to have been positive for the participants. Most of the women expressed regret that they had not worked to initiate more of the community-improvement ideas they had written about in their photostories, but they seemed hopeful that they might still be able to act upon some of those ideas in the future.

Conclusion

This chapter has provided an overview of what took place within the five Photovoice communities during the eight-month project. The data I have presented here have mostly focused on the project outcomes that were related to how Photovoice participants' perceptions of the coal industry changed during the course of the project, and how in Community E speaking out against the coal industry was censored both during the interactions I observed in the Photovoice meetings and in events that took place in the wider community.

Why did the Photovoice groups in Communities A and B become more successful micromobilization contexts against coal-mining-related injustices than the groups in Communities C, D, and E? There are two major factors that I believe influenced the difference. First, Communities A and B are both located in the top coal-producing county in West Virginia. Some Photovoice participants in Community A were dealing with coal slurry in their water wells, and others with mountaintop-removal mine blasts that shook their homes. In Community B, flooding, mudslides, and smoke from underground mine fires were frequent reminders of the dominating power of the coal industry. Thus, people in those two communities had particularly good reasons to speak out against the coal industry.

The second important factor, which I believe may have been even more important than the first, is that the Photovoice groups in Communities A and B each had two activist participants, while the groups in Communities C, D, and E each only had one. Having a second group member who was critical of the coal industry most likely gave the activist participants more confidence to speak openly about their opinions of the industry. Furthermore, starting out with more than one group member who was outwardly critical of the coal industry probably lent more credibility to coal-critical opinions among the rest of the participants because more than one person was expressing them. Whereas one coal-critical person in the group could easily be dismissed as a lone wolf, two people sharing similar opinions about the injustice of coal industry practices may have made those grievances seem more acceptable opinions to hold—and to disclose to others in the community. Having more than one activist participant in the group also increased the likelihood that coal-critical photographs would be shared during reflection meetings. Discussions about the problems with the coal industry in these small-group settings helped to raise consciousness among group members and increased the likelihood that participants would share and create coal-critical photographs and photostories themselves. In Communities A and B, photographs representing problems with the coal industry were openly discussed for great lengths of time. Moreover, it seemed to have become a social norm within those two communities to create photostories that aired grievances about practices of the coal industry.

However, when it came to the point of moving from being critical of the coal industry in photostories to actually taking action against the industry, that was the stage at which most potential activists pulled back, even in Communities A and B. Interestingly, instead of becoming involved in environmental justice activism, a number of participants became involved with what I call *non-contentious advocacy issues*—that is, community problems, such as poor road conditions or litter, that did not challenge the power structure but still gave participants the satisfaction of taking action on behalf of their communities.

Another important finding from this portion of the research is the way in which the statuses of "insider" and "outsider" were manipulated to the benefit of the coal industry, even among people who were "locals." The case of Eve from Community E provides an important example. Eve was clearly marked with an "outsider" stigma in her own community because of her activism against irresponsible coal-industry practices and her association with environmental justice organizations in the area. Eve's treatment by powerful residents in the community sent a clear message to others in the Photovoice group that speaking negatively against coal was not acceptable. The non-activist participants Emily and Elise both shared coal-critical photographs and spoke of problems caused by the coal industry during reflection meetings, but most of the photostories they created were muted in their criticism of the coal industry. This toning down of their photostories probably was done so as not to trigger a label of being "against coal," which would have put Emily and Elise at risk for acquiring the outsider stigma that Eve bore. This reaction is entirely understandable considering the impoverishment of social capital in Central Appalachian coal-mining communities (discussed in chapter 3). Social connections within the community are all the more precious in view of these social losses, and the risk of damaging those connections probably was a bigger risk than Emily and Elise were willing to take.

The fear of an "outsider" stigma could also be seen functioning in important ways within the other Photovoice communities. For instance, I believe that the reason I had such difficulty recruiting participants in Community B was that Betty, who was heavily involved in the recruiting process, was a known and outspoken environmental justice activist in the community.

We were able to recruit only three non-activist participants in Community B, one of whom was Betty's own daughter, Bonnie. Betty and I tried to recruit at least fifteen women in the community to participate in the Photovoice project, but the vast majority of the women we tried to recruit declined. It is quite possible that Betty's open and frequent criticism of the coal industry marked the project as socially risky and deterred other potential recruits from joining.

In the next chapter, I move my analysis into a discussion of the five participants who began the Photovoice project as non-activists but who, during the eight-month project, became engaged with the environmental justice movement. Here again, the "outsider stigma" will become a salient theme for understanding the processes that hinder participation in the environmental justice movement among local residents in Central Appalachia.

10 Becoming, and Un-Becoming, an Activist

During the course of the Photovoice project, five of the non-activist participants became involved with the environmental justice movement: Arlene, Amber, and Aileen from Community A, Bonnie from Community B, and Dorothy from Community D. In this chapter I describe the events and interactions that led to their participation in the environmental justice movement and how the changing collective identity of the movement eventually caused three of the five to disassociate from the organizations in which they had participated.

Bonnie and the Toxic Fish

I had expected Bonnie—the daughter of Betty, an outspoken environmental justice activist in Community B—to come to the Photovoice project already critical of the coal industry. However, Bonnie informed me that before starting the Photovoice project she hadn't been interested in her mother's activist organizations. Bonnie had been one of the few women coal miners in West Virginia in the 1970s, and she had worked underground for almost ten years. Since becoming involved in environmental justice activism in 2003, Betty had tried many times to talk with her daughter about the devastation the coal industry was causing to the area, but Bonnie was not interested in discussing it. Bonnie told me:

> My mom, she was doing all that stuff with [the environmental justice movement], and she'd tell me this and this and this, and, "The strip mines are bad," and this and this, and I was always like, "Mom, they've gotta get the coal." I just ... I was a coal miner, that's what I thought they did—just get the coal! I didn't really realize what they were *doing*.

Bonnie became involved in the Photovoice project because she enjoyed taking pictures. An avid ATV rider, Bonnie had spent much of her free time exploring old logging roads in the mountains and taking photographs of the trees and wildflowers, deer, birds, bear tracks, and old and forgotten punch-hole mines. She came to the project thinking that Photovoice was a photo contest. Once she realized that the project wasn't just about taking beautiful photographs but was also a way to expose some of the problems and issues facing her community, she set out on her ATV with a new eye for her surroundings:

> I went out there [looking for things to photograph], and I was like, "Whoa, can you believe some of that?" And I wanted to bring pictures back to show people, you know, where the mountain was gone, and, where did all the animals go? And then I started noticin' like where [the coal companies] were doing things that would probably be dangerous to us, and like a flood could come and those chemicals [in the slurry ponds]—you can't even, you can't walk past them at 20 yards and breathe—what else is that doing to us?

Bonnie claimed that being involved in the Photovoice project caused her to "wake up to this community and what's going on in it." In particular, she was stunned to learn how polluted her favorite fishing streams were and that the coal companies were the primary cause of the pollution. Through Photovoice, Bonnie says, she was able to see the problems in her community, and she became politicized, wanting to tell other people about those problems.

During the Photovoice project, Bonnie became especially interested in water contamination in the coalfields, because she enjoys fishing and eating the fish she catches. Recently she had begun to get ill after eating fish she had caught from the stream in front of her house. During the January reflection meeting, Bonnie shared a series of photographs of large trout she had caught the preceding summer and autumn. She told the group that she had begun experiencing some alarming symptoms after eating these fish: dizziness, nausea, loss of balance, and memory loss, lasting weeks. "Do you think the fish could have caused that?" she asked. The women turned to me, and I replied:

> Well, I've heard that a lot of the fish in West Virginia are contaminated with toxic [chemicals] like dioxin and selenium and PCBs and mercury. You know, there are so many coal mines and coal-preparation plants close by—a lot of their waste does end up in creeks and groundwater. Especially since you got so sick, I really don't think you should eat any more of the fish you catch around here.

"This water around here is not safe," Betty interjected. "My husband's doctor told me that he believed the reason my husband got pancreatic cancer was the water here. This water killed my husband."

After becoming aware of the likely connection between her sickness and the fish she had consumed, Bonnie told me she wanted to tell everyone about the hazard. "Why isn't somebody telling us not to eat the fish?" she asked. As her way of trying to spread the word about the unsafe water, Bonnie created a photostory about her experience; it is shown here as figure 10.1.

Because water contamination became a prevalent theme across the Photovoice communities, I put together a booklet of photostories that various participants had created to express their concerns about water pollution in southern West Virginia. I had these booklets professionally printed so the women could share the collection of photostories with their legislators if they chose to become politically engaged during the 2009 legislative session. After meeting an organizer from one of the environmental justice organizations at our regional Photovoice meeting in January, Bonnie decided that she wanted to go to Charleston and lobby the state legislature about the water contamination in her community. Bonnie attended a "lobby day" organized by one of the environmental justice organizations and brought along copies of the photostory booklet to share with the legislators with whom she talked. After the project ended, Bonnie continued to be interested and involved in the environmental justice movement and sometimes accompanied her mother to events associated with environmental justice organizations.

Arlene, Amber, and Aileen and the Attempt to Save Heritage Rock

Arlene, Amber, Aileen, and Adelle from Community A were all members of the same family and all lived in the same hollow. Although Adelle stopped attending Photovoice meetings after Meeting 3 because of child-care issues, and though Aileen did not begin attending meetings until Meeting 8 because of her work schedule, both of them remained connected to the Photovoice project for the duration of the eight months through Arlene and Amber. In fact, Arlene jointly created photostories with both Aileen and Adelle for the public exhibits that were to be held at the end of the project.

"Toxic Fish"

These are trout caught in [the river by my house] during the Summer of 2008. Fishing is pretty good in this river, but eating them is dangerous. I found that out the hard way. On two different occasions, I have cooked up fish I have caught and gotten extremely sick for a number of weeks afterwards. The first time, I ate a fish that was approximately 2.5 pounds. For about six weeks after eating that fish, I was so dizzy that I found it hard to walk, and when I lay down, my head spun to the point of nausea. I also experienced short term memory loss during that time. Eventually, the symptoms went away, but I had no idea what had caused the illness. Then, later that summer, I ate another fish weighing about 1.5 pounds, and the dizziness, nausea, and memory loss came back, lasting about four weeks this time. After coming down with the symptoms again, I realized that it was the fish that did it to me. I haven't eaten any fish that I've caught in this area since then, and I've been fine. With all the coal mining in this area, I wonder if there are heavy metals or chemicals in the water from the mining activity that are contaminating the fish and making them toxic.

Figure 10.1
Bonnie's photostory of toxic fish in Community B.

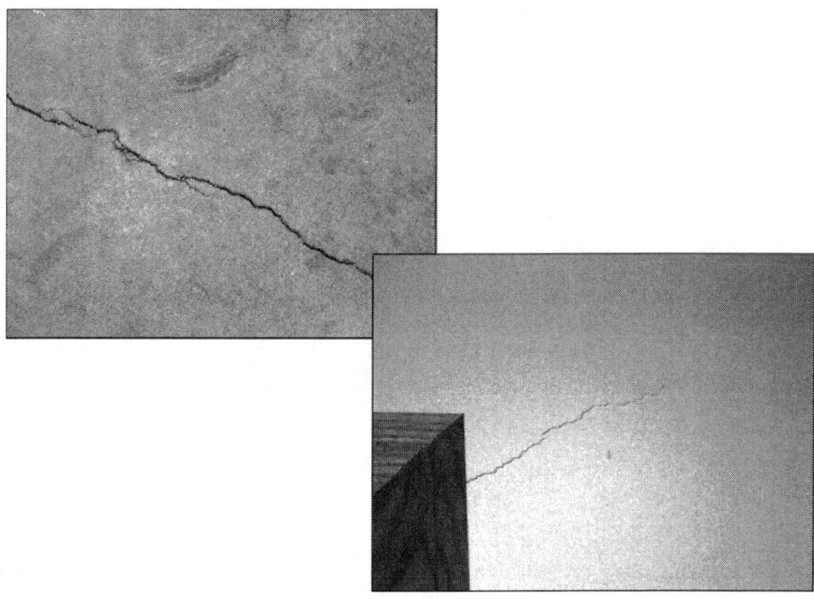

"Mining Blasts Crack Me Up—Literally"

These pictures are of my home, which was built in 2005. The cracks you see are in our walls, as well as our porch and our garage. Though the mining companies claim that they are from the "settling" of our house, the cracks only appeared after intense blasting from the mountaintop removal mine behind our house began less than a year ago.

Figure 10.2
A coal-critical photostory created by Amber in Community A.

Of all the non-activist participants in Community A, Arlene and Amber shared the greatest number of coal-critical photographs during the meetings, created the most coal-critical photostories, and then selected the greatest number of coal-critical photostories for inclusion in the public exhibits. Figure 9.5 is an example of one of Arlene's coal-critical photostories, and figure 10.2 is an example of one of Amber's.

Arlene and Amber first became involved with the environmental justice movement at the beginning of January, when the West Virginia Department of Environmental Protection (DEP) held a public hearing to receive comments on a renewal application for a mountaintop-removal mining permit in the hollow in which Arlene, Amber, Adelle, and Aileen lived. The four women were particularly hopeful that the permit would not be renewed because an important community landmark—which I will call Heritage Rock here—fell within the boundaries of the permit and would be destroyed if mining operations continued.

Amber attended the DEP hearing and spoke against the renewal of the mining permit. During our post-project interview, she cited the Photovoice project as having helped her find the courage to speak out against the coal industry: "I felt like Photovoice gave, you know, gave me the backbone to stand up at the town meeting where we were talking about mountaintop removal."

At the January reflection meeting, Amber and Arlene told me with sadness and anger that they felt the permit hearing had been "in name only" because, despite the public outcry against renewing the permit, the DEP had approved it. The realization that their efforts and passion against the permit could have had so little effect on the DEP's decision shattered their sense of how a democracy is supposed to work. Devastated, they watched as, the day after the permit hearing, the coal company tore down the community's beloved landmark, Heritage Rock. In response to this experience, Arlene and Adelle created a joint photostory called "The Death of a Community Treasure" (figure 10.3), which they selected to be displayed in the local Photovoice exhibit and in the regional Photovoice exhibit in Charleston.

During the first regional Photovoice meeting, held two weeks after the failed attempt to stop the mining permit, the participants from all five Photovoice groups came together for the first time and learned about the issues of concern in the other Photovoice communities. I had invited an organizer from one of the environmental justice groups to give a presentation about the work her organization was doing to advocate on behalf of communities experiencing water contamination caused by coal industry practices. Amber and Arlene expressed interest in becoming involved with the organization and gave the organizer their contact information.

About two months later, when a reporter from a prominent national newspaper contacted environmental justice groups in the area about scheduling a visit to interview local people about mountaintop-removal mining, Amber and Arlene were invited to meet with him during his visit. They agreed to do so, and so did Aileen. The reporter spent part of a day with the three women, who took him to see the mountaintop-removal mine in their hollow and told him about the damage that the mine had caused to their

"The Death of a Community Treasure"

The rock formation in the top two photographs was called [Heritage] Rock. As children in [our] elementary school, we would go on field trips to this rock. It has been a landmark to our community for generations. On January 6, 2009, we met with the Department of Environmental Protection (DEP) and the CEO of Pritchard Mining Company to try to save "our rock." Community members were invited to attend a "town forum" to (supposedly) give us the opportunity to provide in-put about whether the DEP should renew Pritchard Mining Company's expired mining permit, which included the area of [Heritage] Rock. There were about 100 people total at this meeting. At least 10-12 community members spoke out against renewing the permit, while only one community person spoke for it. Despite our time and effort, the day after this meeting - January 7th - the mining company tore down one of the rocks, and the others soon followed. Obviously, this meeting was in name only. We now feel that the DEP doesn't take the input of the community seriously.

Figure 10.3

A photostory created by Arlene and Adelle about a failed attempt to stop the renewal of a permit for a mountaintop-removal mine in Community A.

homes and their community. The next day, a news photographer arrived, and Arlene and Aileen again helped by acting as "tour guides" for him. They invited me to come along for the day, and I gladly accepted the invitation. We drove and hiked to three different locations in the area that offered clear views of mountaintop-removal mine sites. There was some risk involved in taking us to these sites, for almost as soon as we reached one of the locations, which came right up to the edge of the mine property, an armed guard drove up in a pick-up truck and told us to leave (despite the fact that we were on the property of a local resident who had granted us permission to be there).

Toward the end of the day, when I was riding back with Arlene from the last "viewing spot," she told me how excited she was about finding her voice and having the power to speak out against something she thought was wrong. "Shannon," she told me, "I think I'm becoming one of those 'radical environmentalists'!"

A few weeks later, the newspaper article was printed. Aileen was quoted twice, first as having said "You know 'Almost heaven, West Virginia'? Well, now it's 'Almost level, West Virginia'" and second as having asked "Who said it's okay to bury streams, it's okay to cut the tops off mountains to get coal?" Almost as soon as the article came out, so did the backlash. One of the leaders of a civic organization in which Aileen was heavily involved admonished her, telling her that she really ought to watch what she said publicly because their organization often asked coal companies for donations for projects and that the article could really hurt their relationships with those companies. As a result, Aileen backed away from her involvement in the environmental justice movement.

When our project ended in May, Arlene and Amber were still in contact with environmental justice groups. When I called Arlene four months later in order to arrange a post-project interview, I expected to be met with the same level of enthusiasm she had expressed in the spring about finding the courage to speak out against the mining practices that were destroying her community. Instead, however, I heard slightly hesitant responses to my questions. Toward the end of our interview, when I asked her if there was anything that she would have liked to have gone differently with the project, she responded:

> Well, I really hadn't intended for it to be ... so much against the mining industry as a whole. You know, I was, I was against the mountaintop thing, but it seemed

like, you know, it kinda went to bein' against miners totally. ... It seems like there's, there's just so much against it right now. And I kinda feel bad because ... I voiced my opinion on it, and maybe, you know, helped it to go that way, I don't know. ... That wasn't my plans, in taking the mountaintop-removal pictures, you know. But it just seems like ... a bunch (of people), are going against the mining industry. And, you know, that's the way we made our living. My husband worked in the mines for twenty-some years, and I wasn't against it all together, just against the mountaintop part. ... After we saw the way it was going, we did back off.

I interviewed Amber immediately after her mother, Arlene. When I asked her if she was still involved with any of the environmental justice groups with which she had made contact during the project, she replied:

Some people took it to the extreme with things. ... I've just kind of retracted myself from certain groups and everything because I just felt like I didn't want my name to be out there with that group because of some of the things that they were doing that I totally didn't agree with. I mean, I agree with their cause, but I think there's a way to go about things. ... They're taking stuff a little farther than what I'm comfortable with. I know Mom's feeling that way too, you know what I mean? We're all about change and everything, but I think there's a line that you gotta, especially as a Christian, I think there's a line there that you, you know, that you can be for a cause without being, you know, *nuts* about it, I guess.

When I asked Amber if she could expand on what in particular was making her feel uncomfortable about the environmental justice groups, she responded as follows:

We have to live here. And, you know, I respect their causes, and I understand for a lot of them, that's kind of what they've dedicated their life to, but don't, don't try to *force*, you know? I mean, it had gotten to the point with Mom where she's like, "Don't even answer the phone if this person calls," don't answer the phone. Because, I mean, it was just crazy stuff.

From the "othering" language that both Amber and Arlene used to describe the individuals associated with the environmental justice organizations, it became clear that there was a disjuncture between their personal identities and what they viewed to be the collective identity of the movement. In fact, Amber actually said "I don't want to be involved with something like that, it's just not me." According to Amber, it wasn't the *reasons* for the actions that troubled her, but the tactics they used to accomplish their goals. She explained:

That felt real good to have the allies and everything, but like I said, there's a way to go about things, I think, that's more Christ-like than what I've seen. So, like I said,

> I've just kinda separated myself from that sort of thing, and, you know, there's still, that's not going to change the fact that, you know, I want to educate my kids to be mindful of their communities and everything, and let them know that they do have a voice in order to make changes and everything, but you don't have to be extreme about it. People will listen, if you just, you know ... just have a kind voice rather than, you know, one that's shouting hateful words and everything.

Although the environmental justice movement in Central Appalachia was indeed started by *local* people fighting for the protection of their communities (Bell 2013), in recent years, as the movement has gained national attention and organizers have reached out to others who may be able to help, more and more non-local environmentalists have come to the region to join the fight against mountaintop-removal mining. However, this may be happening at the expense of the local identity of the Central Appalachian environmental justice movement—an identity that may be crucial to the successful recruitment of new local participants.

My follow-up interview with Dorothy from Community D helped illuminate a particular protest event in the summer of 2009 that may have contributed to Amber's and Arlene's decision to disassociate from the environmental justice organizations. That event, though a successful tactic in gaining national media coverage, deepened the perception among many coalfield residents that the Central Appalachian environmental justice movement is an "outsider's movement." Describing her own observations of the after-effects of the protest, Dorothy exclaimed:

> They got—who was it—Daryl Hannah—*Daryl Hannah* came in and got arrested. Well, that was, that put it into national [news], which really makes people talk and get upset, and it opened a big can of worms because words got harsh. It put people back away from that negotiating line. It really is difficult to get them up to that point because there's so much history behind it. It takes a lot, it takes a lot of work to get the confidence, to get people to open up to even just listen to you. And then when you get people like that that come in, that just are used to having–in the big city, you need to stir it up to get people talking, because no one notices anything. But if you come out [in the rural area] where nothing's going on and you stir things up, I mean, it just, it puts everybody in fighting mode, and then they back away, and you've added another layer to that history and mistrust .... I don't know how they'll get them to open up again, it'll be someone that has to come in very quietly and win the confidence, and it'll take a lot of work.

Here Dorothy suggests that perhaps the attention-gaining tactics that the Central Appalachian environmental justice movement has used more widely in recent years (such as inviting celebrities to protests) may be contributing to the perception among non-activist coalfield residents that this movement is not really a movement of *their* people. As Meyer and Gamson (1995, p. 187) argue, enlisting celebrities to help draw attention to a social movement can be a double-edged sword: though celebrities may help gain media coverage, resources, and higher attendance at protest events, they may also "drown out some movement claims and constituents," overshadowing the causes they are trying to help. As a result, celebrities often make it difficult for social movements to control their collective identity and public image (ibid.; Meyer 1990).

My follow-up interviews with Adah and Amanda from Community A confirm the notion that there is a disconnect between local residents' personal identities and how they perceive the non-local activists who have come into the region to help the environmental justice movement. As Adah told me, many in her community wonder "How can you possibly, how can you be here in southern West Virginia protesting a coal-mining operation in the middle of the week?" She continued:

> What are you doing for a living? How can you do that? ... People don't understand—and most of the people around here are at the point of "OK, look. Here's what you are *supposed* to do: you're supposed to have a job, you're supposed to go to work, you're supposed to pay your bills. And, yes, you can be concerned about these issues, but no matter what you're concerned about, you go to work, you do your job, and you take care of your family." [Thumps her hand on the table for emphasis.] And if you're somewhere doing this when you're supposed to be working, how are you [doing what you're supposed to be doing]?

Here Adah makes clear that most local residents she knows prioritize formal employment over environmental concerns. She also alludes to perceived class divisions between many local residents and the non-local activists who have come into the community. Local residents view the alternative lifestyle that many of the non-local activists have chosen—a lifestyle that allows them to protest during "the middle of the week" when others are working—as foreign, if not downright objectionable.

The difference in lifestyles is also reflected in appearance. As Amanda explained, there is a "difference in the way they dress and take care of theirself." "The protesters, or the environmentalists," Adah further explained, "sometimes ... do it to themselves, because they come in and ... they *deliberately* make themselves *look* completely different from the norm." Both Amanda and Adah acknowledged that not all the non-local activists seemed different in lifestyle and appearance. However, in a way similar to the way

Dorothy described the effect of the protest involving Daryl Hannah, Amanda commented: "It only takes just one person like that, and then they're like, 'You tree-huggin' people!' And then any help that they've brought to the situation is evaporated."

Dorothy and Renewable Energy

Dorothy's description of the protest with celebrity Daryl Hannah is interesting in that it included "othering" language, but not just concerning the people Dorothy observed participating in the protest. Dorothy also spoke of *local* residents as "them" and "they," instead of "we" and "us." Through this language, Dorothy seemed to place herself outside the local context, as an external observer.

Though Dorothy lived in Community D, at the time of this project she had lived there only 13 years. Originally from California, Dorothy had spent most of her life far from the coalfields of southern West Virginia. Thus, her perspective was, in many ways, that of an external observer. Dorothy's non-local history also explains why the story of her involvement with the environmental justice movement was so different from that of the three women in Community A. As was described in chapter 9, Community D was the least coal-critical of the five communities in the study. Insofar as no more than 1 percent of the photographs shared at Community D's reflection meetings were related to the coal industry, it is all the more surprising that Dorothy would have become involved with the environmental justice organizations in the area. However, I believe that attending the regional Photovoice meeting and seeing the effects of the coal industry on other communities may have raised Dorothy's awareness of coal-related issues in Community D. Soon after the regional meeting, Dorothy submitted two photostories that were vaguely critical of the coal industry. (See figures 9.20 and 10.4.) Although they were worded somewhat ambiguously, Dorothy explicitly told me that she had written these photostories as statements about mountaintop-removal mining and coal-related water contamination.

It was at the local community exhibit and presentation that Dorothy made her connection with the environmental justice movement. In attendance at the event were two young non-local environmental justice organizers who were working on a campaign to bring "green jobs" to the

"River Access at [River] Bridge"

It looks so peaceful. Makes you want to jump in...and then you think about what is in the water.

Figure 10.4
A vaguely coal-critical photostory created by Dorothy from Community D.

coalfields. Specifically, they were trying to find landowners in the area who might be interested in working together to develop a wind-farm cooperative in the county. At the end of the Photovoice presentation, one of the organizers made an announcement about a field trip they were organizing to a large wind farm in the eastern part of the state and urged anyone who was interested to talk with him. Dorothy talked with the organizers for quite some time that evening, and later she told me that she had gone on the trip to the wind farm and had had a great time.

Soon after the Photovoice project ended, Dorothy also attended a "green jobs" picnic, and, at the request of one of the environmental justice organizations sponsoring the event, she had brought photostories from Community D to display there. During my follow-up interview with Dorothy, she was still very much interested in what various groups were doing to try to bring renewable energy and green jobs to the coalfields. Unlike the participants from Community B, Dorothy did not indicate a desire to retract her association with the environmental justice groups.

Social Networks, Identity, "Cultural Holes," and Social- Movement Disengagement

The Photovoice project began with a total of 54 women living in five different coal-mining communities in southern West Virginia. Forty-seven were non-activists, and seven were involved in environmental justice activism. I aimed to create a micromobilization context in each of these Photovoice groups by recruiting the seven local activists to join the project and by attempting to control for the four barriers to local participation I had identified in my previous research. The fact that only five of the 47 non-activist participants became involved in the environmental justice movement points to an often-overlooked actuality of social movements: mobilization is, in fact, a very *infrequent* occurrence among individuals experiencing injustice (McAdam and Boudet 2012).

But there were five women who *did* become mobilized through this project. Three of these women—Arlene, Amber, and Aileen, who were all members of the same family in Community A—became especially vocal against the coal-related injustices taking place in their community. Most notably, Amber spoke out at a public hearing against a permit for a mountaintop-removal mine, and Arlene, Aileen, and Amber helped a reporter and photographer from a prominent national newspaper with a story on the problems mountaintop-removal mining was causing in Appalachian communities. All three of these women seemed invigorated by their experiences and eager to continue speaking out against the problems the coal industry was causing for their communities and families. But their mobilization was short-lived. Within a few months, Arlene, Aileen, and Amber had disassociated themselves from the environmental justice movement, explaining that the groups were using tactics that were too "extreme" for their comfort level. Amber stated she didn't want her name "to be out there" in association with one of the activist groups, "because of some of the things that they were doing." Moreover, she said, the movement is "just not me."

Much of Doug McAdam's research on the Mississippi Freedom Summer campaign has focused on the importance of networks to social-movement recruitment and participation. As McAdam and Paulsen (1993) assert, however, social ties do not only draw people *into* social movements; they can also deter and prevent involvement. It is very likely that the close family ties and the social capital that bound Arlene, Aileen, and Amber to one another brought them into the environmental justice movement together. But it is also likely that the same ties pulled them out of the movement together. Thus, Aileen's being reprimanded for speaking out against mountaintop-removal mining in an article appearing in a national newspaper not only affected her own willingness to continue participating in the movement; it also affected Arlene and Amber's willingness to participate, leading them to view the movement more critically. As was discussed in chapters 3 and 9, the depletions of social capital felt in the Central Appalachian coalfields means that those community bonds that *are* present are all the more precious. If there is a fear that speaking out against an environmental injustice could damage these relationships, it seems logical that a person would choose to withdraw her involvement.

Indeed, during an interview I conducted with Arlene in 2013, four years after the project ended, she told me that, because of her association with environmental justice groups during the Photovoice project, she had "even had family members tell me that I would [have to] take their children in and feed them if they lost their jobs." The dilemma that Arlene faced in reconciling her own feelings about coal-industry practices with economic realities in her community was obvious as she continued: "The mountaintop removal, it's a heartbreak. It's a heartbreak to any hillbilly, I would think. But if that's the only way some people can work, their work means more, I guess." Aileen and Amber also expressed feeling a need to choose community and family ties over a moral, emotional, or intellectual stance against irresponsible mining practices. As Aileen put it while reflecting on her involvement in the movement: "It backlashed on us. ... We had repercussions over it."

Though it is clear that networks are important to both participation in and disengagement from social movements, McAdam and Paulsen (1993) argue that social networks *and* identity function synergistically to encourage (and, it follows, *dis*courage) participation in social movements. My data suggest that another major factor influencing Aileen's, Amber's, and Arlene's decision to disengage from the movement was an inability to reconcile their personal identities with the collective identity of the environmental justice organizations, which they perceived to be at odds with many of their own values and cultural expectations. Aileen was the first to pull back, worrying that her participation would affect her status within a civic group that was important to her, but Arlene and Amber soon followed once they began to question the decisions, tactics, and culture of the activist groups. As Amber and Aileen indicated, they could not reconcile their feelings about what entailed "Christian-like" behavior with the actions of the environmental justice activists. In Amber's words, "It's just not me." Thus, networks and identity functioned synergistically to cause Arlene, Aileen, and Amber to break their affiliation with the movement.

The way in which identity and networks intersected to prompt these three women's disassociation from the movement points to the importance of the cultural context of a social network to determining the success or failure of recruitment into social movements. Pachucki and Brieger's (2010) concept of "cultural holes" is important for interpreting the withdrawal of Arlene, Aileen, and Amber from the movement. According to Vilhena et al. (2014, p. 221), the absence of shared cultural connections and understandings within a social network creates a cultural hole, the presence of which impoverishes existing network ties and makes the creation of new ties "improbable or impossible." The cultural hole that emerged with regard to the protest tactics the environmental justice actors were using and what Arlene, Aileen, and Amber believed to be "appropriate" behavior bankrupted the network connection between the Photovoice women and the environmental justice activists they had met, leading Arlene, Aileen, and Amber to cut their ties with the movement.

That Dorothy and Bonnie remained associated with the environmental justice organizations may also be attributable to their social networks. Dorothy's social network stretched over a vast geographic area because she had lived in California for much of her life. She and her husband regularly traveled to Seattle and to southern California to visit relatives and friends. Similarly, Bonnie, the daughter of an environmental justice activist and a person whose social network primarily consisted of individuals living outside of southern West Virginia, was not nearly as embedded in the local networks of the coalfields as the women in Community A. Thus, though Dorothy and Bonnie were both "locals" in the sense that they lived in the coal-mining region of Central Appalachia, they had non-local networks that may have offered them some protection from the social sanctions associated with speaking out against the coal industry. Moreover, these diverse networks may have also allowed them to more readily achieve identity correspondence with the changing collective identity of the coalfield environmental justice movement than the other women in the study. The "cultural holes" that the three Photovoice participants in Community A felt so deeply did not seem to be an issue for Dorothy and Bonnie. Here again, we see that the cultural context of network connections matters to social-movement participation and retention.

In chapter 9 I discussed how the power of the local elite and the fear of an "outsider stigma" contributed to the anti-mobilization context that emerged in Community E. Those two processes also seem to have deterred some of the women described in the present chapter from continuing to participate in the activities of the environmental justice movement. The way in which Arlene's civic organization was beholden to local coal companies for donations parallels the Jackson family's power within the church in Community E. Furthermore, the othering language that the Photovoice women used to describe actors in the environmental justice movement indicates that they viewed those activists as "outsiders," despite the local roots of the social movement. As the women in Community A and Community E revealed, there was a fear that being associated with this outsider stigma could have threatened their standing in the community. When I asked Amber what was making her uncomfortable with the actions of the environmental justice groups, her response—"We have to live here"—revealed her concern that there could be serious social consequences for her if she were to continue her association with those groups. Simultaneously, Amber's words signaled her belief that those organizations were made up of people who did *not* "have to live here"—in other words, outsiders. My data suggest that there is a *perception* among some (and perhaps many) residents that the movement is an "outsiders' movement," and this perception may have profound consequences for recruiting new local participants into the environmental justice organizations working in the coalfields of Central Appalachia.

Conclusion

This book began with a puzzle: Why do so many local citizens who are affected by industry-produced environmental hazards and toxics not participate in movements to bring about social justice and industry accountability? By asking my research question in this way—and not as "Why do certain citizens who are affected by industry-produced environmental hazards and toxics *participate* in movements to bring about social justice and industry accountability"—I correct for a common problem associated with research on social movements: selecting on the dependent variable (McAdam and Boudet 2012). In the case of the environmental justice movement in Central Appalachia, I instead examine the barriers that prevent so many local coalfield residents from becoming involved in collective action against the myriad injustices the people of this region suffer in the name of "cheap energy" for the rest of the nation.

I study this question of non-participation in social movements by drawing on data gathered from field research conducted in southern West Virginia between July of 2006 and May of 2009 and then again in August and September of 2013.

Part I of the book draws on social-movement theory to connect the low levels of local participation in the Central Appalachian environmental justice movement to possible barriers inhibiting the micro-level processes of solidarity building, identity correspondence, consciousness transformation, and micromobilization. Through a series of four discrete studies in the coal-mining region of Central Appalachia, I identify four major factors suppressing local participation in the environmental justice movement:

- depleted social capital in coal-mining communities, indicating high levels of isolation, sparse social networks, and few formal organizations in the region

• the gendering of activist involvement—that is, the underrepresentation of men involved in environmental justice activism, owing to the coal industry's influence on the local hegemonic masculinity of the region
• the coal industry's ideology-construction efforts to maintain and amplify the perception that coal is both the economic backbone of the state and the cultural identity of the citizenry
• the fact that the majority of the coal industry's environmental destruction is not visible to most local residents.

While these four factors are constraining local participation in the Central Appalachian environmental justice movement, do they make up the entire story? One of the challenges we face in studying social movements is that it is difficult to observe the process of "becoming an activist" because such a transition is difficult to find and difficult to recognize. However, observing individuals making or not making this transition could provide significant insights into the factors facilitating and constraining an individual actor's decision to become involved in a social movement. Part II of the book attempts to create a situation in which observing this process is possible. Through using the feminist participatory-action research method of Photovoice with women living in five coal-mining communities in southern West Virginia, I attempted to create a micromobilization context among five groups of non-activist coalfield residents in order to study the factors that prevent and facilitate the process of "becoming an activist" in this context.

I recruited 54 women to participate in the Photovoice project, 47 of whom had had no previous involvement in the environmental justice movement and seven of whom were associated with environmental justice organizations in the area. In the design of this research, I attempted to control for the four barriers outlined above, creating a micromobilization context that could potentially facilitate these participants' recruitment into the environmental justice movement. Through analyzing the experiences of the women who chose to become involved in environmental justice activism and those who did not, I investigated the additional social factors that hinder local residents' participation in the movement.

My analysis of the Photovoice portion of this research suggests that there are two additional barriers to social-movement participation among local residents. The first is the power of members of the local elite, who benefit from the maintenance of the status quo. The pressure that these individuals can exert to stifle other community members' willingness to speak out against environmental injustice is a strong force in the small communities I studied. This was most apparent in Community E, where Photovoice participants' questions or criticisms of the coal industry were met with censure, both from other members of the Photovoice group and through actions that took place outside the meeting space. Similarly, in Community A, when Aileen was quoted in a prominent national newspaper in a story about the problems associated with mountaintop-removal mining, a member of her civic organization told her that her public criticisms of the coal industry might cost the organization much-needed donations from local coal companies. As a result of this reprimand, Aileen pulled back from her involvement with the environmental justice movement. Gaventa (1980, pp. vi–vii) recognizes such instances of repression as integral to power holders' ability to maintain their position of dominance: "Power works to develop and maintain the quiescence of the powerless. ... Together, patterns of power and powerlessness can keep issues from arising, grievances from being voiced, and interests from being recognized."

The second barrier revealed through the Photovoice study is that the collective identity of the environmental justice movement is changing in ways that have made potential local recruits less likely to view the movement as being compatible with their own personal identities. The recent influx of non-local environmental groups, college students, and celebrities into the environmental justice movement—and particularly the protest tactics they have chosen—may be changing the collective identity of the movement such that the process of identity correspondence is becoming increasingly difficult among local would-be recruits.

The influx of non-locals into the Appalachian coalfields has helped draw attention to the injustices taking place and has given the environmental justice movement a strong and deep base of support. At the same time, however, many supporters of the coal industry have been quick to condemn the newcomers—and the environmental justice organizations by association—as groups of "outsider extremists" who, if successful, will close all the coal mines and leave the "locals" without a source of income. Thus, although the environmental justice movement was *started* by local coalfield residents, and those local residents are *still* central to the leadership of the movement, the surge of non-local people joining the movement has provided an opportunity for the opposition to capitalize on an "insider-outsider" dichotomy, effectively challenging the collective identity of the movement so that many no longer perceive it as a "local" struggle.

As was discussed in chapter 5, one way the coal industry maintains its power is by actively constructing ideology that furthers its interests. The decline in mining jobs, the increase in the supply of cheap natural gas from the environmentally contentious process of hydraulic fracturing, and the rising tide of protest against the ecological, public-health, and social damage that the coal industry is causing in Central Appalachia have converged to cause a crisis for the industry, challenging its hold on political power. The industry has responded to this challenge by engaging in cultural manipulation in order to maintain and amplify the perception of Central Appalachia as being both economically dependent on coal and culturally defined by coal. As part of its ongoing ideology-construction efforts, the coal industry also endeavors to manipulate the public's perception of the environmental justice movement so that supporters of the movement will be viewed as "outsiders."

The cultural manipulation of the statuses of "insider" and "outsider" can be seen in various forms of coal-industry propaganda, such as a television commercial produced by the coal company Massey Energy (now Alpha Natural Resources) in 2009. The opening scene of the commercial is video footage from the June 2009 protest that Dorothy described in chapter 10, during which the actress Daryl Hannah was arrested. Prominently displayed in the opening scene is a hand-painted sign held by a counter-protester that reads "WV Miners Say Go Home Treehuggers." The narrator begins:

Tree-hugging extremists and self-serving politicians,

[image of Al Gore]

all jumping up and down, claiming they can save the planet.

["Extremists Threaten Our Jobs" appears below an image of a male miner operating heavy equipment.]

What about the real endangered species—the American worker?

["American Jobs at Risk" appears below an image of two male coal miners walking on a mine site]

We at Massey Energy are fighting hard for Appalachian jobs and *our* way of life.

[image of two men in blaze orange vests and a dog walking through the woods carrying hunting rifles]

It's not easy to fight for what's right,

[image of man in Marine Corps uniform saluting in front of war memorial]

But the people of Appalachia aren't known for backing down.

[image of coal train]

Massey Energy: we work here and we give here, because we live here, too.

["We Work Here. We Give Here. We Live Here" appears across the image of a coal train]

In this commercial, Massey Energy is clearly attempting to brand participants in the environmental justice movement as outsiders by referring to them as "tree-hugging extremists" and by showing a protest sign that tells the tree-huggers to "go home." In addition, we again see the coal industry appropriating the local masculine cultural icons described in chapter 5: the "American worker," the "avid outdoorsman," and the "military hero." Through these appropriations, the company aims to position itself as the ultimate "insider." Massey Energy claims to be fighting to protect "Appalachian jobs" from outsiders, who are purportedly threatening those jobs through environmentalism.

Along with Appalachian jobs, Massey also claims to be fighting to protect the Appalachian way of life, which the company calls "*our* way of life," in another attempt to position itself as a cultural insider. The coal industry attempts to manipulate the public's perception so that the coal *company* is seen as being interchangeable with the coal *miner*. There is, of course, great irony in the coal industry's attempts to brand itself as an "insider" to Central Appalachia. The coal companies have *always* been outsiders to the region, ever since the first coal barons swindled local residents out of their mineral resources in the early 1900s. In fact, until Massey Energy was bought by Alpha Natural Resources after the horrific Upper Big Branch Mine Disaster of 2010, its headquarters were in Richmond, Virginia, hundreds of miles from the coalfields of Appalachia, in one of the largest metropolitan and financial centers of the southeast. As if signaling the absurdity of this coal company's attempts to portray itself as an "insider" to Central Appalachia, the narrator of the commercial even pronounces the word *Appalachia* in the non-local way. Instead of saying "A-puh-*latch*-uh," as Central and Southern Appalachians will tell you is the correct way to pronounce it, he says, "A-puh-*lay*-shuh," which some say is a sure-fire way to tell that someone is "not from around here."

Despite the non-localness of the multinational coal companies that are extracting resources in Central Appalachia, my data suggest that the coal industry's ideology-construction efforts to manipulate the public's perception about the environmental justice organizations have been relatively successful. Whether or not local people really believe that the coal companies are "insiders" to Central Appalachia, there seem to be significant fears about becoming involved with the environmental justice organizations. In particular, the fear of acquiring an "outsider stigma" by associating with these groups appears to be especially salient because it could have negative consequences for an individual's local networks and relationships. In a region that has suffered severe depletions in social capital (discussed in chapter 3), the fear of isolation and damaging important relationships may be a particularly strong deterrent against participation in the environmental justice movement.

Attaching an "outsider stigma" to those who challenge the power of local elites is a strategy that has been observed in other contexts and locations as well. For instance, Shriver (2000) found in his study of the resistance movement against the nuclear weapons testing site in Oak Ridge, Tennessee that local residents who expressed grievances against the Department of Energy were branded "communist" and bad for the community. Similarly, Shriver, Adams, and Messer (2014) found that activist women who were fighting legacy pollution from a decommissioned zinc smelter facility in rural Blackwell, Oklahoma were vilified and publicly stigmatized by members of the local elite. The fear of ostracism and social isolation served as a deterrent to others in the community who might otherwise have been likely to speak out. Mobilizing an "outsider" stigma against local activists is one tactic among a suite of "coercive measures" that Shriver, Adams, and Messer (ibid.) identify as integral to efforts by elite groups to stymie resistance efforts once they emerge. Thus, it should not be altogether surprising that the coal industry would perceive and amplify the tensions around "insiderness" and "outsiderness" within the environmental justice movement in an effort to hinder local recruitment efforts.

This insight presents a significant dilemma for the future of the environmental justice movement in Central Appalachia, and undoubtedly other contexts as well. On the one hand, organizing high-profile social-movement protests that lead to the arrests of celebrities and other non-locals draws a great deal of media coverage. The non-locals who have joined the fight for justice in Central Appalachia in recent years have been a primary reason why mountaintop-removal mining is no longer the region's "dirty little secret." It is likely that the increased scrutiny that this form of coal extraction has received from the Environmental Protection Agency and other federal agencies is in part attributable to the efforts of the many dedicated non-locals who have joined the movement to stand in solidarity with local coalfield residents fighting to protect their families, communities, and heritage from the consequences of irresponsible mining practices. On the other hand, the fact that participants in the Photovoice project disassociated themselves from the environmental justice movement because they felt that the movement's tactics didn't agree with their own personal values indicates that the changing face of the coalfield movement may actually be deterring—and disempowering—a group of potential recruits. Particularly because the roots of this movement are deeply embedded in the lives and history of the people of Central Appalachia, it seems important that a balance be struck between actions that draw national media attention and tactics that correspond more readily with the personal identities of the local coalfield residents. Although the recent high-profile protest activities taking place in the coalfields are quite reminiscent of the direct actions initiated by local people involved in the anti-strip-mining movement of the 1960s and the 1970s,[1] much has changed since that first attempt to protect the Appalachian region from surface mining. The earlier movement emerged during an era defined by social activism. Not only were wildcat strikes rampant throughout the coalfields during that time period, but the Civil Rights Movement, the Women's Liberation Movement, and the Antiwar Movement were part of the social fabric of the United States. Thus, the militant actions that local coalfield residents initiated to try to end surface mining in Appalachia in the 1960s and the 1970s should be considered within the context of the period. With Central Appalachia largely de-unionized, and with a more subdued current political culture across the nation, high-profile protest activities may seem somewhat shocking and foreign to local coalfield residents today. Opportunistically, the coal industry has aggressively sought to propagandize the "foreignness" of such activities, manipulating the public's perception of the environmental justice movement such that it is increasingly viewed as an "outsider's movement," rather than as a local struggle.

The high-profile protest activities that have been organized in the coal-mining region of Central Appalachia are not the only tactics—or even the main tactics—that the environmental justice movement is employing to bring an end to irresponsible mining practices in the area. Grassroots organizations such as Coal River Mountain Watch, Ohio Valley Environmental Coalition, Kentuckians For The Commonwealth, and Appalachian Voices are all devoting a great deal of energy toward developing campaigns and strategies that would bring a sustainable future to Central Appalachia and reduce the region's dependence on the coal industry. These organizations' efforts to develop "green jobs," wind farms, and small local businesses in the region offer hope for achieving a more gentle balance between the collective identity of the environmental justice movement and the personal identities of many local residents. However, these more quiet strategies seem to be drowned out by the din of high-profile protest, which, as Dorothy articulates in chapter 10, "puts everybody in fighting mode" and causes them to "back away ... add[ing] another layer to that history and mistrust" in the region. Drawing more local residents into the environmental justice movement will, as Dorothy suggests, require organizers who will "come in very quietly" and will gently, and more deliberately, try to win the confidence of the community.

But *should* the Central Appalachian environmental justice movement be concerned with ensuring that its collective identity is aligned with the personal identities of non-activist local coalfield residents? If actions such as occupying mountaintop-removal mines and staging large demonstrations at which celebrities are arrested are successfully drawing national political attention, what does it matter if new local participants are not recruited into the movement? The movement was *started* by local coalfield residents, many of whom are still leaders in the struggle. Furthermore, the end goal of the movement is to protect the Appalachian people from the negative effects of irresponsible coal-mining practices. Isn't that enough?

As a feminist scholar, I would argue that *all* social movements aiming to "help" a group of people should attend to matters of disempowerment and underrepresentation. But I believe that there are also other compelling reasons, beyond normative considerations, why the movement should focus its efforts on recruiting more local people. The environmental justice platform is particularly influential because it is grounded in a struggle for human rights: seeking social justice for people who live, work, play, and learn in the most polluted environments in the world (Cole and Foster 2001). The focus is on protecting *people*, which makes it possible for environmental justice movements to cross political boundaries more readily than mainstream environmental movements, allowing for a wider base of support. Moreover, local people also bring critical experiential knowledge of injustices to the movement; they know firsthand how pollution and contamination have compromised the health and safety of their families and communities. Thus, these movements need local voices—*many* local voices—to give credibility to the claims of injustice that form the basis of the environmental justice platform. If these movements lose their local identities, they may also lose their power.

Given the increasing globalization of grassroots environmental justice movements throughout the world, questions about the relevance of local identities to the ultimate success of environmental justice struggles may be significant for many movements outside of Central Appalachia as well. Because environmental justice movements evolve and draw non-locals into their efforts, new tactics and ideas are also introduced that may unintentionally affect the local identities of those social movements. Furthermore, as was seen in the case of the coal industry in Central Appalachia, the opposition can—and does—use this changing identity to its advantage. How can a grassroots movement avoid losing its local identity as its support base becomes more diverse? It is my hope that future studies will help elucidate possible solutions to this dilemma, as the outcomes of many struggles for environmental justice throughout the world may hinge on this challenge.

Appendix A: Data-Collection Methods and Tables for Chapter 3

Data-Collection Methods for the Social-Capital Study

I conducted forty face-to-face interviews with randomly selected individuals, twenty in each of the study towns (Coalville and Farmstead). In order to select my respondents, I obtained aerial photographs and street maps of each town and divided the towns into one-block-square quadrants. Not all areas of the towns could be neatly divided into such quadrants, however, and in those cases I created a "quadrant" out of a street or two streets linked together. In both Coalville and Farmstead, every part of the town was incorporated into one of these numbered quadrants so that all housing units in the town had an equal chance of selection. To determine the counting interval necessary to achieve a random sample of twenty housing units, I took the total number of housing units in each town (gleaned from census data) and divided that number by 20 to obtain a number *n*. Next, I picked a random quadrant and began at the southwestern corner of the quadrant, walking clockwise and counting housing units until I reached the *n*th unit. At the *n*th housing unit, I requested an interview with one or more adults living there. If no one was home, I returned up to three more times on different days and at different times. In the case of a refusal, I went to the next housing unit and requested an interview. After finishing my interview at that home, I continued around the quadrant, counting, until I reached the next *n*th housing unit. Once there were no more homes to count in a particular quadrant, I went to the southwestern corner of the next quadrant and picked up my counting where I had left off. In this way, every housing unit in each town was counted and thus had an equal chance of selection. This method allowed me to obtain a random sample of individuals living in each town.

Each research participant was asked to take part in an anonymous, audio-recorded, face-to-face interview. These interviews ranged in length from 35 minutes to 150 minutes. The interview was semi-structured, but I encouraged respondents to expand on their answers. I asked my interviewees to provide details of their own experiences within their towns that reflected trusting behavior, social norms, and reciprocity within their community, and they were also asked about their formal and informal networks. Six people in Farmstead refused to be interviewed (a refusal rate of 23.1 percent), thirteen in Coalville (a refusal rate of 39.4 percent).

The comparative demographics of the respondents in the two towns are quite similar. Fifty percent of Farmstead respondents reported having a high school diploma or a higher degree, 58 percent of Coalville respondents. In Farmstead the respondents' rate of home ownership was 80 percent; in Coalville the rate was 71 percent. The median age for Farmstead respondents was 61 years, that of Coalville respondents was 59. The median household income for both Farmstead and Coalville respondents was between $20,000 and $30,000. In each town, fourteen of the respondents were women and six were men.

Though the median household income for the respondents was close to the census data reported in table 3.1 ($24,178 for Farmstead and $19,250 for Coalville), the median ages were higher than the census data reports for the populations, as was the number of women represented in each sample. Though some of the age skewing can be explained by the fact that only people aged 18 and older were included in this sample (and the census-reported median age includes children), the characteristics of those who declined to be interviewed are also significant. Individuals who appeared to be in their twenties or their thirties had a refusal rate twice that of middle-aged and older adults. This may have been due to a perceived "lack of time" to participate in an hour-long interview, as most of these individuals worked and had children at home. The gender imbalance can also be explained by those who declined: men were more than twice as likely to refuse to grant me an interview as women were. This gender bias may have been due to the fact that I am a woman, and perhaps women were more comfortable talking with me in their homes than the men I approached. However, because these patterns were consistent between both Farmstead and Coalville, any bias the age and gender skewing introduced to the data was introduced equally.

Table A.1

Components of the Social Capital Index.

Network of closest friends and family (informal networks)	In this item, I asked individuals to list up to twenty people who were most important in their lives, creating a "most important people network" list. These individuals could be friends or family and could live close by or far away. For the purposes of the index, however, I examined the number of adults in each respondents' "most important people network" that live in their town. A score of –1 was assigned if the respondent had zero or one adults in their "most important people network" living in their town; a score of 0 indicates two or three adults in the network living in their town; a score of 1 indicates four or more individuals.
Degree to which respondents are vested in the community (social trust, networks, social norms)	This component indicates respondents' level of identification with and commitment to their community. This was assessed through examining respondents' descriptions of their towns and their expressed desire either to be living there or to be living somewhere else. A clear connection to the community and desire to be there was given a score of 1; an ambiguous connection—neither entirely positive or negative—was given a score of 0; a clear desire to live elsewhere was given a score of –1.
Engagement with neighbors (social norms, informal networks, social trust)	In this category I coded for recent stories indicating reciprocity (favor exchange) with neighbors. A score of 1 indicates favor exchange with neighbors; a score of –1 indicates no favor exchange with neighbors.
Social trust	In this category, I combined answers to specific questions about trust (e.g., Are there people in this town that you don't trust? Is there any group or organization that you don't trust?) with stories that respondents told elsewhere in the interview indicating trust or a lack of trust within the community. A score of 1 indicates the respondent was clearly trusting of others in the community; a score of 0 indicates an ambiguity about level of trust; a score of –1 indicates a clear mistrust of others in the town.
Received assistance from community in times of difficulty (social norms, informal networks)	This component measures whether the social norms of helpfulness and reciprocity have been accessible to respondents in times of need. A score of 1 indicates that respondents have received assistance from others in the town during a difficult time; a score of 0 indicates that they have not needed assistance; a score of –1 indicates that they had a need, but no one in the town helped.

Table A.1 (continued)

Recently helped someone in community during a difficult time (social norms, informal networks)	In this category, I coded for stories of respondents' own contribution to the social norms of helpfulness and reciprocity within the town in the form of assisting a fellow resident in a time of crisis. A respondent who provided stories of assisting others in the town received a score of 1 for this category; one who could not provide stories of assisting others received a score of –1.
Volunteering (social norms, formal networks)	This category indicates whether respondents regularly volunteer in their own town (a score of 1) or outside their town (a score of 0), either formally (with a group) or informally (on their own). A score of –1 was given to a respondent who did no volunteering, either in his or her community or elsewhere.
Non-religious group membership/ involvement (formal networks)	Reported in this category is a resident's involvement in organizations or groups within his or her town (score of 1) and outside the town (score of 0). A score of –1 was assigned to a respondent who was not involved in any organizations.
Church/religious group involvement (formal networks)	I coded for respondents' religious group involvement within their town (score of 1) and outside their town (score of 0). Respondents receiving a score of –1 were not involved in any church or religious groups.

Table A.2

Experiences of social capital by town, including age.

	Social Capital Index value	Farmstead	Coalville
High Social Capital (N = 10 Farmstead; N = 2 Coalville)	9	Nancy (44) Ann (66)	
	8		
	7		
	6	*David (72) Ron (48) Tonya (40)	*Vincent (76)
	5	*Beulah (99) *William (72) Lucinda (58) *John (75) Harriet (65)	*Alice (70)

Table A.2 (continued)

Moderate Social Capital (N = 8 Farmstead; N = 7 Coalville)	4	*Bonnie (74) *Mildred (79)	*Evelyn (92) *Mabel (80)
	3	*Sylvia (73) Tracy (42) Amber (41) Greta (40) Eddie (37)	*Charles (82) *Helen (71)
	2		Amy (26)
	1	Gail (55)	*Linda (67) Tina (53)
Low Social Capital (N = 2 Farmstead; N = 5 Coalville)	0	*Tilly (78)	Ricky (51) Herb (60) Mark (57)
	–1	Pepe (33)	
	–2		June (58)
	–3		
	–4		Robin (54)
Very Low Social Capital (N = 0 Farmstead; N = 6 Coalville)	–5		Annette (23) Bob (52)
	–6		
	–7		Sandy (52) Elsie (60) *Ruth (79)
	–8		Gloria (38)
	–9		

* Age 70 or older. Linda (67) is borderline, but she follows the social-capital pattern of the older cohort. Because the person to whom she is closest in age is in the older cohort, and because she follows the older cohort pattern, that is the group in which I place her for the analysis.

Table A.3

Coalville and Farmstead residents' experiences of social capital by birth cohort.

	Coalville		Farmstead	
	Born before 1940	Born after 1940	Born before 1940	Born after 1940
High Social Capital	$N = 2$ Vincent (76) Alice (70)		$N = 4$ David (72) Beulah (99) William (72) John (75)	$N = 6$ Ron (48) Nancy (44) Tonya (40) Lucinda (58) Ann (66) Harriet (65)
Moderate Social Capital	$N = 5$ Evelyn (92) Mabel (80) Charles (82) Helen (71) Linda (67)	$N = 2$ Amy (26) Tina (53)	$N = 3$ Bonnie (74) Mildred (79) Sylvia (73)	$N = 5$ Tracy (42) Eddie (37) Gail (55) Amber (41) Greta (40)
Low Social Capital		$N = 5$ Ricky (51) Herb (60) Mark (57) June (58) Robin (54)	$N = 1$ Tilly (78)	$N = 1$ Pepe (33)
Very Low Social Capital	$N = 1$ Ruth (79)	$N = 5$ Annette (23) Bob (52) Sandy (52) Elsie (60) Gloria (38)		

Appendix B: Interview Methods and Demographics of the Study Sample for Chapter 4

Data and Analysis

The twenty in-depth interviews referred to in chapter 4 were all audio-recorded and ranged in length from 45 minutes to 4 hours. During the consent process, each participant was asked if she or he would like to be assigned a pseudonym for the study; all the interviewees declined, preferring to have their real names used in any publications. The interview protocol was open ended, focusing on activists' narratives of entry into the environmental justice movement, the challenges they had faced in their protest activities, and what sustained and motivated their continued involvement. I also conducted participant observation with two different environmental justice organizations in southern West Virginia during the summers of 2006 and 2007. Participant-observation activities included attending various events, such as protests, permit hearings for mountaintop-removal mines, media tours, press conferences, and picnics, as well as volunteering in the office of one of the environmental justice organizations and living in two different coalfield communities.

Data analysis was undertaken in an inductive manner, first by reading through the interview transcripts and field notes line by line to develop a list of themes and a detailed coding scheme and then by applying the coding scheme to the data in order to examine thematic patterns across and within gender categories.

Table B.1
Characteristics of activists.

	Women (N = 12)	Men (N = 8)
Median age in 2007	52 (range: 38–77)	53 (range: 26–71)
Race	100% white	100% white
Class	83% working class, 17% professional class	50% working class, 50% professional class
Percent who had lived outside the coalfields for five or more years	25%	75%
Percent who had never worked for the coal industry or whose partners never had worked for the coal industry	25%	50%

Appendix C: Creation of the Coal-Critical Index and Analysis of Pre-Project and Post-Project Results in Photovoice Groups and Control Groups

The Photovoice-group and control-group questionnaires included the following coal-critical questions, numbered as shown here:

11. G) Most of the time we can trust the coal company executives to do what is right.
    a. Strongly agree—1
    b. Agree—2
    c. Neither agree nor disagree—3
    d. Disagree—4
    e. Strongly disagree—5
13. E) How much confidence do you have in the coal companies to keep the best interests of your community in mind when making decisions?
    a. Complete confidence—1
    b. A great deal of confidence—2
    c. Some confidence—3
    d. Very little confidence—4
    e. No confidence at all—5
14. C) Do you feel that coal companies have too much or too little power in West Virginia?
    a. Too much power—5
    b. About the right amount of power—3
    c. Too little power—1

15. D) Do you trust the coal companies to give you correct information about the causes of pollution?
    a. Yes—1
    b. No—5
    c. Not sure—3

I combined these four questions to create a "Coal-Critical Index" that would allow me to compare changes in participants' attitudes toward the coal industry over the time period of the project.

The first step in creating the index was to assign numerical values to the possible responses to each of the four questions, ranging from 1 to 5. Responses that were critical of the coal industry received higher values than responses that were favorable to it. For instance, in question 11G the respondent was asked to indicate a level of agreement with the statement "Most of the time we can trust the coal company executives to do what is right." A response of "strongly agree" was assigned a value of 1; a response of "strongly disagree" was assigned a value of 5. Question 13E was coded in the same way as question 11G. For questions 14C and 15D, the three-point scale was stretched to a five-point scale (receiving a value of 1, 3, or 5) in order to match the scale in questions 11G and 13E, so that every item had the same weight in the index. I determined the total index score for each respondent by adding the scores for the four questions for a combined value ranging from 4 to 20.

I next tested three hypotheses, presented below, through a series of one-tailed *t*-tests.[1]

Hypothesis 1 Non-activist Photovoice participants will become more critical of the coal industry during the course of the project, as measured through the change in the mean of the Coal-Critical Index values for these participants.

Through conducting a one-tailed *t*-test on non-activist participants in the Photovoice groups, I found that the mean Coal-Critical Index value for the pre-questionnaires was 14.92 and that the mean index value for the post-questionnaires was 16.20. This represents a 1.28 unit increase in the mean Index score from the start of the project to the end of the project. This difference was statistically significant at the 0.05 level ($t = 2.03$; d.f. = 24; $p = 0.026$).

Hypothesis 2 Control Group participants will *not* have become more critical of the coal industry during the course of the project, as measured through the change in the mean of the Coal-Critical Index values for these participants.

By conducting a one-tailed *t*-test on Control Group participants, I found that the mean Coal-Critical Index value on the pre-questionnaires was 14.18 and the mean index value on the post-questionnaires was 14.09. This represented a 0.09 decrease in the Coal-Critical Index from the start of the project to the end of the project. The difference in Coal-Critical Index values was not statistically significant. ($t = -0.20$; d.f. = 21; $p = 0.577$).

Hypothesis 3 The change in Photovoice participants' Coal-Critical Index value from the start of the project to the end of the project will be greater than the change in Control Group participants' Coal-Critical Index value during the same time period.

By conducting a one-tailed *t*-test comparing the change in non-activist Photovoice participants' Coal-Critical Index value with the change in Control Group participants' Coal-Critical Index value, I found that the data do support Hypothesis 3. The mean difference in the Coal-Critical Index for these two groups was significant at the 0.05 level ($t = 1.71$; d.f. = 45; $p = 0.047$). Thus, Photovoice participants did become more critical of the coal industry than Control Group participants during the project.

Appendix C

1. I am aware that the variables I use in this analysis are ordinal-level variables and that by using a *t*-test I am treating them as interval-level variables. However, using a *t*-test on this type of survey data is common practice, and similar analyses using non-parametric tests yielded similar results.

Appendix D: Photovoice Participation, Coal-Critical Photographs Shared, and Coal-Critical Photostories Created

Table D.1

Participants' attendance at photovoice meetings and events in Community A.

	Meeting 1† (9/8)	Meeting 2 (first reflection meeting) (9/29)	Meeting 3 (second reflection meeting) (11/10)	Meeting 4 (third reflection meeting) (12/1)	Meeting 5 (fourth reflection meeting) (1/12)	Regional meeting (1/24)	Meeting 6 (fifth reflection meeting) (2/2)	Meeting 7 (sixth reflection meeting) (2/23)	Meeting 8 (seventh reflection meeting) (3/16)	Local exhibit (3/30)	Regional exhibit (4/17)	Regional meeting (5/2)	Total local meetings	Total events
Alice*	X	X	X	—	X	X	X	X	X	X	X	X	7 (88%)	11 (92%)
Agnes*	—	X	—	—	—	X	—	X	X	X	X	X	3 (38%)	7 (58%)
Arlene	X	X	X	—	X	X	—	X	X	X	X	X	6 (75%)	10 (83%)
Adah	X	X	X	X	X	X	—	X	X	X	X	—	7 (88%)	10 (83%)
Amanda	X	X	—	X	X	X	—	X	—	X	X	X	5 (63%)	9 (75%)
Andrea	X	X	X	—	X	X	X	—	—	X	X	X	5 (63%)	9 (75%)
Annette	—	X	X	X	X	X	X	X	X	X	—	—	7 (88%)	9 (75%)
Amber	X	X	X	—	X	X	—	—	X	X	—	—	5 (63%)	7 (58%)
Angie	X	—	—	X	—	X	X	X	—	X	—	—	4 (50%)	6 (50%)
Annemarie	X	X	—	—	X	—	—	—	X	X	—	—	4 (50%)	5 (42%)
Aileen	—	—	—	—	—	—	—	—	X	X	X	—	1 (13%)	3 (25%)
Audrey	—	—	—	X	—	X	—	—	—	—	—	—	1 (13%)	2 (17%)
Adelle	—	X	X	—	—	—	—	—	—	—	—	—	2 (25%)	2 (17%)
Total	8 (62%)	10 (77%)	7 (54%)	5 (38%)	8 (62%)	10 (77%)	4 (31%)	7 (54%)	8 (62%)	11 (85%)	7 (54%)	5 (38%)		

*activist participant

†Photovoice orientation

Table D.2

Photographs shared and coal-critical photographs shared during reflection meetings in Community A, and percentages that were coal critical.

<table>
<tr><th></th><th>Meeting 1† (9/8)</th><th>Meeting 2 (first reflection meeting) (9/29)</th><th>Meeting 3 (second reflection meeting) (11/10)</th><th>Meeting 4 (third reflection meeting) (12/1)</th><th>Meeting 5 (fourth reflection meeting) (1/12)</th><th>Meeting 6 (fifth reflection meeting) (2/2)</th><th>Meeting 7 (sixth reflection meeting) (2/23)</th><th>Meeting 8 (seventh reflection meeting) (3/16)</th><th>Total</th></tr>
<tr><td>Alice*</td><td>No photos shared</td><td>4 | 3 (75%)</td><td>8 | 1 (13%)</td><td>—</td><td>73 | 45 (62%)</td><td>25 | 1 (4%)</td><td>90 | 20 (22%)</td><td>0 | 0 (0%)</td><td>200 | 70 (35%)</td></tr>
<tr><td>Agnes*</td><td></td><td>4 | 3 (75%)</td><td>—</td><td>—</td><td>—</td><td>—</td><td>0 | 0 (0%)</td><td>0 | 0 (0%)</td><td>4 | 3 (75%)</td></tr>
<tr><td>Arlene</td><td></td><td>1 | 1 (100%)</td><td>49 | 16 (33%)</td><td>—</td><td>42 | 26 (62%)</td><td>—</td><td>0 | 0 (0%)</td><td>31 | 2 (6%)</td><td>123 | 45 (37%)</td></tr>
<tr><td>Adah</td><td></td><td>5 | 0 (0%)</td><td>81 | 0 (0%)</td><td>10 | 0 (0%)</td><td>46 | 0 (0%)</td><td>—</td><td>0 | 0 (0%)</td><td>0 | 0 (0%)</td><td>142 | 0 (0%)</td></tr>
<tr><td>Amanda</td><td></td><td>14 | 1 (7%)</td><td>—</td><td>28 | 0 (0%)</td><td>0 | 0 (0%)</td><td>—</td><td>33 | 6 (18%)</td><td>—</td><td>75 | 7 (9%)</td></tr>
<tr><td>Andrea</td><td></td><td>0 | 0 (0%)</td><td>6 | 0 (0%)</td><td>—</td><td>11 | 1 (9%)</td><td>1 | 0 (0%)</td><td>—</td><td>—</td><td>18 | 1 (6%)</td></tr>
<tr><td>Annette</td><td></td><td>5 | 0 (0%)</td><td>14 | 0 (0%)</td><td>13 | 0 (0%)</td><td>16 | 0 (0%)</td><td>16 | 0 (0%)</td><td>3 | 0 (0%)</td><td>0 | 0 (0%)</td><td>67 | 0 (0%)</td></tr>
<tr><td>Amber</td><td></td><td>4 | 0 (0%)</td><td>24 | 0 (0%)</td><td>—</td><td>10 | 1 (10%)</td><td>—</td><td>0 | 0 (0%)</td><td>13 | 13 (100%)</td><td>51 | 14 (27%)</td></tr>
<tr><td>Angie</td><td></td><td>—</td><td>—</td><td>25 | 0 (0%)</td><td>—</td><td>11 | 0 (0%)</td><td>0 | 0 (0%)</td><td>—</td><td>36 | 0 (0%)</td></tr>
<tr><td>Annemarie</td><td></td><td>0 | 0 (0%)</td><td>—</td><td>—</td><td>39 | 0 (0%)</td><td>—</td><td>—</td><td>—</td><td>39 | 0 (0%)</td></tr>
<tr><td>Aileen</td><td></td><td>—</td><td>—</td><td>—</td><td>—</td><td>—</td><td>—</td><td>0 | 0 (0%)</td><td>0 | 0 (0%)</td></tr>
<tr><td>Audrey</td><td></td><td>—</td><td>—</td><td>62 | 5 (8%)</td><td>—</td><td>—</td><td>—</td><td>—</td><td>62 | 5 (8%)</td></tr>
<tr><td>Adelle</td><td></td><td>5 | 2 (40%)</td><td>39 | 10 (26%)</td><td>—</td><td>—</td><td>—</td><td>—</td><td>—</td><td>44 | 12 (27%)</td></tr>
<tr><td>Total</td><td></td><td>42 | 10 (24%)</td><td>221 | 27 (12%)</td><td>138 | 5 (4%)</td><td>237 | 73 (31%)</td><td>53 | 1 (2%)</td><td>126 | 26 (21%)</td><td>44 | 15 (34%)</td><td>861 | 157 (18%)</td></tr>
</table>

*activist participant

†Photovoice orientation

Table D.3

Photostories created and selected for public exhibits in Community A.

	Photostories created			Photostories selected for local exhibit			Photostories selected for regional exhibit		
	Total	Explicitly critical of coal	Vaguely critical of coal	Total	Explicitly critical of coal	Vaguely critical of coal	Total	Explicitly critical of coal	Vaguely critical of coal
Alice*	38 (1 joint)	14	4	11 (1 joint)	6	2	4 (1 joint)	1	1
Agnes*	10	4	0	10	4	0	3	2	0
Arlene	14 (2 joint)	2 (1 joint)	1	12 (2 joint)	2 (1 joint)	1	4 (1 joint)	2 (1 joint)	0
Adah	10 (2 joint)	1 (joint)	1	10 (2 joint)	1 (joint)	1	4 (1 joint)	1 (joint)	0
Amanda	13	1	2	10	1	2	3	0	1
Andrea	11 (1 joint)	1	0	11 (1 joint)	1	0	4 (1 joint)	1	0
Annette	20 (1 joint)	2	0	11 (1 joint)	0	0	4 (1 joint)	0	0
Amber	11	3	0	10	3	0	3	2	0
Angie	5	0	0	5	0	0	3	0	0
Annemarie	10	0	0	10	0	0	3	0	0
Aileen	2 (2 joint)	0	0	2 (2 joint)	0	0	2 (all joint)	0	0
Audrey	2 (2 joint)	1 (joint)	0	2 (2 joint)	1 (joint)	0	2 (all joint)	1 (joint)	0
Adelle	3 (3 joint)	1 (joint)	0	3 (3 joint)	1 (joint)	0	3 (all joint)	1 (joint)	0
Total	141	28 (20%)	8 (6%)	99	18 (18%)	5 (5%)	35	9 (26%)	2 (6%)

*activist participant

Note: Jointly created photostories are counted only once in totals. Two of of the photostories that were not explicitly or vaguely critical of the coal industry were created jointly by three participants. (All of the other jointly created photostories were created by two participants.)

Table D.4

Participants' attendance at photovoice meetings and events in Community B.

	Meeting 1[†] (9/11)	Meeting 2 (first reflection meeting) (10/2)	Meeting 3 (second reflection meeting) (11/13)	Meeting 4 (third reflection meeting) (12/4)	Meeting 5 (fourth reflection meeting) (1/15)	Regional meeting (1/24)	Meeting 6 (fifth reflection meeting) (2/5)	Meeting 7 (sixth reflection meeting) (2/26)	Meeting 8 (seventh reflection meeting) (3/19)	Meeting 9 (eighth reflection meeting) (4/16)	Local exhibit (4/30)	Regional exhibit (4/17)	Regional meeting (5/2)	Total local meetings	Total events
Betty*	X	X	—	—	X	X	X	—	X	X	X	X	X	6 (67%)	10 (77%)
Belinda*	X	X	—	X	X	X	—	—	—	X	X	X	X	5 (56%)	9 (69%)
Bonnie	X	X	X	—	X	X	—	X	X	X	X	X	X	7 (78%)	11 (85%)
Barbara	X	X	—	X	X	X	X	X	X	X	X	X	X	8 (89%)	12 (92%)
Brandy	X	X	X	—	X	X	X	X	X	X	X	X	—	8 (89%)	11 (85%)
Total	5 (100%)	5 (100%)	2 (40%)	2 (40%)	5 (100%)	5 (100%)	3 (60%)	3 (60%)	4 (80%)	5 (100%)	5 (100%)	5 (100%)	4 (80%)		

*activist participant

† Photovoice orientation

Table D.5

Photographs shared and coal-critical photographs shared during reflection meetings in Community B, and percentages that were coal-critical.

<table>
<tr><th></th><th>Meeting 1†</th><th>Meeting 2 (first reflection meeting) (10/2)</th><th>Meeting 3 (second reflection meeting) (11/13)</th><th>Meeting 4 (third reflection meeting) (12/4)</th><th>Meeting 5 (fourth reflection meeting) (1/15)</th><th>Meeting 6 (fifth reflection meeting) (2/5)</th><th>Meeting 7 (sixth reflection meeting) (2/26)</th><th>Meeting 8 (seventh reflection meeting) (3/19)</th><th>Meeting 9 (eighth reflection meeting) (4/16)</th><th>Total</th></tr>
<tr><td>Betty*</td><td>No photos shared</td><td>9 | 2 (22%)</td><td>—</td><td>—</td><td>46 | 23 (50%)</td><td>No photos shared</td><td>—</td><td>0 | 0 (0%)</td><td>No photos shared</td><td>55 | 25 (45%)</td></tr>
<tr><td>Belinda*</td><td></td><td>19 | 11 (58%)</td><td>—</td><td>19 | 15 (79%)</td><td>10 | 6 (60%)</td><td></td><td>—</td><td>—</td><td></td><td>48 | 32 (67%)</td></tr>
<tr><td>Bonnie</td><td></td><td>46 | 16 (35%)</td><td>53 | 20 (38%)</td><td>—</td><td>10 | 6 (60%)</td><td></td><td>77 | 30 (39%)</td><td>44 | 27 (61%)</td><td></td><td>230 | 99 (43%)</td></tr>
<tr><td>Barbara</td><td></td><td>68 |0 (0%)</td><td>—</td><td>54 | 0 (0%)</td><td>65 | 0 (0%)</td><td></td><td>55 | 7 (13%)</td><td>0 | 0 (0%)</td><td></td><td>242 | 7 (3%)</td></tr>
<tr><td>Brandy</td><td></td><td>0 | 0 (0%)</td><td>78 | 4 (5%)</td><td>—</td><td>11 | 10 (91%)</td><td></td><td>7 | 0 (0%)</td><td>0 | 0 (0%)</td><td></td><td>96 | 14 (15%)</td></tr>
<tr><td>Total</td><td></td><td>142 | 29 (20%)</td><td>131 | 24 (18%)</td><td>73 | 15 (21%)</td><td>142 | 45 (32%)</td><td></td><td>139 | 37 (27%)</td><td>44 | 27 (61%)</td><td></td><td>671 | 177 (26%)</td></tr>
</table>

*activist participant

† Photovoice orientation

Table D.6
Photostories created and selected for public exhibits in Community B.

	Photostories created			Photostories selected for local exhibit			Photostories selected for regional exhibit		
	Total	Explicitly critical of coal	Vaguely critical of coal	Total	Explicitly critical of coal	Vaguely critical of coal	Total	Explicitly critical of coal	Vaguely critical of coal
Betty*	27 (1 joint)	17 (1 joint)	0	10 (1 joint)	8 (1 joint)	0	4 (1 joint)	3 (1 joint)	0
Belinda*	12	7	0	10	5	0	3	1	0
Bonnie	27 (1 joint)	12 (1 joint)	0	11 (1 joint)	8 (1 joint)	0	4 (1 joint)	3 (1 joint)	0
Barbara	33	2	0	10	1	0	3	1	0
Brandy	30	3	2	10	2	1	3	1	0
Total	128	40 (31%)	2 (2%)	50	23 (46%)	1 (2%)	16	8 (50%)	0 (0%)

*activist participant

Note: Jointly created photostories are counted only once in totals.

Table D.7

Participants' attendance at photovoice meetings and events in Community C.

	Meeting 1[†] (9/8)	Meeting 2 (first reflection meeting) (9/29)	Meeting 3 (second reflection meeting) (11/10)	Meeting 4 (third reflection meeting) (12/1)	Meeting 5 (fourth reflection meeting) (1/12)	Reg. meeting (1/24)	Meeting 6 (fifth reflection meeting) (2/2)	Meeting 7 (sixth reflection meeting) (2/23)	Meeting 8 (seventh reflection meeting) (3/16)	Reg. exhibit (4/17)	Meeting 9 (eighth reflection meeting) (4/20)	Local exhibit (4/23)	Regional meeting (5/2)	Total local meetings	Total events
Carolyn*	X	X	X	—	—	X	X	X	X	X	X	—	X	7 (78%)	10 (77%)
Cora	X	X	—	X	X	X	X	X	X	—	X	X	—	8 (89%)	10 (77%)
Cecilia	X	—	X	X	X	—	X	X	X	—	—	X	—	7 (78%)	8 (62%)
Constance	X	X	—	—	X	—	X	X	X	—	X	X	—	7 (78%)	8 (62%)
Carla	X	X	—	X	—	X	—	—	X	—	X	X	X	5 (56%)	8 (62%)
Carrie	—	—	—	X	X	—	—	X	X	—	—	X	—	4 (44%)	5 (38%)
Cindy	X	X	X	—	X	X	—	X	X	—	X	X	X	7 (78%)	10 (77%)
Colleen	—	X	X	X	X	X	X	X	X	X	X	X	—	8 (89%)	11 (85%)
Charity	—	X	—	—	X	—	—	X	—	—	—	—	—	3 (33%)	3 (23%)
Cathleen	X	X	X	Dropped out of project											
Claudia	X	Dropped out of project													
Christa	—	X	Dropped out of project												
Total	8 (67%)	9 (82%)	5 (50%)	5 (56%)	7 (78%)	5 (56%)	5 (56%)	8 (89%)	8 (89%)	2 (22%)	6 (67%)	7 (78%)	3 (33%)		

*activist

† Photovoice orientation

Note: Claudia, Christa, and Cathleen all dropped out of the group during the first half of the project. I have only included them in the attendance rate calculations for the meetings that took place before they dropped out.

Table D.8

Photographs shared and coal-critical photographs shared during reflection meetings in Community C, and percentages that were coal critical.

<table>
<tr><th></th><th>Meeting 1†</th><th>Meeting 2 (first reflection meeting) (9/29)</th><th>Meeting 3 (second reflection meeting) (11/10)</th><th>Meeting 4 (third reflection meeting) (12/1)</th><th>Meeting 5 (fourth reflection meeting) (1/12)</th><th>Meeting 6 (fifth reflection meeting) (2/2)</th><th>Meeting 7 (sixth reflection meeting) (2/23)</th><th>Meeting 8 (seventh reflection meeting) (3/16)</th><th>Meeting 9 (eighth reflection meeting) (4/20)</th><th>Total</th></tr>
<tr><td>Carolyn*</td><td rowspan="10">No photos shared</td><td>11 | 0 (0%)</td><td>10 | 0 (0%)</td><td>—</td><td>—</td><td>0 | 0 (0%)</td><td>9 | 0 (0%)</td><td>0 | 0 (0%)</td><td rowspan="10">No photos shared</td><td>30 | 0 (0%)</td></tr>
<tr><td>Cora</td><td>9 | 0 (0%)</td><td>—</td><td>16 | 1 (6%)</td><td>20 | 0 (0%)</td><td>19 | 0 (0%)</td><td>17 | 0 (0%)</td><td>10 | 0 (0%)</td><td>91 | 1 (1%)</td></tr>
<tr><td>Cecilia</td><td>—</td><td>33 | 1 (3%)</td><td>9 | 3 (33%)</td><td>32 | 0 (0%)</td><td>3 | 0 (0%)</td><td>0 | 0 (0%)</td><td>0 | 0 (0%)</td><td>77 | 4 (5%)</td></tr>
<tr><td>Constance</td><td>10 | 0 (0%)</td><td>—</td><td>—</td><td>13 | 0 (0%)</td><td>0 | 0 (0%)</td><td>0 | 0 (0%)</td><td>9 | 1 (11%)</td><td>32 | 1 (3%)</td></tr>
<tr><td>Carla</td><td>9 | 0 (0%)</td><td>—</td><td>—</td><td>—</td><td>—</td><td>—</td><td>0 | 0 (0%)</td><td>9 | 0 (0%)</td></tr>
<tr><td>Carrie</td><td>—</td><td>—</td><td>11 | 0 (0%)</td><td>15 | 0 (0%)</td><td>—</td><td>0 | 0 (0%)</td><td>7 | 0 (0%)</td><td>33 | 0 (0%)</td></tr>
<tr><td>Cindy</td><td>13 | 0 (0%)</td><td>36 | 0 (0%)</td><td>—</td><td>0 | 0 (0%)</td><td>—</td><td>24 | 0 (0%)</td><td>11 | 0 (0%)</td><td>84 | 0 (0%)</td></tr>
<tr><td>Colleen</td><td>27 | 0 (0%)</td><td>50 | 0 (0%)</td><td>4 | 0 (0%)</td><td>4 | 0 (0%)</td><td>0 | 0 (0%)</td><td>41 | 0 (0%)</td><td>0 | 0 (0%)</td><td>126 | 0 (0%)</td></tr>
<tr><td>Charity</td><td>0 | 0 (0%)</td><td>—</td><td>—</td><td>9 | 1 (11%)</td><td>—</td><td>0 | 0 (0%)</td><td>—</td><td>9 | 1 (11%)</td></tr>
<tr><td>Cathleen</td><td>21 | 0 (0%)</td><td>32 | 0 (0%)</td><td>—</td><td>—</td><td>—</td><td>—</td><td>—</td><td>53 | 0 (0%)</td></tr>
<tr><td>Total</td><td></td><td>100 | 0 (0%)</td><td>161 | 1 (0.6%)</td><td>40 | 4 (10%)</td><td>93 | 1 (1%)</td><td>22 | 0 (0%)</td><td>91 | 0 (0%)</td><td>37 | 1 (3%)</td><td></td><td>544 | 7 (1%)</td></tr>
</table>

*activist participant

† Photovoice orientation

Note: Claudia and Christa, who both dropped out of the project, are not included in this table because they did not share any photographs at any of the meetings.

Table D.9
Photostories created and selected for public exhibits in Community C.

	Photostories created			Photostories selected for local exhibit			Photostories selected for regional exhibit		
	Total	Explicitly critical of coal	Vaguely critical of coal	Total	Explicitly critical of coal	Vaguely critical of coal	Total	Explicitly Critical of coal	Vaguely critical of coal
Carolyn*	9	4	2	9	4	2	3	2	1
Cora	31	0	1	10	0	1	3	0	0
Cecilia	20 (1 joint)	3	1	11 (1 joint)	2	1	3	2	1
Constance	10	0	1	10	0	1	3	0	0
Carla	7	0	0	5	0	0	3	0	0
Carrie	13 (1 joint)	0	0	10 (1 joint)	0	0	3	0	0
Cindy	13	0	0	10	0	0	3	0	0
Colleen	9	0	0	9	0	0	3	0	0
Charity	12	0	1	10	0	1	3	0	0
Total	123	7 (6%)	6 (5%)	83	6 (7%)	6 (7%)	27	4 (15%)	2 (7%)

*activist participant
† Photovoice orientation

Table D.10

Attendance at photovoice meetings and events in Community D.

	Meeting 1† (9/9)	Meeting 2 (first reflection meeting) (9/30)	Meeting 3 (second reflection meeting) (11/11)	Meeting 4 (third reflection meeting) (12/2)	Meeting 5 (fourth reflection meeting) (1/13)	Regional meeting (1/24)	Meeting 6 (fifth reflection meeting) (2/10)	Meeting 7 (sixth reflection meeting) (2/24)	Meeting 8 (seventh reflection meeting) (3/17)	Meeting 9 (eighth reflection meeting) (4/7)	Regional exhibit (4/17)	Local exhibit (4/21)	Regional meeting (5/2)	Total local meetings	Total events
Diane*	—	X	X	X	X	X	—	—	X	X	X	X	—	6 (67%)	9 (69%)
Dorothy	X	X	—	X	X	X	X	X	X	X	X	X	X	8 (89%)	12 (92%)
Deidre	X	X	X	X	X	X	X	—	X	X	X	X	X	8 (89%)	12 (92%)
Dixie	X	X	X	X	X	X	—	X	X	X	X	X	X	8 (89%)	12 (92%)
Darlene	X	—	X	—	X	X	—	X	X	X	X	X	X	6 (67%)	10 (77%)
Dawn .	X	X	X	X	X	X	—	X	X	—	—	X	X	7 (78%)	10 (77%)
Deanna	X	X	X	X	X	X	—	X	X	X	—	X	X	8 (89%)	11 (85%)
Denise	—	X	X	Dropped out of project										2 (22%)	2 (15%)
Doreen	X	—	X	Dropped out of project										2 (22%)	2 (15%)
Delores	X	Dropped out of project													
Darcie	X	Dropped out of project													
Delphine	X	Dropped out of project													
Danielle	—	X	Dropped out of project												
Total	10 (77%)	8 (80%)	8 (89%)	6 (86%)	7 (100%)	7 (100%)	2 (29%)	5 (71%)	7 (100%)	6 (86%)	5 (71%)	7 (100%)	6 (86%)		

*activist participant

† Photovoice orientation

Note: Delores, Darcie, Delphine, Danielle, Denise, and Doreen all dropped out during the first half of this project. I have only included them in the attendance rate calculations for the meetings that took place before they dropped out.

Table D.11

Photographs shared and coal-critical photographs shared during reflection meetings in Community D, and percentages that were coal critical.

<table>
<tr><th></th><th>Meeting 1†</th><th>Meeting 2 (first reflection meeting) (9/30)</th><th>Meeting 3 (second reflection meeting) (11/11)</th><th>Meeting 4 (third reflection meeting) (12/2)</th><th>Meeting 5 (fourth reflection meeting) (1/13)</th><th>Meeting 6 (fifth reflection meeting) (2/10)</th><th>Meeting 7 (sixth reflection meeting) (2/24)</th><th>Meeting 8 (seventh reflection meeting) (3/17)</th><th>Meeting 9 (eighth reflection meeting) (4/7)</th><th>Total</th></tr>
<tr><td>Diane*</td><td>No photos shared</td><td>0 | 0 (0%)</td><td>15 | 1 (7%)</td><td>5 | 0 (0%)</td><td>0 | 0 (0%)</td><td>—</td><td>—</td><td>0 | 0</td><td>No photos shared</td><td>20 | 1 (5%)</td></tr>
<tr><td>Dorothy</td><td></td><td>43 | 0 (0%)</td><td>—</td><td>55 | 0 (0%)</td><td>47 | 0 (0%)</td><td>10 | 0 (0%)</td><td>0 | 0 (0%)</td><td>6 | 0 (0%)</td><td></td><td>161 | 0 (0%)</td></tr>
<tr><td>Deidre</td><td></td><td>45 | 0 (0%)</td><td>52 | 0 (0%)</td><td>11 | 0 (0%)</td><td>0 | 0 (0%)</td><td>65 | 2 (3%)</td><td>—</td><td>44 | 0 (0%)</td><td></td><td>217 | 2 (1%)</td></tr>
<tr><td>Dixie</td><td></td><td>7 | 0 (0%)</td><td>25 | 0 (0%)</td><td>7 | 0 (0%)</td><td>14 | 0 (0%)</td><td>—</td><td>0</td><td>17 | 0 (0%)</td><td></td><td>70 | 0 (0%)</td></tr>
<tr><td>Darlene</td><td></td><td>—</td><td>69 | 0 (0%)</td><td>—</td><td>35 | 0 (0%)</td><td>—</td><td>36 | 0 (0%)</td><td>18 | 0 (0%)</td><td></td><td>158 | 0 (0%)</td></tr>
<tr><td>Dawn .</td><td></td><td>8 | 0 (0%)</td><td>18 | 0 (0%)</td><td>26 | 0 (0%)</td><td>99 | 0 (0%)</td><td>—</td><td>1 | 0 (0%)</td><td>17 | 0 (0%)</td><td></td><td>169 | 0 (0%)</td></tr>
<tr><td>Deanna</td><td></td><td>18 | 0 (0%)</td><td>65 | 0 (0%)</td><td>19 | 0 (0%)</td><td>130 | 0 (0%)</td><td>—</td><td>41 | 0 (0%)</td><td>79 | 0 (0%)</td><td></td><td>352 | 0 (0%)</td></tr>
<tr><td>Denise</td><td></td><td>22 | 0 (0%)</td><td>—</td><td>—</td><td>—</td><td>—</td><td>—</td><td>—</td><td></td><td>22 | 0 (0%)</td></tr>
<tr><td>Doreen</td><td></td><td>—</td><td>10 | 0 (0%)</td><td>—</td><td>—</td><td>—</td><td>—</td><td>—</td><td></td><td>10 | 0 (0%)</td></tr>
<tr><td>Total</td><td></td><td>143 | 0 (0%)</td><td>254 | 1 (0.4%)</td><td>123 | 0 (0%)</td><td>325 | 0 (0%)</td><td>75 | 2 (3%)</td><td>78 | 0 (0%)</td><td>181 | 0 (0%)</td><td></td><td>1179 | 3 (0.3%)</td></tr>
</table>

*activist participant

† Photovoice orientation

Note: Delores, Darcie, Delphine, and Danielle, who all dropped out of the project, are not included in this table because they did not share photographs at any of the meetings.

Table D.12

Photostories created and selected for public exhibits in Community D.

	Photostories created			Photostories selected for local exhibit			Photostories selected for regional exhibit		
	Total	Explicitly critical of coal	Vaguely critical of coal	Total	Explicitly critical of coal	Vaguely critical of coal	Total	Explicitly critical of coal	Vaguely critical of coal
Diane*	7	1	1	7	1	1	3	1	0
Dorothy	12	0	2	10	0	2	3	0	2
Deidre	16	0	0	10	0	0	3	0	0
Dixie	15	0	0	10	0	0	3	0	0
Darlene	7	0	0	7	0	0	3	0	0
Dawn .	8	0	0	8	0	0	3	0	0
Deanna	16	0	0	10	0	0	3	0	0
Total	81	1 (1%)	3 (4%)	62	1 (2%)	3 (5%)	21	1 (5%)	2 (10%)

*activist participant

Table D.13

Participants' attendance at photovoice meetings and events in Community E.

	Meeting 1† (9/10)	Meeting 2 (first reflection meeting) (10/1)	Meeting 3 (second reflection meeting) (11/12)	Meeting 4 (third reflection meeting) (12/6)	Meeting 5 (fourth reflection meeting) (1/14)	Regional Meeting (1/24)	Meeting 6 (fifth reflection meeting) (2/4)	Meeting 7 (sixth reflection meeting) (2/26))	Meeting 8 (seventh reflection meeting) (3/18)	Local exhibit (4/23)	Regional exhibit (4/17)	Regional meeting (5/2)	Total reflection meetings	Total events
Eve*	X	X	Dropped out of project							(X)			2 (25%)	3 (25%)
Emily	X	X	X	X	X	X	X	—	X	X	X	X	7 (88%)	11 (92%)
Elaine	X	X	X	X	X	—	X	X	X	X	X	—	8 (100%)	10 (83%)
Edna	X	X	—	X	X	X	X	X	X	X	X	—	7 (88%)	10 (83%)
Elise	X	X	—	X	—	X	—	X (late)	X	X	—	—	5 (63%)	7 (58%)
Ethel	X	X	X	—	—	—	—	X	X	—	—	—	5 (63%)	5 (41%)
Eloise	—	X	—	—	—	—	X	Dropped out of project					2 (25%)	2 (17%)
Ericka	—	X	—	—	X	Dropped out of project							2 (25%)	2 (17%)
Erin	—	X	—	X	Dropped out of project								2 (25%)	2 (17%)
Elyssa	—	X	Dropped out of project										1 (13%)	1 (8%)
Esther	—	X	Dropped out of project										1 (13%)	1 (8%)
Total	6 (55%)	11 (100%)	3 (38%)	5 (63%)	4 (57%)	3 (50%)	4 (67%)	4 (80%)	5 (100%)	4 (80%)	3 (60%)	1 (20%)		

*activist participant

† Photovoice orientation

Note: This is the only group in which the activist participant dropped out of the project. Eve did not participate in any of the local meetings after the first reflection session, nor did she create any photostories for the exhibit. She did attend the local Photovoice exhibit and presentation, but not as a member of the group (although she did end up agreeing to read another participants' slides for the presentation when she had to cancel at the last minute). Additionally, the six participants who dropped out of the project are only included in the attendance rate calculations for the meetings that took place before they dropped out.

Table D.14

Photographs shared and coal-critical photographs shared during reflection meetings in Community E, and percentage that were coal critical.

	Meeting 1†	Meeting 2 (first reflection meeting) (10/1)	Meeting 3 (second reflection meeting) (11/12)	Meeting 4 (third reflection meeting) (12/6)	Meeting 5 (fourth reflection meeting) (1/14)	Meeting 6 (fifth reflection meeting) (2/4)	Meeting 7 (sixth reflection meeting) (2/26)	Meeting 8 (seventh reflection meeting) (3/18)	Total
Eve*	No photos shared	39 | 22 (56%)	—	—	—	—	—	—	39 | 22 (56%)
Emily		55 | 1 (2%)	21 | 9 (43%)	34 | 0 (0%)	54 | 3 (6%)	34 | 0 (0%)	0 | 0 (0%)	3 | 0 (0%)	201 | 13 (6%)
Elaine		6 | 0 (0%)	62 | 0 (0%)	0 | 0 (0%)	34 | 0 (0%)	0	7 | 0 (0%)	0 | 0 (0%)	109 | 0 (0%)
Edna		34 | 0 (0%)	—	36 | 0 (0%)	17 | 0 (0%)	0	0 | 0 (0%)	0 | 0 (0%)	87 | 0 (0%)
Elise		19 | 0 (0%)	—	15 | 4 (27%)	—	—	13 | 0 (0%)	0 | 0 (0%)	47 | 4 (9%)
Ethel		0 | 0 (0%)	15 | 0 (0%)	—	—	—	0 | 0 (0%)	0 | 0 (0%)	15 | 0 (0%)
Eloise		8 | 0 (0%)	—	—	—	0	—	—	8 | 0 (0%)
Ericka		10 | 0 (0%)	—	—	7 | 0 (0%)	—	—	—	17 | 0 (0%)
Erin		10 | 0 (0%)	—	66 | 0 0%	—		—	—	76 | 0 (0%)
Total		181 | 23 (13%)	98 | 9 (9%)	151 | 4 (3%)	112 | 3 (3%)	34 | 0 (0%)	20 | 0 (0%)	3 | 0 (0%)	599 | 39 (7%)

*activist participant

† Photovoice orientation

Note: Elyssa and Esther, who both dropped out of the project, are not included in this table because they did not share photographs during any of the meetings.

Table D.15

Photostories created and selected for public exhibits in Community E.

	Photostories created			Photostories selected for local exhibit			Photostories selected for regional exhibit		
	Total	Explicitly critical of coal	Vaguely critical of coal	Total	Explicitly critical of coal	Vaguely critical of coal	Total	Explicitly critical of coal	Vaguely critical of coal
Emily	16 (1 joint)	2	2	11 (1 joint)	0	3	4 (1 joint)	0	1
Elaine	20	0	0	10	0	0	3	0	0
Edna	17 (1 joint)	0	0	11(1 joint)	0	0	4 (1 joint)	0	0
Elise	22	0	1	10	0	1	3	0	1
Ethel	7	0	0	5	0	0	3	0	0
Erin	11	0	0	8	0	0	3	0	0
Total	92	2 (2%)	3 (3%)	54	0 (0%)	4 (7%)	19	0 (0%)	2 (10%)

*activist participant

Note: Eve, Eloise, Ericka, Elyssa and Esther, who all dropped out of the project, are not included in this table because they did not submit any photostories to me during the project. Jointly created photostories are counted only once in totals.

Notes

Introduction

1. For notable exceptions, see Gaventa 1980, Cable, Shriver, and Hastings 1999, Shriver 2000, McAdam and Boudet 2012, and Shriver, Adams, and Messer 2014. On the related and also understudied concept of demobilization, see Lapegna 2013, Lapegna 2015, and Lapegna forthcoming.

2. I use the term *non-action,* rather than *inaction,* to signal the intentionality of the quiescence. In other words, it is an active choice not to act.

3. Although this method of coal extraction is also called "mountaintop mining" in industry-produced publications and in much of the scientific literature, I have chosen to use the term used by the environmental justice movement: *mountaintop-removal mining.* As a number of activists have told me, "mountaintop mining" does not adequately capture the magnitude of the land disturbance that this method entails. Many in the environmental justice community say that an even more accurate term would be *mountain range removal mining.*

4. Among residents of Central Appalachia, there is a very clear distinction between "local" residents (people who are "from" there) and "non-local" residents (often called "outsiders"). Although non-local residents may be deeply committed to the coalfield region and the community in which they live, they are distinct from local residents in that they spent their formative years elsewhere and/or have not spent the majority of their lives living in the area. I myself am a "non-local."

5. Photovoice is a form of participatory-action research in which participants take photographs that represent important aspects of their lives and communities over the course of multiple months or years. Participants meet for regular group reflection sessions to discuss their photos and to write short narratives about them. The Photovoice method is discussed in detail in chapter 8.

6. Micromobilization contexts can be defined as small-group settings and interactions that facilitate the social-psychological processes necessary for recruitment into a social movement.

7. Structural availability is, of course, also a major constraint on individual participation in *any* social movement. However, I controlled for this barrier by studying individuals who had the time and the availability to participate in Photovoice. The project required that participants commit to taking photographs, writing about them, and attending regularly scheduled local and regional meetings over the course of eight months. Thus, those who weren't "structurally available" self-selected out of the study.

Chapter 1

1. This chapter contains some excerpts from Bell and York 2010 and Bell 2009.

2. There are three regions of Appalachia: Northern, Central, and Southern. Central Appalachia is made up of 60 counties in southern West Virginia, eastern Kentucky, southwest Virginia, and northeastern Tennessee. The entire state of West Virginia is considered to be in Appalachia, but it is split between Central and Northern Appalachia (Gaventa 1980, p. 33).

3. It is important to note, however, that some members of the local elite participate in and benefit from the region's exploitation, so not all the "exploiters" are from outside the region.

4. However, West Virginia's population declined by only about 10 percent over this period, owing to natural increase.

5. My data-collection-methods for these interviews are described in detail in chapters 3–5.

6. Slurry impoundments are not limited to the coal-preparation process. When coal is burned at coal-fired power plants, coal fly-ash slurry is also generated and is stored in impoundments. In December of 2008, 1.1 billion gallons of coal fly-ash slurry broke through an impoundment at the Tennessee Valley Authority's Kingston Fossil Plant in Harriman, Tennessee, contaminating a branch of the Emory River and approximately 300 acres of the surrounding land (U.S. Environmental Protection Agency 2009). In 2014 a similar coal ash spill happened on the Dan River in North Carolina.

Chapter 2

1. There are many different definitions of social capital. (See, for instance, Bourdieu 1985; Coleman 1988; Portes 1998.) Most theorizations of this concept fall within two major categories: those that define social capital from a social-structural perspective (focusing on the resources that emanate from network connections) and those that articulate a more normative understanding of the concept (Foley and Edwards 1999). Representing the second perspective is the work of Robert Putnam, who defines social capital as "the features of social organization, such as networks,

norms, and social trust that facilitate coordination and cooperation for mutual benefit (1995, p. 67). Although social networks are important in this understanding of social capital, they do not constitute the totality of this feature of social life. Rather, it is the three components taken together—networks, trust, and social norms (such as civic engagement)—that comprise the major dimensions of social capital (Coleman 1988; Putnam 1995; Silverman 2004). In both the social-structural and the normative conceptualizations, social capital can be an important resource for citizens, providing access to jobs, child care, safety, and assistance in times of need, among other benefits. However, Putnam's definition (quoted above) captures an important aspect of social capital that most in the social-structural perspective do not acknowledge: its role in facilitating collective action. Other scholars also have recognized the collective-action function of social capital (Alder and Kwon 2002; Fukuyama 1995; Paxton 1999), and many have pointed to social capital as a factor influencing citizens' ability to cooperatively address problems in their communities (Brehm and Rahn 1997).

2. Although McAdam's (1982) theorization of cognitive liberation re-introduced the significance of social psychology into the literature on social movements, his conceptualization of this consciousness change has been critiqued for seeming to omit the role of emotions in this process. As Emirbayer and Goldberg point out (2005, p. 479), by attributing this process to a "set of cognitive cues" (McAdam 1982, p. 49) this transformation is rendered coldly rational when in fact, "by its very nature," it entails "a complex synthesis of strategic reasoning and passionate assessment." In a conversation I had with Doug McAdam in May of 2010, he fully agreed that emotions are integral to the consciousness transformation that cognitive liberation theorizes, acknowledging that the term he chose to describe this process does not sufficiently capture the complexities of the process. He maintains that consciousness change takes place when the "two perceptions of injustice and efficacy are linked to the emotions of anger and hope, and sometimes fear" in this process. While I seek to build on McAdam's important theory of cognitive liberation, I maintain (as he does) that it is not strictly a "cognitive" process and that emotion is tightly woven into any transformation in consciousness among would-be insurgents. In fact, not only is emotion important to the process of cognitive liberation; it is also central to solidarity and collective identity, for, as Jasper has argued (1998, p. 404), emotions are "an integral part of all social action," entering into protest activities "at every stage." Despite the shortcomings of the term "cognitive liberation," I have chosen to use it throughout the book to signal my intention to contribute to our understanding of this concept.

Chapter 3

1. This chapter incorporates and expands upon excerpts and empirical findings reported in Bell 2009.

2. Although, this is changing in certain counties in the state, for in the years after this study was conducted, hydraulic fracturing for natural gas has become a dominant industry in north central West Virginia counties.

3. This study was conducted in 2006; thus, I used data from the 2000 census to select my communities.

4. My interviews suggest that the trust in Farmstead crossed racial lines, at least with regard to the African American population that had lived there for generations. The two African Americans I interviewed expressed high levels of trust and satisfaction within the community and indicated a belief that their African American friends and family members felt the same way. However, it is also important to note that at the time of my study, Farmstead had recently experienced an influx of immigrants from Mexico and Central and South America, who had moved to the area to work in the two poultry factories. Pepe, the one Mexican immigrant who was part of my sample, indicated that he trusted people in Farmstead and also exchanged favors with his neighbors. However, as I note below, he wasn't well integrated into formal networks within the community or into informal networks outside of his family and immediate neighbors. Thus, it is unclear whether the recent immigrant population in Farmstead experienced the same levels of community social capital as the rest of the population.

5. Admittedly, the use of an index has an inherent limitation in that all components are assigned equal weights, whether or not they truly are theoretically equivalent. However, because the concept of social capital is made up of, and contributes to, so many different aspects of community life, generating an index is an efficient way to categorize levels of social capital and to order the interviews for further analysis. Thus, the index should be viewed as a heuristic tool that allowed me to compare the interviews using a common categorical language; the interviewees' stories and words substantiate and describe the experiences of people that fell within the categories that I generated from the index. It is also important to note that, although for stylistic reasons I do not always use the word *bonding* to modify the term *social capital* in my analysis, the type of social capital that this index measures is, in fact, bonding social capital within each town, as the indicators I use were selected to represent the network linkages, trust, connectedness, and shared social norms among residents within each community.

Chapter 4

1. This chapter incorporates and expands upon excerpts and empirical findings reported in Bell and Braun 2010.

2. Yvonne A. Braun is an associate professor of Women's and Gender Studies and International Studies at the University of Oregon. Her research focuses on gender,

development, environment, globalization, and inequality, with current projects in Lesotho and Costa Rica. Her scholarship has recently appeared in *Social Problems*, in *Gender & Society*, in the *International Feminist Journal of Politics*, and in the *Cambridge Journal of Regions, Economy, and Society*. Dr. Braun was the chair of my PhD dissertation committee and was a co-author of the 2010 study that is woven into this chapter. I conceptualized the study, recruited the research participants, conducted the interviews, and analyzed the data; Dr. Braun contributed to the analysis of the findings, helped connect these findings to the literature, and helped write the 2010 article.

3. Because portions of this chapter draw on co-authored material, I use "we" instead of "I" in certain sections.

4. Readers will notice the use of "women" and "men" (terms describing gender identity) rather than "female" and "male" (terms describing biological sex) throughout the text. This reflects the fact that this chapter examines the ways in which coalfield activists' social location in the gender hierarchy affects their activism—not now their biological sex affects it.

5. It is worth noting that this is a change in the performance of coalfield masculinity. As Yarrow (1990) describes, in the days when the union was strong, standing up to the "coal boss" was a marker of manliness. Since the decline of the union in the early 1980s, though, "the definition of masculinity has become less class-combative" and more focused on "how hard a worker one is" (ibid., p. 49).

Chapter 5

1. This chapter incorporates and expands on excerpts and empirical findings reported in Bell and York 2010.

2. Richard York is a professor of sociology and environmental studies at the University of Oregon. His research merges human ecology and political economy to examine how the structural characteristics of societies, including demographic, economic, and technological factors, influence levels of resource consumption and pollution emissions. Dr. York was a member of my dissertation committee and was co-author of the 2010 study that is woven into this chapter. I conceptualized the study, collected the data, and analyzed the data; Dr. York contributed to interpreting the findings, helped articulate this study's contributions to the literature, and helped write the 2010 article.

3. A severance tax is a tax levied on the extraction of natural resources, such as coal.

4. Net out-migration accounts for births and deaths and not just population change. Simply looking at the population change over time does not give an accurate picture

of out-migration, as it does not account for the number of people being born into the area or who have died.

5. First introduced by Allan Schnaiberg (1980) in order to explain why environmental degradation in the United States had grown dramatically since World War II, the treadmill-of-production theory asserts that ecological destruction is intrinsic to capitalist (and some other) modes of production. The theory argues that the pattern of increasing extraction and degradation in order to generate greater and greater profits has become the central operating framework of the global market. It is widely held that the treadmill of production, along with the ecological degradation it generates, is unavoidable unless the relations of production under corporate capitalism are changed (Buttel 2004; Foster 2005; Foster and York 2004; Gould, Pellow, and Schnaiberg 2004; Schnaiberg 1980). The treadmill of production's effects aren't limited to the ecological, however. Displaced workers are another result. "Improvements" in technology lead to an increase in "worker productivity," which accelerates the treadmill, "producing higher production and profits with fewer workers" (Gould, Pellow, and Schnaiberg 2004, p. 306).

6. Because portions of this chapter draw on co-authored material, I use "we" instead of "I" in certain sections.

Chapter 6

1. Sean P. Bemis is an assistant professor of earth and environmental sciences at the University of Kentucky. His research focuses on the geologic study of active faults and related deformation, both as a means of recognizing potential seismic hazards and as a tool for understanding the processes of tectonic deformation of fault systems through time. For the study presented in this chapter, I developed the research questions, contextualized the study within the literature, collected and analyzed the background interviews and participant observation data, and chose the county that would be the focus of the analysis. Dr. Bemis developed the idea of using a geographic information system (GIS) to address the research question, conducted the GIS viewshed analysis, created the maps depicting that analysis, and contributed to the interpretation of the findings.

Because this chapter is co-authored, I use "we" instead of "I" throughout.

2. Surface mining includes both "strip mining" and "mountaintop-removal" mining. However, because the majority of surface mining is actually mountaintop removal, these terms are used interchangeably in this chapter.

3. An individual driving on a road within the borders of Boone County may be able to see parts of the landscape that are in adjacent counties. By creating a buffer around the county line, we controlled for certain landscape features that may be in a different county but still visible from within Boone County.

Chapter 7

1. Research undertaken in collaboration with research subjects in order to simultaneously address a social problem and contribute to knowledge within an academic field has been called *action research, participatory research,* and *participatory-action research.* Within this book, I have used the term *participatory-action research* to describe the Photovoice methodology, in recognition of the fact that the method has two purposes: to foster a collaborative relationship with the people studied and to address a social problem that is relevant to their lives.

Chapter 8

1. The Photovoice process I employ was first articulated in the public health literature by Caroline Wang and colleagues in the mid 1990s. Although others have used modified versions of this method and still called it Photovoice, Wang's original conceptualization of the process is explicitly feminist (Wang and Redwood-Jones 2001). This is why I refer to Photovoice as a "feminist method."

2. However, it is important to note that a PAR project, in its purest form, is entirely collaborative, from the development of the research questions to the data collection to the dissemination of the results. Thus, the fact that I did not involve my research participants in the development of my *academic* research questions (although they had control over the photo-taking, sharing, and dissemination components of the *activist* portion of the project) means that the Photovoice project I implemented was technically a modified version of PAR. I am not alone in having made such a decision, however; in her 1993 study of successful scholar-activists, Francesca Cancian found that each of her research participants acknowledged adapting the "exclusively collaborative" aspect of PAR in order to meet their academic institution's publication expectations. Thus, although at its core my desire for this Photovoice project was for it to be a project that would benefit communities and local residents while helping me understand the social forces limiting activism, it is important to acknowledge that, because of the research questions I was asking, there are some aspects of the academic research component of this project that were not fully collaborative.

3. The Photovoice project, and all other data-collection procedures involving human subjects reported in this book, were approved by the Institutional Review Board at the University of Oregon and/or the University of Kentucky.

Chapter 9

1. All the participants in the control group are considered non-activist.

2. Bullet Mountain is a pseudonym.

3. The "Wild and Wonderful" welcome signs along the highways and interstates at the West Virginia border were replaced with "Open for Business" welcome signs in the mid 2000s by Governor Joe Manchin. The newer signs were highly unpopular and sparked a great deal of criticism from the public. Following this backlash, the governor's office conducted a telephone and online poll that allowed residents to vote on what slogan should appear on the welcome signs. Overwhelmingly, the public voted for "Wild and Wonderful West Virginia." The "Open for Business" signs were replaced in 2008.

4. Jackson is a pseudonym.

Conclusion

1. I am indebted to Ryan Wishart for pointing this out to me.

References

Ahern, Melissa M., and Michael Hendryx. 2008. Health Disparities and Environmental Competence: A Case Study of Appalachian Coal Mining. *Environmental Justice* 1 (2): 81–86.

Ahern, Melissa M., Michael Hendryx, Jamison Conley, Evan Fedorko, Alan Ducatman, and Keith J. Zullig. 2011. The Association between Mountaintop Mining and Birth Defects among Live Births in Central Appalachia, 1996–2003. *Environmental Research* 111 (6): 838–846.

Alder, Paul S., and Seok-Woo Kwon. 2002. Social Capital: Prospects for a New Concept. *Academy of Management Review* 27 (1): 17–40.

Anglin, Mary K. 1992. A Question of Loyalty: National and Regional Identity in Narratives of Appalachia. *Anthropological Quarterly* 65 (3): 105–116.

Anglin, Mary K. 2002. *Women, Power, and Dissent in the Hills of Carolina*. University of Illinois Press.

Appalachian Land Ownership Taskforce. 1983. *Who Owns Appalachia? Landownership and Its Impact*. University Press of Kentucky.

Appalachian Voices. 2007. What Are the Economic Consequences of Mountaintop Removal in Appalachia? (http://www.appvoices.org/index.php?/mtr/economics/).

Batteau, Allen W. 1990. *The Invention of Appalachia*. University of Arizona Press.

Beckwith, Karen. 2001. Gender Frames and Collective Action: Configurations of Masculinity in the Pittston Coal Strike. *Politics & Society* 29: 297–330.

Bell, Shannon Elizabeth. 2008. Photovoice as a Tool for Community Organizing in the Appalachian Coalfields. *Journal of Appalachian Studies* 14 (1–2): 34–48.

Bell, Shannon Elizabeth. 2009. "There Ain't No Bond in Town Like There Used to Be": The Destruction of Social Capital in the West Virginia Coalfields. *Sociological Forum* 24 (3): 631–657.

Bell, Shannon Elizabeth. 2013. *Our Roots Run Deep as Ironweed: Appalachian Women and the Fight for Environmental Justice*. University of Illinois Press.

Bell, Shannon Elizabeth. 2014. "Sacrificed So Others Can Live Conveniently": Social Inequality, Environmental Injustice, and the Energy Sacrifice Zone of Central Appalachia. In *Understanding Diversity: Celebrating Difference, Challenging Inequality*, ed. Claire M. Renzetti and Raquel Kennedy Bergen. Allyn and Bacon.

Bell, Shannon Elizabeth. 2015. Bridging Activism and the Academy: Exposing Environmental Injustices through the Feminist Ethnographic Method of Photovoice. *Human Ecology Review* 21 (1): 27–58.

Bell, Shannon Elizabeth, and Yvonne A. Braun. 2010. Coal, Identity, and the Gendering of Environmental Justice Activism in Central Appalachia. *Gender & Society* 24 (6): 794–813.

Bell, Shannon Elizabeth, and Richard York. 2010. Community Economic Identity: The Coal Industry and Ideology Construction in West Virginia. *Rural Sociology* 75 (1): 111–143.

Bell, Shannon Elizabeth, Alicia Hullinger, and Lilian Brislen. 2015. Manipulated Masculinities: Agribusiness, Deskilling, and the Rise of the Businessman-Farmer in the United States. *Rural Sociology* 80 (3): 285–313.

Billings, Dwight. 1974. Culture and Poverty in Appalachia: A Theoretical Discussion and Empirical Analysis. *Social Forces* 53: 315–323.

Billings, Dwight B., and Kathleen M. Blee. 2000. *The Road to Poverty: The Making of Wealth and Hardship in Appalachia*. Cambridge University Press.

Billings, Dwight B., Gurney Norman, and Katherine Ledford, eds. 1999. *Back Talk from Appalachia: Confronting Stereotypes*. University Press of Kentucky.

Blaaker, Debra, Joshua Woods, and Christopher Oliver. 2012. How Big Is Big Coal? Public Perceptions of the Coal Industry's Impact in West Virginia. *Organization & Environment* 25 (4): 385–401.

Bluestone, Barry, and Bennett Harrison. 1982. *The Deindustrialization of America: Plant Closings, Community Abandonment, and the Dismantling of Basic Industry*. Basic Books.

Bonskowski, Rich. 2004. EIA Coal Statistics, Projections, and Analyses: What They Say about Changes in the Coal Industry. Presentation at SME Central Appalachian Section Spring Meeting (www.eia.doe.gov/cneaf/coal/page/f_p_coal/coalstats.ppt).

Bonskowski, Richard, William Watson, and Fred Freme. 2006. Coal Production in the United States: An Historical Overview (http://www.eia.doe.gov/cneaf/coal/page/coal_production_review.pdf).

Bourdieu, Pierre. 1985. Forms of Capital. In *Handbook of Theory and Research for the Sociology of Education*, ed. John G. Richardson. Greenwood.

Braun, Yvonne A. 2008. "How Can I Stay Silent?" One Woman's Struggles for Environmental Justice in Lesotho. *Journal of International Women's Studies* 10 (1): 5–20.

Brehm, John, and Wendy Rahn. 1997. Individual-Level Evidence for the Causes and Consequences of Social Capital. *American Journal of Political Science* 41: 999–1023.

Brown, Phil, and Faith I.T. Ferguson. 1995. "Making a Big Stink": Women's Work, Women's Relationships, and Toxic Waste Activism. *Gender & Society* 9 (2): 145–172.

Bullard, Robert D. 1990. *Dumping in Dixie: Race, Class, and Environmental Quality*. Westview.

Bullard, Robert D. 1996. *Unequal Protection: Environmental Justice and Communities of Color*, second edition. Sierra Club Books.

Bullard, Robert D., Paul Mohai, Robin Saha, and Beverly Wright. 2007. *Toxic Wastes and Race at Twenty: 1987–2007*. United Church of Christ.

Burns, Shirley Stewart. 2007. *Bringing Down the Mountains: The Impact of Mountaintop Removal on Southern West Virginia Communities*. West Virginia University Press.

Buttel, Frederick. 2004. The Treadmill of Production: An Appreciation, Assessment, and Agenda for Research. *Organization & Environment* 17 (3): 323–336.

Cable, Sherry. 1992. Women's Social Movement Involvement: The Role of Structural Availability in Recruitment and Participation Processes. *Sociological Quarterly* 33 (1): 35–50.

Cable, Sherry. 1993. From Fussin' to Organizing: Individual and Collective Resistance at Yellow Creek. In *Fighting Back in Appalachia: Traditions of Resistance and Change*, ed. Stephen L. Fisher. Temple University Press.

Cable, Sherry, Thomas E. Shriver, and Donald W. Hastings. 1999. The Silenced Majority: Governmental Social Control on the Oak Ridge Nuclear Reservation. *Research in Social Problems and Public Policy* 7:59–81.

Cancian, Francesca M. 1993. Conflicts between Activist Research and Academic Success: Participatory Research and Alternative Strategies. *American Sociologist* 24 (1): 92–106.

Čapek, Stella. 1993. The "Environmental Justice" Frame: A Conceptual Discussion and an Application. *Social Problems* 40 (1): 5–24.

Capous-Desyllas, Moshoula. 2013. Using photovoice with sex workers: The power of art, agency and resistance. *Qualitative Social Work: Research and Practice* 13 (4): 477–501.

Catalani, Caricia, and Meredith Minkler. 2010. Photovoice: A Review of the Literature in Health and Public Health. *Health Education & Behavior* 37 (3): 424–451.

"Cedar of Southern West Virginia." 2005. *Coal Leader: Coal's National Newspaper*, September (http://www.coalleader.com/).

Coal Impoundment Location and Information System. 2005. Listing of Coal Impoundments: West Virginia. Wheeling Jesuit University (http://www.coalimpoundment.org/locate/list.asp).

Coal Leader . 2003."Friends of Coal."

Cole, Luke. W. and Sheila R. Foster. 2001. *From the Ground Up: Environmental Racism and the Rise of the Environmental Justice Movement.* New York University Press.

Coleman, James S. 1988. Social Capital in the Creation of Human Capital. *American Journal of Sociology* 94: 95–120.

Collins, Patricia Hill. 1990. *Black Feminist Thought: Knowledge, Consciousness, and the Politics of Empowerment.* Routledge.

Connell, R. W. and James W. Messerschmidt. 2005. Hegemonic Masculinity: Rethinking the Concept. *Gender & Society* 19: 829–859.

Cook, Samuel R. 2000. *Monacans and Miners: Native American and Coal Mining Communities in Appalachia.* University of Nebraska Press.

Culley, Marci R., and Holly L. Angelique. 2003. Women's Gendered Experiences as Long-Term Three Mile Island Activists. *Gender & Society* 17 (3): 445–461.

Cunningham, Rodger. 2010. Reflections on Identity and the Roots of Prejudice. In Appalachian Identity: A Roundtable Discussion. *Appalachian Journal* 38 (1): 74–76.

Dahal, Ganga Ram, and Krishna Prasad Adhikari. 2008. Bridging, Linking, and Bonding Social Capital in Collective Action: The Case of Kalahan Forest Reserve in the Philippines. Collective Action and Property Rights Working Paper 79, International Food Policy Research Institute.

DeSena, Judith. 2004. Mobilizing Social Capital through Community Struggle. In *Community-Based Organizations: The Intersection of Social Capital and Local Context in Contemporary Urban Society*, ed. Robert Silverman. Wayne State University Press.

Ducre, K. A. 2012. *A Place We Call Home: Gender, Race, and Justice in Syracuse.* Syracuse University Press.

Dunaway, Wilma A. 2001. The Double Register of History: Situating the Forgotten Woman and Her Household in Capitalist Commodity Chains. *Journal of World-systems Research* 7 (1): 2–29.

Dunaway, Wilma A. 2003. *Slavery in the American Mountain South*. Cambridge University Press.

Eades, Rick. 2000. Brushy Fork Slurry Impoundment: A Preliminary Report (http://www.ohvec.org/issues/slurry_impoundments/articles/brushy_fork.pdf).

Eagleton, Terry. 1994. Ideology and Its Vicissitudes in Western Marxism. In *Mapping Ideology*, ed. S. Žižek. Verso.

Eller, Ronald D. 1982. *Miners, Millhands, and Mountaineers: Industrialization of the Appalachian South, 1880–1930*. University of Tennessee Press.

Eller, Ronald D. 2008. *Uneven Ground: Appalachia since 1945*. University Press of Kentucky.

Emirbayer, Mustafa, and Chad Alan Goldberg. 2005. Pragmatism, Bourdieu, and Collective Emotions in Contentious Politics. *Theory and Society* 34 (5–6): 469–518.

Energy Information Administration. 2002, 2004, 2006. U.S. Coal Production by Coal-Producing Region and State (http://www.eia.doe.gov/cneaf/coal/page/acr/backissues.html).

Epstein, Barbara. 1995. Grassroots Environmentalism and Strategies for Change. *New Political Science* 32: 1–24.

Erikson, Kai T. 1976. *Everything in Its Path: Destruction of Community in the Buffalo Creek Flood*. Simon and Schuster.

Faber, Daniel. 2008. *Capitalizing on Environmental Injustice: The Polluter-Industrial Complex in the Age of Globalization*. Rowman & Littlefield.

Ferree, Myra Marx, and Frederick D. Miller. 1985. Mobilization and Meaning: Some Social Psychological Contributions to the Resources Mobilization Perspective on Social Movements. *Sociological Inquiry* 55 (1): 38–61.

Finger, John R. 1986. *The Eastern Band of Cherokees, 1819–1900*. University of Tennessee Press.

Fisher, Stephen L. 1977. Folk Culture or Folk Tale: Prevailing Assumptions About the Appalachian Personality. In *An Appalachian Symposium*, ed. J. W. Williamson. Appalachian State University Press.

Fisher, Stephen L. 1993. *Fighting Back in Appalachia: Traditions of Resistance and Change*. Temple University Press.

Fisher, Stephen L. 2010. Claiming Appalachia—and the Questions That Go with It." In Appalachian Identity: A Roundtable Discussion. *Appalachian Journal* 38 (1): 58–61.

Fisher, Stephen L., and Barbara Ellen Smith, eds. 2012. *Transforming Places: Lessons from Appalachia*. University of Illinois Press.

Flood Advisory Technical Taskforce. 2002. Runoff Analyses of Seng, Scrabble, and Sycamore Creeks, Part I (http://www.epa.gov/region3/mtntop/pdf/Appendices/Appendix%20H%20Engineering/WV%20Flooding%20Study/Flooding_Study__Part_01.pdf).

Foley, Michael, and Bob Edwards. 1999. Is It Time to Disinvest in Social Capital? *Journal of Public Policy* 19 (2): 141–173.

Fortin, Rebecca, Suzanne F. Jackson, Jessica Maher, and Catherine Moravac. 2014. I WAS HERE: Young Mothers Who Have Experienced Homelessness Use Photovoice and Participatory Qualitative Analysis to Demonstrate Strengths and Assets. *Global Health Promotion* 22 (1): 8–20.

Foster, John Bellamy. 2005. The Treadmill of Accumulation: Schaiberg's Environment and Marxian Political Economy. *Organization & Environment* 18 (1): 7–18.

Foster, John Bellamy, and Richard York. 2004. Political Economy and Environmental Crisis: Introduction to the Special Issue. *Organization & Environment* 17 (3): 293–294.

Foster, Stephen William. 1988. *The Past Is Another Country: Representation, Historical Consciousness, and Resistance in the Blue Ridge*. University of California Press.

Fox, Julia. 1999. Mountaintop Removal in West Virginia: An Environmental Sacrifice Zone. *Organization & Environment* 12 (2): 163–183.

Freire, Paulo. 1970. *Pedagogy of the Oppressed*. Continuum, 2000.

Friedman, D., and D. McAdam. 1992. Collective Identity and Activism: Networks, Choices, and the Life of a Social Movement. In *Frontiers in Social Movement Theory*, ed. A. D. Morris and C. M. Mueller. Yale University Press.

Friends of Coal. 2007. Welcome Friends of Coal (www.friendsofcoal.org).

Frohmann, Lisa. 2005. The Framing Safety Project: Photographs and Narratives by Battered Women. *Violence Against Women* 11 (11): 1396–1419.

Fukuyama, Francis. 1995. *Trust: Social Virtues and the Creation of Prosperity*. Free Press.

Gamson, William A. 1992. The Social Psychology of Collective Action. In *Frontiers in Social Movement Theory*, ed. Aldon D. Morris and Carol McClurg Mueller. Yale University Press.

Gaventa, John. 1978. Property, Coal, and Theft. In *Colonialism in Modern America: The Appalachian Case*, ed. Helen Matthews Lewis, Linda Johnson, and Donald Askins. Appalachian Consortium Press.

Gaventa, John. 1980. *Power and Powerlessness: Quiescence and Rebellion in an Appalachian Valley*. University of Illinois Press.

Geredien, Ross. 2009. Assessing the Extent of Mountaintop Removal in Appalachia: An Analysis using Vector Data. Technical Report for Appalachian Voices (availsble at http://ilovemountains.org).

Giesen, Carol A. B. 1995. *Coal Miners' Wives: Portraits of Endurance*. University Press of Kentucky.

Gould, Kenneth A., David N. Pellow, and Allan Schnaiberg. 2004. Interrogating the Treadmill of Production: Everything You Wanted to Know About the Treadmill but Were Afraid to Ask. *Organization & Environment* 17 (3): 296–316.

Gramsci, Antonio. 1971. *Selections from the Prison Notebooks*. International, 2010

Habermas, Jürgen. 1975. *Legitimation Crisis*. Translated by T. McCarthy. Beacon.

Hall, Jacquelyn Dowd. 1986. Disorderly Women: Gender and Labor Militancy in the Appalachian South. *Journal of American History* 73 (2): 354–382.

Hansen, Evan, Alan Collins, Michael Hendryx, Fritz Boettner, and Anne Hereford. 2008. *The Long-Term Economic Benefits of Wind Versus Mountaintop Removal Coal on Coal River Mountain*. West Virginia: Downstream Strategies.

Haynes, Ada. 1997. *Poverty in Central Appalachia*. Garland.

Hendryx, Michael. 2008. Mortality Rates in Appalachian Coal Mining Counties: 24 Years Behind the Nation. *Environmental Justice* 1 (1): 5–11.

Hendryx, Michael, and Melissa M. Ahern. 2008. Relations Between Health Indicators and Residential Proximity to Coalmining in West Virginia. *American Journal of Public Health* 98: 669–671.

Hendryx, Michael, Melissa M. Ahern, and Timothy R. Nurkiewicz. 2007. Hospitalization Patterns Associated with Appalachian Coal Mining. *Journal of Toxicology and Environmental Health* 70: 2064–2070.

Hendryx, Michael, Leah Wolfe, Juhua Luo, and Bo Webb. 2012. Self-Reported Cancer Rates in Two Rural Areas of West Virginia with and without Mountaintop Coal Mining. *Journal of Community Health* 37 (2): 320–327.

Hohmann, George. 2005. Capitol rallies to reflect divergent opinions on coal." *Charleston Daily Mail*, March 20.

Holtby, Alix, Kate Klein, Katie Cook, and Robb Travers. 2015. To be seen or not to be seen: Photovoice, queer and trans youth, and the dilemma of representation. *Action Research*. doi:.10.1177/1476750314566414

Hufford, Mary. 1999. Landscape and History at the Headwaters of the Big Coal River Valley (http://memory.loc.gov/ammem/collections/tending/essay5.pdf).

Jasper, James M. 1998. The Emotions of Protest: Affective and Reactive Emotions in and around Social Movements. *Sociological Forum* 13 (3): 397–424.

Jennings, Derek, and John Lowe. 2014. Photovoice: Giving Voice to Indigenous Youth. *Pimatisiwin* 11 (3): 521–537.

Kaplan, Temma. 1997. *Crazy for Democracy: Women in Grassroots Movements*. Routledge.

Kingsolver, Ann E. 1992. Five Women Negotiating the Meaning of Negotiation: Introduction to the Special Issue on Negotiating Identity in Southeastern U.S. Uplands. *Anthropological Quarterly* 65 (3): 101–104.

Krauss, Celine. 1993. Women and Toxic Waste Protest: Race, Class, and Gender as Resources of Resistance. *Qualitative Sociology* 16 (3): 247–262.

Krieg, Brigette, and Lana Roberts. 2007. Photovoice: Insights Into Marginalisation through a "Community Lens" in Saskatchewan, Canada. In *Participatory Research Action Approaches and Methods: Connecting People, Participation and Place*, ed. S. Kindon, R. Pain and M. Kesby. Routledge.

Lancee, Bram. 2010. The Economic Returns of Immigrants' Bonding and Bridging Social Capital: The Case of the Netherlands. *International Migration Review* 44 (1): 202–206.

Lapegna, Pablo. 2013. Social Movements and Patronage Politics: Processes of Demobilization and Dual Pressure. *Sociological Forum* 28 (4): 842–863.

Lapegna, Pablo. 2015. Popular Demobilization, Agribusiness Mobilization, and the Agrarian Boom in Post-Neoliberal Argentina. *Journal of World-systems Research* 21 (1): 69–87.

Lapegna, Pablo. Forthcoming. *Soybeans and Power: Genetically Modified Crops, Environmental Politics, and Social Movements in Argentina*. Oxford University Press.

Legerski, Elizabeth Miklya, and Marie Cornwall. 2010. Working-Class Job Loss, Gender, and the Negotiation of Household Labor. *Gender & Society* 24:447–474.

Leonard, Madeline. 2004. Bonding and Bridging Social Capital: Reflections from Belfast. *Sociology* 38 (5): 927–944.

Lewis, Helen M., and Edward E. Knipe. 1978. The Colonialism Model: The Appalachian Case. In *Colonialism in Modern America: The Appalachian Case*, ed. Helen Matthews Lewis, Linda Johnson, and Donald Askins. Appalachian Consortium Press.

Lewis, Ronald L. 1987. *Black Coal Miners in America: Race, Class, and Community Conflict, 1780–1980*. University Press of Kentucky.

Lewis, Ronald L. 1999. Beyond Isolation and Homogeneity: Diversity and the History of Appalachia. In *Back Talk from Appalachia: Confronting Stereotypes*, ed. Dwight B. Billings, Gurney Norman and Katherine Ledford. University Press of Kentucky.

Lockard, Duane. 1998. *Coal: A Memoir and Critique*. University Press of Virginia.

Loeb, Penny. 2003. The Floods of 2001 (www.wvcoalfield.com).

Maggard, Sally Ward. 1987. Women's Participation in the Brookside Coal Strike: Militance, Class, and Gender in Appalachia. *Frontiers* 9 (3): 16–21.

Maggard, Sally Ward. 1990. Gender Contested: Women's Participation in the Brookside Coal Strike. In *Women and Social Protest*, ed. Guida West and Rhoda Lois Blumberg. Oxford University Press.

Maggard, Sally Ward. 1994. From Farm to Coal Camp to Back Office and McDonald's: Living in the Midst of Appalachia's Latest Transformation. *Journal of the Appalachian Studies Association* 6 (1): 14–38.

Maggard, Sally Ward. 1999. Gender, Race, AND Place: Confounding Labor Activism in Central Appalachia. In *Neither Separate nor Equal: Women, Race, and Class in the South*, ed. Barbara Ellen Smith. Temple University Press.

Mann, Michael. 1970. The Social Cohesion of Liberal Democracy. *American Sociological Review* 35 (3): 423–439.

Martin, Patricia Yancey. 2001. "Mobilizing Masculinities": Women's Experiences of Men at Work. *Organization* 8:587–618.

McAdam, Doug. 1982. *Political Process and the Development of Black Insurgency, 1930–1970*. University of Chicago Press.

McAdam, Doug. 1986. Recruitment to High-Risk Activism: The Case of Freedom Summer. *American Journal of Sociology* 92 (1): 64–90.

McAdam, Doug. 1988 a. Micromobilization Contexts and Recruitment to Activism. *Conflicts and Change* 1: 125–154.

McAdam, Doug. 1988 b. *Freedom Summer*. Oxford University Press.

McAdam, Doug. 2002. Beyond Structural Analysis: Toward a More Dynamic Understanding of Social Movements. In *Social Movement Analysis: The Network Perspective*, ed. Mario Diani and Doug McAdam. Oxford University Press.

McAdam, Doug, and Hilary Schaffer Boudet. 2012. *Putting Social Movements in Their Place: Explaining Opposition to Energy Projects in the United States, 2000–2005*. Cambridge University Press.

McAdam, Doug, and Ronelle Paulsen. 1993. Specifying the Relationship between Social Ties and Activism. *American Journal of Sociology* 99 (3): 640–667.

McAdam, Doug, Sidney Tarrow, and Charles Tilly. 2001. *The Dynamics of Contention*. Cambridge University Press.

McIlmoil, Rory, Evan Hansen, Ted Boettner, and Paul Miller. 2010. Coal and Renewables in Central Appalachia: The Impact of Coal on the West Virginia State Budget.

Downstream Strategies (http://www.downstreamstrategies.com/documents/reports_publication/DownstreamStrategies-coalWV.pdf).

McIlmoil, Rory, Evan Hansen, Nathan Askins, and Meghan Betcher. 2013. The Continuing Decline in Demand for Central Appalachian Coal: Market and Regulatory Influences. Downstream Strategies (http://www.downstreamstrategies.com/documents/reports_publication/the-continuing-decline-in-demand-for-capp-coal.pdf).

McKinney, Gordon B. 1977. Industrialization and Violence in Appalachia in the 1890s. In *An Appalachian Symposium*, ed. J.W. Williamson. Appalachian State University Press.

McKinney, Gordon B. 1980. Political Uses of Appalachian Identity After the Civil War. *Appalachian Journal* 7 (3): 200–209.

McNeil, Bryan T. 2005. Searching for Home Where Mountains Move: The Collision of Economy, Environment, and an American Community. PhD dissertation, University of North Carolina, Chapel Hill.

McNeil, Bryan T. 2012. *Combating Mountaintop Removal: New Directions in the Fight against Big Coal.* University of Illinois Press.

Megyesi, Boldizsár, Eszter Kelemen, and Markus Schermer. 2011. Social Capital as a Success Factor for Collective Farmers Marketing Initiatives. *International Journal of Sociology of Agriculture and Food* 18 (1): 89–103.

Meyer, David S. 1990. *A Winter of Discontent: The Nuclear Freeze and American Politics.* Praeger.

Meyer, David S. 2005. Scholarship That Might Matter. In *Rhyming Hope and History: Activism and Social Movement Scholarship*, ed. David Crouteau, Bill Hoynes, and Charlotte Ryan. University of Minnesota Press.

Meyer, David S. 2007. *The Politics of Protest: Social Movements in America.* Oxford University Press.

Meyer, David S., and Joshua Gamson. 1995. The Challenge of Cultural Elites: Celebrities and Social Movements. *Sociological Inquiry* 65 (2): 181–206.

Miewald, Christiana E., and Eugene J. McCann. 2004. Gender Struggle, Scale, and the Production of Place in the Appalachian Coalfields. *Environment & Planning A* 36: 1045–1064.

Miller, Tom. 1974. Who Owns West Virginia? Reprint from *Herald-Advertiser* and *Herald-Dispatch*, Huntington, West Virginia, December 1974. Cited in Barbara Rasmussen, *Absentee Landowning and Exploitation in West Virginia, 1760–1920* (University Press of Kentucky, 1994).

Mohai, Paul. 1992. Men, Women and the Environment: An Examination of the Gender Gap in Environmental Concern and Activism. *Society & Natural Resources* 5: 1–9.

Montrie, Chad. 2003. *To Save the Land and People: A History of Opposition to Surface Mining in Appalachia*. University of North Carolina Press.

Morrow, Elizabeth. 2013. Activist Groups: Bridging or Bonding Social Capital? Presented at session on Social Capital, Civic Society and Politics, Political Studies Association Conference, Cardiff, Wales.

Naples, Nancy A. 1992. Activist Mothering: Cross-Generational Continuity in the Community Work of Women from Low-Income Urban Neighborhoods. *Gender & Society* 6: 441–463.

Naples, Nancy A. 1998. *Grassroots Warriors: Activist Mothering, Community Work, and the War on Poverty*. Routledge.

Narayan, Deepa. 1999. Bonds and Bridges: Social Capital and Poverty. Policy Research Working Paper 2167, World Bank.

National Mining Association. 2008. Trends in U.S. Coal Mining 1923–2007 (http://www.nma.org/pdf/c_trends_mining.pdf).

Neal, Arthur G., and Melvin Seeman. 1964. Organizations and Powerlessness: A Test of the Mediation Hypothesis. *American Sociological Review* 29 (2): 216–226.

Norris, Randall, and Jean-Philippe Cyprès. 1996. *Women of Coal*. University Press of Kentucky.

Nyden, Paul J. 2002. Heaviest Trucks Carrying Coal; Most Stopped Trucks Above Limit Sought by Industry, Group Says. *Charleston Gazette*, February 25.

Obermiller, Phillip J., M. Kathryn Brown, Donna Jones, Michael E. Maloney, and Thomas E. Wagner. 2012. Identity Matters: Building an Urban Appalachian Movement in Cincinnati. In *Transforming Places: Lessons from Appalachia*, ed. Stephen L. Fisher and Barbara Ellen Smith. University of Illinois Press.

Oliveiraa, Elsa, and Jo Vearey. 2015. Images of Place: Visuals from Migrant Women Sex Workers In South Africa. *Medical Anthropology* 34 (4): 305–318.

Olson, Mancur, Jr. 1965. *The Logic of Collective Action: Public Goods and the Theory of Groups*. Harvard University Press.

Onyx, Jenny, and Paul Bullen. 2000. Measuring Social Capital in Five Communities. *Journal of Applied Behavioral Science* 36 (1): 23–42.

Orem, William H. 2006. Coal Slurry: Geochemistry and Impacts on Human Health and Environmental Quality. U.S. Geological Survey, Eastern Energy Resources Team,

PowerPoint Presentation to Coal Slurry Legislative Subcommittee of the Senate Judiciary Committee, West Virginia Legislature, November 15.

Ostrom, Elinor, and T. K. Ahn. 2009. The Meaning of Social Capital and its Link to Collective Action. In *Handbook of Social Capital: The Troika of Sociology, Political Science, and Economics*, ed. Gert T. Svedsen and Gunnar L. Svedsen. Edward Elgar.

Pachucki, Mark A., and Ronald L. Breiger. 2010. Cultural Holes: Beyond Relationality in Social Networks and Culture. *Annual Review of Sociology* 36: 205–224.

Palmer, M. A., E. S. Bernhardt, W. H. Schlesinger, K. N. Eshleman, E. Foufoula-Georgiou, M. S. Hendryx, A. D. Lemly, 2010. Mountaintop Mining Consequences. *Science* 327 (5962): 148–149.

Paxton, Pamela. 1999. Is Social Capital Declining in the United States? A Multiple Indicator Assessment. *American Journal of Sociology* 105 (1): 88–127.

Peeples, J. A., and K. M. DeLuca. 2006. The Truth of the Matter: Motherhood, Community, and Environmental Justice. *Women's Studies in Communication* 29 (1): 59–87.

Pellow, David Naguib. 2004. *Garbage Wars: The Struggle for Environmental Justice in Chicago*. MIT Press.

Pellow, David Naguib. 2007. *Resisting Global Toxics: Transnational Movements for Environmental Justice*. MIT Press.

Pena, Maria-Valeria Junho, and Hector Lindo-Fuentes. 1998. Community Organization, Values and Social Capital in Panama. In Central America Country Management Unit Economic Notes No. 9, World Bank.

Pinard, Maurice. 1971. *The Rise of a Third Party: A Study in Crisis Politics*. Prentice-Hall.

Piven, Frances Fox, and Richard Cloward. 1977. *Poor People's Movements: How They Succeed, Why They Fail*. Pantheon.

Polletta, F., and J. Jasper. 2001. Collective Identities and Social Movements. *Annual Review of Sociology* 27: 283–305.

Portes, Alejandro. 1998. Social Capital: Its Origins and Applications in Modern Sociology. *Annual Review of Sociology* 24: 1–24.

Putnam, Robert D. 1995. Bowling Alone: America's Declining Social Capital. *Journal of Democracy* 6: 65–78.

Putnam, Robert D. 2000. *Bowling Alone: The Collapse and Revival of American Community*. Simon & Schuster.

Rasmussen, Barbara. 1994. *Absentee Landowning and Exploitation in West Virginia, 1760–1920*. University Press of Kentucky.

Reid, Bill. 2003. Editorial. *Coal Leader: Coal's National Newspaper,* March __ (http://www.coalleader.com/).

Reid, Herbert, and Betsy Taylor. 2010. *Recovering the Commons: Democracy, Place, and Global Justice.* University of Illinois Press.

Roberts, J. Timmons, and Melissa M. Toffolon-Weiss. 2001. *Chronicles from the Environmental Justice Frontline.* Cambridge University Press.

Rome, Adam. 2006. "Political Hermaphrodites": Gender and Environmental Reform in Progressive America. *Environmental History* 11: 440–463.

Schifflett, Crandall A. 1991. *Coal Towns: Life, Work, and Culture in Company Towns of Southern Appalachia. 1880–1960.* University of Tennessee Press.

Schnaiberg, Allan. 1980. *The Environment: From Surplus to Scarcity.* Oxford University Press.

Schussman, Alan, and Sarah A. Soule. 2005. Process and Protest: Accounting for Individual Protest Participation. *Social Forces* 84 (2): 1083–1108.

Scott, Rebecca R. 2010. *Removing Mountains: Extracting Nature and Identity in the Appalachian Coalfields.* University of Minnesota Press.

Scott, Shaunna L. 1995. *Two Sides to Everything: The Cultural Construction of Class Consciousness in Harlan County, Kentucky.* State University of New York Press.

Seitz, Virginia Rinaldo. 1995. *Women, Development, and Communities for Empowerment in Appalachia.* State University of New York.

Seitz, Virginia Rinaldo. 1998. Class, Gender, and Resistance in the Appalachian Coalfields. In *Community Activism and Feminist Politics: Organizing Across Race, Class, and Gender,* ed. Nancy A. Naples. Routledge.

Shanghai Zoom Intelligence Co. Ltd.: China Energy Competitive Intelligence Provider. "Making Friends: West Virginia Coal Needs You," *Coal and Electric Power—April News,* April 14, 2006 (http://www.zoomchina.com.cn/new/content/view/4301/197/).

Shapiro, Henry D. 1977. Appalachia and the Idea of America: The Problem of the Persisting Frontier. In *An Appalachian Symposium,* ed. J. W. Williamson. Appalachian State University.

Shapiro, Henry D. 1978. *Appalachia on Our Mind: The Southern Mountains and Mountaineers in the American Consciousness, 1870–1920.* University of North Carolina Press.

Shriver, Thomas E. 2000. Risk and Recruitment: Patterns of Social Movement Mobilization in a Government Town. *Sociological Focus* 33 (3): 321–337.

Shriver, Thomas E., Alison E. Adams, and Rachel Einwohner. 2013. Motherhood and Opportunities for Activism Before and After the Czech Velvet Revolution. *Mobilization* 18 (3): 267–288.

Shriver, Thomas E., Alison E. Adams, and Chris M. Messer. 2014. Power, Quiescence, and Pollution: The Suppression of Environmental Grievances. *Social Currents* 1 (3): 275–292.

Silverman, Robert. 2004. Social Capital and Community Development. In *Community-Based Organizations: The Intersection of Social Capital and Local Context in Contemporary Urban Society*, ed. Robert Silverman. Wayne State University Press.

Silverman, Robert, and Kelly Patterson. 2004. Paradise Lost: Social Capital and the Emergence of a Homeowners Association in a Suburban Detroit Neighborhood. In *Community-Based Organizations: The Intersection of Social Capital and Local Context in Contemporary Urban Society*, ed. Robert Silverman. Wayne State University Press.

Smallacombe, Patricia Stern. 2006. Rootedness, Isolation, and Social Capital in an Inner-City White Neighborhood. In *Social Capital in the City: Community and Civic Life in Philadelphia*, ed. Richardson Dilworth. Temple University Press.

Snow, David A., and Doug McAdam. 2000. Identity Work Processes in the Context of Social Movements: Clarifying the Identity/Movement Nexus. In *Self, Identity, and Social Movements*, ed. S. Stryker, T. Owens, and R. White. University of Minnesota Press.

State of West Virginia. 2014. Executive Budget Fiscal Year 2013: Volume I Budget Report (http://www.budget.wv.gov/executivebudget/archives/Documents/VIBR2013.pdf).

Stockman, Vivian. 2006. Jack Spadaro: Former Top MSHA Safety Trainer Fights the Tragic Consequences of Mountaintop Removal Mining. *Appalachian Voices*, spring (http://appvoices.org/2007/04/page/15/).

Stryker, Sheldon, Timothy J. Owens, and Robert W. White, eds. 2000. *Self, Identity, and Social Movements*. University of Minnesota Press.

Szreter, S., and M. Woolcock. 2004. Health by Association? Social Capital, Social Theory and the Political Economy of Public Health. *International Journal of Epidemiology* 33: 650–667.

Taylor, Dorceta E. 2014. *Toxic Communities: Environmental Racism, Industrial Pollution, and Residential Mobility*. New York University Press.

Turner, William H., and Edward J. Cabbell, eds. 1985. *Blacks in Appalachia*. University Press of Kentucky.

U.S. Bureau of Economic Analysis. 2014. Regional Data, Real GDP by State. Query: All Industries, West Virginia, 2011 (http://www.bea.gov/iTable/iTable.cfm?reqid=70&step=1&isuri=1&acrdn=1#reqid=70&step=1&isuri=1).

U.S. Census Bureau. 2000 a. Census 2000 Summary File 1, Table P27: Relationship by Household Type—Universe: Total, State Data, added Geographic Components: Rural (http://factfinder.census.gov).

U.S. Census Bureau. 2000 b. Fact Sheet: [Farmstead] town, West Virginia (http://factfinder.census.gov).

U.S. Census Bureau. 2000 c. Fact Sheet: [Coalville] town, West Virginia (http://factfinder.census.gov).

U.S. Census Bureau. 1971, 1981, 1991, 1994, 2000, 2005. Mining and Mineral Products. *Statistical Abstract of the United States.*

U.S. Census Bureau. 2010. 2005–2009 American Community Survey 5-Year Estimates. American Fact Finder Fact Sheet: Pike, Perry, Harlan, Letcher, Knott, Leslie, Martin, and Floyd Counties, Kentucky and McDowell County, West Virginia (http://factfinder.census.gov/).

U.S. Environmental Protection Agency. 2003. Affected Environment and Consequences of MTM/VF. In Draft Environmental Impact Statement: Mountaintop Mining/Valley Fills in Appalachia (http://www.epa.gov/region3/mtntop/eis.htm).

U.S. Environmental Protection Agency. 2005. Mountaintop Mining/Valley Fills in Appalachia Final Programmatic Environmental Impact Statement (http://www.epa.gov/region03/mtntop/).

U.S. Government Accountability Office. 2009. Surface Coal Mining: Characteristics of Mining in Mountainous Areas of Kentucky and West Virginia. Report to Congressional Requestors (http://www.gao.gov/products/GAO-10-21).

Vilhena, Daril A., Jacob G. Foster, Martin Rosvall, Jevin D. West, James Evans, and Carl T. Bergstrom. 2014. Finding Cultural Holes: How Structure and Culture Diverge in Networks of Scholarly Communication. *Sociological Science* 1: 221–238.

Walls, David S. 1978. Internal Colony or Internal Periphery? A Critique of Current Models and an Alternative Formulation. In *Colonialism in Modern America: The Appalachian Case*, ed. Helen Matthews Lewis, Linda Johnson, and Donald Askins. Appalachian Consortium Press.

Walsh, Caroline, Brigette Krieg, Gayle Rutherford, and Meaghan Bell. 2013. Aboriginal Women's Voices: Breaking the Cycle of Incarceration and Homelessness. *Pimatisiwin* 11 (3): 377–394.

Wang, Caroline, and Mary Anne Burris. 1994. Empowerment through Photo Novella: Portraits of Participation. *Health Education Quarterly* 21 (2): 171–186.

Wang, Caroline, and Yanique Redwood-Jones. 2001. Photovoice Ethics: Perspectives from Flint Photovoice. *Health Education & Behavior* 28 (5): 560–572.

Wang, Caroline, Kun Yi Wu, Wen Tao Zhan, and Kathryn Carorano. 1998. Photovoice as a Participatory Health Promotion Strategy. *Health Promotion International* 13 (1): 75–86.

Weiss, Chris. 1993. Appalachian Women Fight Back: Organizational Approaches to Nontraditional Job Advocacy. In *Fighting Back in Appalachia: Traditions of Resistance and Change*, ed. Stephen L. Fisher. Temple University Press.

Weller, Jack. 1978. Appalachia: America's Mineral Colony. In *Colonialism in Modern America: The Appalachian Case*, ed. Helen Matthews Lewis, Linda Johnson, and Donald Askins. Appalachian Consortium Press.

Wells, Leigh Ann. 2006. Lawsuits Muddy Water Project. *Appalachian News-Express*, August 13 (http://www.newsexpresssky.com/articles/2006/07/30/top_story/01water.txt).

West Virginia Bureau of Employment Programs and Workforce West Virginia. 2005. Monthly Report on the Civilian Labor Force, Employment and Unemployment Data (http://www.wvbep.org/bep/lmi/TABLE2/T205west.htm).

West Virginia Center on Budget and Policy and the American Friends Service Committee. 2013. Who Owns West Virginia? (http://www.wvpolicy.org/wp-content/uploads/2013/12/land-study-paper-final3.pdf).

West Virginia Coal Association. 2007. CEDAR (http://www.wvcoal.com/cedar.html).

West Virginia Coal Association. 2011. Coal Facts 2011 (http://www.wvcoal.com/2011-coal-facts.html).

West Virginia Health Statistics Center. 2002. A Look at West Virginia's Population by Decade, 1950–2000: Statistical Brief Number 8. Office of Epidemiology and Health Promotion, Bureaufor Public Health, Department of Health and Human Resources (http://www.wvdhhr.org/bph/oehp/hsc/briefs/eight/default.htm).

West Virginia Health Statistics Center. 2013. Births, Deaths, Natural Increase or Decrease, and Net Migration, West Virginia Population by County, 1950–2010.

West Virginia Office of Miners' Health, Safety, and Training. 2012 [2003]. West Virginia Coal Mining Facts (http://www.wvminesafety.org/wvcoalfacts.htm).

West Virginia State Treasurer's Office. 2014. Quarterly Distributions: 25% Portion Distributed to Counties and Municipalities (http://www.wvsto.com/dept/Admin/Tax/Pages/CoalSeveranceTax.aspx).

Whisnant, David E. 1983. *All That Is Native and Fine: The Politics of Culture in an American Region*. University of North Carolina Press.

Wilhelm, Gene. 1977. Appalachian Isolation: Fact or Fiction? In *An Appalachian Symposium*, ed. J. W. Williamson. Appalachian State University.

Wilson, Darlene. 1995. The Felicitous Convergence of Mythmaking and Capital Accumulation: John Fox Jr. and the Formation of An(Other) Almost-White American Underclass. *Journal of Appalachian Studies* 1 (1): 5–44.

Wilhelm, Gene. 1977. Appalachian Isolation: Fact or Fiction? In *An Appalachian Symposium*, ed. J. W. Williamson. Appalachian State University Press.

Williams, John Alexander. 1976. *West Virginia and the Captains of Industry*. West Virginia University Press.

Wilson, Darlene. 1995. The Felicitous Convergence of Mythmaking and Capital Accumulation: John Fox Jr. and the Formation of An(Other) Almost-White American Underclass. *Journal of Appalachian Studies* 1:1.

WindLogics. 2006. Coal River Mountain Area, West Virginia Regional Prospecting Analysis. Confidential report produced for BKA Group.

Witt, Tom S., and Mark Fletcher. 2005. Tourism and the West Virginia Economy. Bureau of Business and Economic Research, West Virginia University (http://www.be.wvu.edu/bber/publications.aspx#).

Witt, Tom S., and J. Sebastian Leguizamon. 2007. Tourism and the West Virginia Economy. Bureau of Business and Economic Research, West Virginia University (http://www.be.wvu.edu/bber/publications.aspx#).

Workforce West Virginia. 2000a, 2001, 2002, 2003, 2004, 2005, 2006, 2007. West Virginia—Employment and Wages (www.wvbep.org/bep/lmi/DEFAULT.HTM).

Workforce West Virginia. 2000 b. West Virginia Nonfarm Payroll Employment, By Industry, Annual Averages 1939–1999 (http://www.wvbep.org/bep/lmi/e&e/nf_39-99.htm).

Yarrow, Michael. 1990. Voices from the Coalfields: How Miners' Families Understand the Crisis of Coal. In *Communities in Economic Crisis: Appalachia and the South*, ed. John Gaventa, Barbara Ellen Smith, and Alex Wellingham. Temple University Press.

Yarrow, Michael. 1991. The Gender-Specific Class Consciousness of Appalachian Coal Miners: Structure and Change. In *Bringing Class Back In: Contemporary and Historical Perspectives*, ed. S. G. McNall, R. F. Levine, and R. Fantasia,. Westview.

Index

Urban and Industrial Environments

Series editor: Robert Gottlieb, Henry R. Luce Professor of Urban and Environmental Policy, Occidental College

Maureen Smith, *The U.S. Paper Industry and Sustainable Production: An Argument for Restructuring*

Keith Pezzoli, *Human Settlements and Planning for Ecological Sustainability: The Case of Mexico City*

Sarah Hammond Creighton, *Greening the Ivory Tower: Improving the Environmental Track Record of Universities, Colleges, and Other Institutions*

Jan Mazurek, *Making Microchips: Policy, Globalization, and Economic Restructuring in the Semiconductor Industry*

William A. Shutkin, *The Land That Could Be: Environmentalism and Democracy in the Twenty-First Century*

Richard Hofrichter, ed., *Reclaiming the Environmental Debate: The Politics of Health in a Toxic Culture*

Robert Gottlieb, *Environmentalism Unbound: Exploring New Pathways for Change*

Kenneth Geiser, *Materials Matter: Toward a Sustainable Materials Policy*

Thomas D. Beamish, *Silent Spill: The Organization of an Industrial Crisis*

Matthew Gandy, *Concrete and Clay: Reworking Nature in New York City*

David Naguib Pellow, *Garbage Wars: The Struggle for Environmental Justice in Chicago*

Julian Agyeman, Robert D. Bullard, and Bob Evans, eds., *Just Sustainabilities: Development in an Unequal World*

Barbara L. Allen, *Uneasy Alchemy: Citizens and Experts in Louisiana's Chemical Corridor Disputes*

Dara O'Rourke, *Community-Driven Regulation: Balancing Development and the Environment in Vietnam*

Brian K. Obach, *Labor and the Environmental Movement: The Quest for Common Ground*

Peggy F. Barlett and Geoffrey W. Chase, eds., *Sustainability on Campus: Stories and Strategies for Change*

Steve Lerner, *Diamond: A Struggle for Environmental Justice in Louisiana's Chemical Corridor*

Jason Corburn, *Street Science: Community Knowledge and Environmental Health Justice*

Peggy F. Barlett, ed., *Urban Place: Reconnecting with the Natural World*

David Naguib Pellow and Robert J. Brulle, eds., *Power, Justice, and the Environment: A Critical Appraisal of the Environmental Justice Movement*

Eran Ben-Joseph, *The Code of the City: Standards and the Hidden Language of Place Making*

Nancy J. Myers and Carolyn Raffensperger, eds., *Precautionary Tools for Reshaping Environmental Policy*

Kelly Sims Gallagher, *China Shifts Gears: Automakers, Oil, Pollution, and Development*

Kerry H. Whiteside, *Precautionary Politics: Principle and Practice in Confronting Environmental Risk*

Ronald Sandler and Phaedra C. Pezzullo, eds., *Environmental Justice and Environmentalism: The Social Justice Challenge to the Environmental Movement*

Julie Sze, *Noxious New York: The Racial Politics of Urban Health and Environmental Justice*

Robert D. Bullard, ed., *Growing Smarter: Achieving Livable Communities, Environmental Justice, and Regional Equity*

Ann Rappaport and Sarah Hammond Creighton, *Degrees That Matter: Climate Change and the University*

Michael Egan, *Barry Commoner and the Science of Survival: The Remaking of American Environmentalism*

David J. Hess, *Alternative Pathways in Science and Industry: Activism, Innovation, and the Environment in an Era of Globalization*

Peter F. Cannavò, *The Working Landscape: Founding, Preservation, and the Politics of Place*

Paul Stanton Kibel, ed., *Rivertown: Rethinking Urban Rivers*

Kevin P. Gallagher and Lyuba Zarsky, *The Enclave Economy: Foreign Investment and Sustainable Development in Mexico's Silicon Valley*

David Naguib Pellow, *Resisting Global Toxics: Transnational Movements for Environmental Justice*

Robert Gottlieb, *Reinventing Los Angeles: Nature and Community in the Global City*

David V. Carruthers, ed., *Environmental Justice in Latin America: Problems, Promise, and Practice*

Tom Angotti, *New York for Sale: Community Planning Confronts Global Real Estate*

Paloma Pavel, ed., *Breakthrough Communities: Sustainability and Justice in the Next American Metropolis*

Anastasia Loukaitou-Sideris and Renia Ehrenfeucht, *Sidewalks: Conflict and Negotiation over Public Space*

David J. Hess, *Localist Movements in a Global Economy: Sustainability, Justice, and Urban Development in the United States*

Julian Agyeman and Yelena Ogneva-Himmelberger, eds., *Environmental Justice and Sustainability in the Former Soviet Union*

Jason Corburn, *Toward the Healthy City: People, Places, and the Politics of Urban Planning*

JoAnn Carmin and Julian Agyeman, eds., *Environmental Inequalities Beyond Borders: Local Perspectives on Global Injustices*

Louise Mozingo, *Pastoral Capitalism: A History of Suburban Corporate Landscapes*

Gwen Ottinger and Benjamin Cohen, eds., *Technoscience and Environmental Justice: Expert Cultures in a Grassroots Movement*

Samantha MacBride, *Recycling Reconsidered: The Present Failure and Future Promise of Environmental Action in the United States*

Andrew Karvonen, *Politics of Urban Runoff: Nature, Technology, and the Sustainable City*

Daniel Schneider, *Hybrid Nature: Sewage Treatment and the Contradictions of the Industrial Ecosystem*

Catherine Tumber, *Small, Gritty, and Green: The Promise of America's Smaller Industrial Cities in a Low-Carbon World*

Sam Bass Warner and Andrew H. Whittemore, *American Urban Form: A Representative History*

John Pucher and Ralph Buehler, eds., *City Cycling*

Stephanie Foote and Elizabeth Mazzolini, eds., *Histories of the Dustheap: Waste, Material Cultures, Social Justice*

David J. Hess, *Good Green Jobs in a Global Economy: Making and Keeping New Industries in the United States*

Joseph F. C. DiMento and Clifford Ellis, *Changing Lanes: Visions and Histories of Urban Freeways*

Joanna Robinson, *Contested Water: The Struggle Against Water Privatization in the United States and Canada*

William B. Meyer, *The Environmental Advantages of Cities: Countering Commonsense Antiurbanism*

Rebecca L. Henn and Andrew J. Hoffman, eds., *Constructing Green: The Social Structures of Sustainability*

Peggy F. Barlett and Geoffrey W. Chase, eds., *Sustainability in Higher Education: Stories and Strategies for Transformation*

Isabelle Anguelovski, *Neighborhood as Refuge: Community Reconstruction, Place-Remaking, and Environmental Justice in the City*

Kelly Sims Gallagher, *The Global Diffusion of Clean Energy Technology: Lessons from China*

Vinit Mukhija and Anastasia Loukaitou-Sideris, eds., *The Informal American City: Beyond Taco Trucks and Day Labor*

Roxanne Warren, *Rail and the City: Shrinking Our Carbon Footprint and Reimagining Urban Space*

Marianne Krasny and Keith Tidball, *Civic Ecology: Adaptation and Transformation from the Ground Up*

Julian Agyeman and Duncan McLaren, *Sharing Cities: Enhancing Equity, Rebuilding Community, and Cutting Resource Use*

Jessica Smartt Gullion, *Fracking the Neighborhood: Reluctant Activists and Natural Gas Drilling*

Nicholas Phelps, *Sequel to Suburbia: Glimpses of America's Post-Suburban Future*

Shannon Elizabeth Bell, *Fighting King Coal: The Challenges to Micromobilization in Central Appalachia*